POLITICAL TRAUMA AND HEALING

Political Trauma and Healing

BIBLICAL ETHICS FOR
A POSTCOLONIAL WORLD

Mark G. Brett

WILLIAM B. EERDMANS PUBLISHING COMPANY
GRAND RAPIDS, MICHIGAN

Wm. B. Eerdmans Publishing Co.
2140 Oak Industrial Drive N.E., Grand Rapids, Michigan 49505

© 2016 Mark G. Brett
All rights reserved
Published 2016
Printed in the United States of America

22 21 20 19 18 17 16   1 2 3 4 5 6 7

Library of Congress Cataloging-in-Publication Data

Names: Brett, Mark G., author.
Title: Political trauma and healing: biblical ethics for a postcolonial world / Mark G. Brett.
Description: Grand Rapids, Michigan : Eerdmans Publishing Company, 2016. | Includes
    bibliographical references.
Identifiers: LCCN 2016003797 | ISBN 9780802873071 (pbk.: alk. paper)
Subjects: LCSH: Christianity and politics —Biblical teaching. | Christian ethics—Biblical
    teaching. | Australia—Politics and government—21st century. | Postcolonial theology.
Classification: LCC BR115.P7 B687 2016 | DDC 241/.962—dc23
    LC record available at http://lccn.loc.gov/2016003797

www.eerdmans.com

For the Paulson family,
especially *wapirra*, who led the way.

Contents

Acknowledgments

My first debt of gratitude is to Julia Rhyder, who suggested that my publications over the past twenty-five years could be grouped into three areas: philosophical hermeneutics, inner-biblical dialogue, and public theology. She suggested that I write a book in three sections, demonstrating the connections between these areas, while nevertheless acknowledging that they are separable areas within the hermeneutical enterprise.

Michael Thomson at Eerdmans suggested that this three-dimensional project could be broadly characterized as "postcolonial," and I am grateful to him for bringing this project to fruition as an Eerdmans publication.

Portions of chapters 4, 6, 7, and 9 have appeared in earlier publications:

"Reading as a Canaanite: Paradoxes in Joshua," in *Interested Readers: Essays on the Hebrew Bible in Honor of David J. A. Clines*, ed. Jim K. Aitken, Jeremy M. S. Clines, and Christl M. Maier (Atlanta: Society of Biblical Literature, 2013), 231-46. Reprinted by permission.

"Imperial Imagination in Isaiah 56–66," in *Isaiah and Imperial Context: The Book of Isaiah in Times of Empire*, ed. Andrew Abernethy, Mark G. Brett, Tim Meadowcroft, and Tim Bulkeley (Eugene: Wipf and Stock, 2013), 170-85. Used by permission of Wipf and Stock Publishers. www.wipfandstock.com

"'Speak to the Earth, and She will instruct You' (Job 12.8): An Intersection of Ecological and Indigenous Hermeneutics," in *Where the Wild Ox Roams: Biblical Essays in Honour of Norman C. Habel*, ed. A. Cadwallader (Sheffield: Phoenix, 2013), 1-19.

"Forced Migrations, Asylum Seekers and Human Rights," *Colloquium* 45/2 (2013): 121-36.

I am grateful to the publishers for the opportunity to present substantially revised versions of these essays in the present monograph.

Introduction

The motivation for this book arises from personal engagement with the legacies of political trauma in Australia, but the scope of the discussion necessarily extends well beyond this local context. During the years 2005–2008, I worked with a representative body of traditional Aboriginal owners who negotiated a new policy framework for Indigenous land claims in Victoria — a framework subsequently translated into legislation as the *Traditional Owner Settlement Act (2010)*. The negotiations were in some respects unparalleled in Australian history in so far as the state government of the day did not simply impose a new regime for land claims according to their own legislative lights, or attempt to litigate a new round of cases in the federal court. Part of the acknowledgment of past wrongs included awareness that any new initiatives for reconciliation had to be negotiated with the people who were most affected by the outcomes. The underlying concept of justice at work in this process had more to do with the restoration of relationships than with retributive or distributive justice.

There was also a great irony in these negotiations: the secular notion of restorative justice on which they relied can be traced back to the same religious tradition that had overwhelmed Indigenous sovereignty in the first place — not just in Australia, but also in the Americas, Africa, and Asia. The colonial doctrines of "discovery" were already secularized by the beginning of the nineteenth century, but they can hardly be understood without reference to their religious roots. Both the notion of "discovery" and the more recent "reconciliation" movements grew out of the same Christian tradition.

In reflecting on this complex history, I came to realize that the Australian experience was simply one of many contemporary histories in which social trauma was addressed by an ethic of political reconciliation, which in turn derived from classical religious traditions. As Daniel Philpott has recently argued, Jewish, Christian, and Islamic leaders have all at various times participated in practices of reconciliation and have explained their motivations in relation to their own scriptural sanctions.[1] I will argue in the present work that the Hebrew Bible itself (whether understood as the Jewish scriptures or the Christian Old Testament) can also be read as a series of reflections on political trauma and healing. In this respect, Philpott's account of political reconciliation can be further developed by closer examination of scriptural roots.

As the succession of ancient empires violently asserted their own forms of sovereignty over ancient Israel, the Israelite leadership discovered reasons why such evils had come to pass, and what restoration or redemption might yet be possible in the divine imagination. In each case, these empires left their marks in the making of Scripture — Egypt, Assyria, Babylon, Persia, Greece, and Rome — and in each case, new pathways toward healing were lived out as history unfolded.

The fact that this same Scripture could later be read in ways that sanctioned the foundation of Christian empires (and subsequently the massive expansion of European colonies in the Americas and the Asia-Pacific regions), demonstrates the need for critical "hermeneutics." The term is overly technical, but the issues at stake are immensely practical. I am referring here to the careful and detailed interpretation of what the biblical texts probably meant in the past, as well as the significance that these texts may yield for those who regard them as in some sense relevant for today. The relevance of biblical literature will be most obvious for faith communities who regard them as canonical, but the history of the Bible's influence extends well beyond narrowly religious traditions. Social reformers like the Rev. Martin Luther King Jr., for example, drew out the significance of biblical motifs in renegotiating the competing norms and interests that would shape public life in the United States from the 1960s to the present.

THE ETHICS OF CONVERSATION

The civil rights movements in the USA, Australia, and South Africa all illustrate the same kind of irony observed at the outset of our discussion: the religious tradition that was woven into the colonial racism in all these countries was the very same tradition that joined cause, for example, with Martin Luther King, Nelson Mandela, and the Christian Aboriginal leader in Australia,

---

1. Daniel Philpott, *Just and Unjust Peace: An Ethic of Political Reconciliation* (New York: Oxford University Press, 2012).

Douglas Nicholls, to address the traumas of the past. These cases demonstrate the validity of Alasdair MacIntyre's claim that "a living tradition is a historically extended, socially embodied argument, and an argument precisely in part about the goods which constitute that tradition."[2] The catalogue of complaints that can be brought against colonial Christianity is so impressive one might wonder why it is still the majority religion of many countries in Africa, Latin America, and Oceania.[3] But precisely this catalogue of trauma affirms the necessity for interpreters to be clear about their hermeneutical philosophy. Ideological and self-serving traditions of interpretation call for detailed critique.

MacIntyre, among many others, has drawn attention to the fact that the postmodern condition is partly constituted by the fraying and fragmentation of most normative traditions, along with often hybridized and conflicted contacts with alternative approaches to ethics. The various norms at issue in public debate have become detached, in some significant ways, from the cultural and religious backgrounds that lend them meaning. Symptomatic of this shift is the fact that cultural studies today are more likely to speak of "social imaginaries" than of "traditions," in part because the very idea of a tradition has become problematic. Not only are commentators less willing to presume the coherence of any particular tradition, they are also less willing to assume that classical authors consciously understood the underlying cultural assumptions of their own text, or the ways in which a single tradition can engage with competing concepts and diverse genres of communication.

It is perhaps no accident that a good number of the intellectuals who have been rereading the Bible in recent public philosophy have been atheists. It appears more acceptable now to treat the scriptures of Judaism and Christianity at a safe distance. When it comes to the politics of academia in the West, the endurance of religious convictions is very often perceived as "a failure of reason, or a culpable self-indulgence."[4] Under these conditions, it is important to appreciate that a religious tradition can itself be seen as a series of debates, and that the life of a tradition exhibits particular kinds of argumentative reasoning.

2. Alasdair MacIntyre, *After Virtue* (Notre Dame: University of Notre Dame Press, 1981), p. 207.

3. Lamin Sanneh, *Whose Religion Is Christianity? The Gospel beyond the West* (Grand Rapids: Eerdmans, 2003).

4. Charles Taylor, *A Secular Age* (Cambridge, Mass.: Belknap Press, 2007), p. 591. On recent atheist discussion of the Bible, see for example John Milbank, Slavoj Žižek and Creston Davis, *Paul's New Moment: Continental Philosophy and the Future of Christian Theology* (Grand Rapids: Brazos, 2010); Julia Kristeva, "Reading the Bible," in her *New Maladies of the Soul* (New York: Columbia University Press, 1995), pp. 115-26.

While some versions of secularity imagine that public order is best served by eliminating religious debates or symbolism from public ethics, this is not how secularity was first invented in the West, and it is not how secularity is most often conceived in non-Western contexts.[5]

In presenting the view that biblical ideas might yet have a role in the public sphere, I will consider in Chapter One a recent proposal for "post-secular discourse" which has been advanced by one of the leading philosophers of democracy in Europe, Jürgen Habermas. In reviewing Habermas's work, we begin with the observation that his influential account of discourse ethics was developed in response to the violence perpetrated by National Socialism in Germany. His procedural account of how every voice in a public debate should be given its due — and how the negotiation of public norms necessarily gives priority to universalizable principles over particular traditions — is conceived as a contribution to the formation of just institutions, capable of protecting the human rights of all citizens. Along with the acknowledgment of past wrongs, reparations, and so on, the establishing of just institutions should be seen as an integral part of the ethics of political reconciliation following political trauma.[6] It therefore becomes necessary for our project to examine Habermas's recent proposals for understanding how religious voices might participate in public institutions.[7]

I will argue that Habermas's approach appears inadequate when it comes to the historic injustices suffered by Indigenous people, and this is an inadequacy that cannot be ignored in the public life of settler colonial states like the USA, Canada, Australia, and Aotearoa / New Zealand. Chapter Two will provide a brief history of the various concepts of justice at work in the history of colonialism, illustrating the need for restorative justice in postcolonial societies as they move towards the healing of past traumas. The pursuit of restorative justice and reconciliation requires, it will be argued, a critique of Habermas on the one hand, and of colonial Christianity on the other hand.

---

5. See José Casanova, "Exploring the Postsecular: Three Meanings of 'the Secular' and Their Possible Transcendence," in *Habermas and Religion*, ed. Craig Calhoun, Eduardo Mendieta, and Jonathan VanAntwerpen (Cambridge: Polity, 2013), pp. 27-48.

6. Philpott, *Just and Unjust Peace*, pp. 4, 175-81.

7. See especially the discussion in Jürgen Habermas, et al., *An Awareness of What Is Missing: Faith and Reason in a Post-secular Age*, trans. Ciaran Cronin (Cambridge: Polity, 2010); Habermas, *Between Naturalism and Religion* (Cambridge: Polity, 2008); Judith Butler, Jürgen Habermas, Charles Taylor, and Cornel West, *The Power of Religion in the Public Sphere* (New York: Columbia University Press, 2011); Calhoun, Mendieta, and VanAntwerpen, *Habermas and Religion*.

In dialogue with recent biblical and theological scholarship, I will outline a critique of the colonial prejudices that lie deeply embedded in the history of Western Christianity. I will argue that the church needs to develop not just a more adequate postcolonial theology, but in addition, to develop a repertoire of postcolonial practices.[8] Prominent among these are the Christian practices of "self-emptying" (or *kenosis*),[9] including the relinquishment of aspirations for political control. We will therefore need to explore the paradoxical combination of *kenosis* and political participation, which I will support through fresh engagements with the scriptures.

To foreshadow the argument at this point, I will suggest that the Christian church's form of social life is not to be characterized by the procedural justice and standards of neutrality required within the institutions of a state, such as those prescribed by Habermas's ethics of public discourse. Rather, the church is called to embody the integration of justice and love (*agape*) in ever-expanding networks of relationship across national and cultural traditions, caring for those in need whether they are inside or outside the Christian community.[10] This understanding of the church maintains a healthy separation from the state, yet goes to the heart of public sociality by giving attention especially to the most vulnerable, a priority that was established already by the Law and Prophets within Scripture.

Chapter Three outlines the approach to biblical interpretation that is required in order to sustain the overall argument. The methodological discussion here engages in particular with the work of Kevin Vanhoozer, an influential theologian who has made a distinguished contribution to Christian hermeneutics. In spite of the subtleties of Vanhoozer's position, he ultimately reduces the complexities of inner-biblical debate to a unified metanarrative of divine self-revelation. His approach not only underestimates the diversity

8. See further Mark G. Brett and Jione Havea, eds., *Colonial Contexts and Postcolonial Theology: Storyweaving in the Asia-Pacific* (New York: Palgrave Macmillan, 2014).

9. Cf. Sarah Coakley, *Powers and Submissions: Spirituality, Philosophy and Gender* (Oxford: Blackwell, 2002); Mark G. Brett, *Decolonizing God: The Bible in the Tides of Empire* (Sheffield: Phoenix, 2008), pp. 178-204; Roger Haydon Mitchell, *Church, Gospel and Empires: How the Politics of Sovereignty Impregnated the West* (Eugene: Wipf & Stock, 2011), pp. 171-239; Sallie McFague, *Blessed Are the Consumers: Climate Change and the Practice of Restraint* (Minneapolis: Fortress, 2013).

10. Here I am building on proposals found in Charles Taylor's *A Secular Age* (Cambridge, Mass.: Belknap Press, 2007); Nicholas Wolterstorff, *Justice in Love* (Grand Rapids: Eerdmans, 2011); cf. Gayatri Chakravorti Spivak's brief but provocative comments on love, *A Critique of Postcolonial Reason: Toward a History of the Vanishing Present* (Cambridge, Mass.: Harvard University Press, 1999), pp. 383-84.

of human discourses in the biblical traditions, but it also makes the Bible less accessible to public scrutiny — a significant problem for those exploring the public dimensions of theology. In order to read Scripture as a series of socially embodied arguments, rather than as a single metanarrative, one must engage with the different paradigms of theology and ethics that are expressed through the complex range of scriptural books, literary sources and redactions. Through a number of case studies in Part Two of this volume, I will show how a critical appreciation of the "social imaginaries" at work within inner-biblical conversation can provide some structure for contemporary reflection — at least among the many faith communities who continue to recognize these scriptures as in some sense foundational for their life before God.[11]

To be clear, this argument does not propose that the Scripture can thereby become an authoritative and universal foundation for politics, as perhaps was the case in the days of Christendom. It is well known that the left wing churches of the Christian Reformation (e.g., the Anabaptists and Mennonites) quite consistently advocated a separation of church and state, explicitly opposing the medieval powers of an established church, and implicitly endorsing the secular trends of modernity. This is the tradition that informs today's "communitarian" theology that maintains a rigorous division of church and state, often configuring the churches as resident aliens within a hostile dominant culture. The New Testament documents, written as they were under generally oppressive conditions within colonies of the Roman Empire, naturally provide support for this approach by strengthening the resolve of the church as a network of worshipping communities but weakening the expectation of its influence in public life. There is no straight line from the New Testament to democratic participation.

The Hebrew Bible can make a substantial contribution to rethinking some of these political issues, and it is the older Scripture that features at some decisive points in the formation of modern democratic "social contract" theories.[12] We find more complex models of political engagement in the Hebrew Bible,

11. At this point I will refrain from the closer analysis of different kinds of normativity helpfully provided by Benjamin D. Sommer, "Unity and Plurality in Jewish Canons," in *One Scripture or Many? Canon from Biblical, Theological and Philosophical Perspectives*, ed. Christine Helmer and Christof Landmesser (Oxford: Oxford University Press, 2004), pp. 108-50.

12. See especially Eric Nelson, *The Hebrew Republic: Jewish Sources and the Transformation of European Political Thought* (Cambridge, Mass.: Harvard University Press, 2010); Yoram Hazony, *The Philosophy of Hebrew Scripture* (Cambridge: Cambridge University Press, 2012), pp. 151-54; Mark G. Brett, "Narrative Deliberation in Biblical Politics," in *The Oxford Handbook of Biblical Narrative*, ed. Danna Nolen Fewell (New York: Oxford University Press, 2016), pp. 540-49.

not least because it reflects periods of Israelite political sovereignty as well as the traumas of imperial subjugation and diaspora. There is a broader range of political models to draw on. While most of Jewish history has embodied diaspora models of social life, Christendom made use of the very imperialism that biblical theology repeatedly resisted. In part because the idiom of this resistance to empires was often borrowed from imperial language and ideas, when the Bible took its place in Christendom in later centuries, it could also easily be turned into a source of sanctions for medieval and colonial political power. Any use of the Bible today needs to reflect critically on this legacy.

In his important work *The Christian Imagination: Theology and the Origins of Race*, Willie James Jennings presents a searing critique of Western colonial theology. In one of his detailed case studies, Jennings analyzes the theological vision of José de Acosta Porres, an influential Spanish Jesuit who first arrived in Peru in 1572. Acosta's story illustrates a much broader history of Christian failures to interrogate the justice of colonial expansions, although it is particularly revealing as an early example of the necessary adjustments to the Catholic intellectual paradigm in his day. Acosta's theology was formed precisely by the philosophical tradition of Aristotle and Aquinas that Alasdair MacIntyre has lately attempted to revive. As the Spanish colonial horizons expanded to incorporate Peru, the Indian world was reduced, indeed eventually into reserves called precisely *reducciones*. But in some respects, these geographical transformations affected both the colonized and colonizer. Acosta acknowledges, "I will confess here that I laughed and jeered at Aristotle's meteorological theories and his philosophy, seeing that in the very place where, according to his rules, everything must be burning and on fire, I and all my companions were cold."[13]

Acosta's laugh, in Jennings's account of this dissonance, points to an epistemological crisis that was only resolved by sacrificing the details of classical geography and reasserting the universality of the doctrine of creation: if God created the whole earth, it was reasoned, the local details of creation in particular places are of lesser significance, but with a little theological pruning the realities of life at the equator could be rendered intelligible inside the world of colonial tradition. Acosta was, for example, able to correct St Augustine's claim that people could not exist in the Antipodes, moving about "upside down"; although Augustine's motives were "taken from the innermost parts

---

13. Quoted in Willie James Jennings, *The Christian Imagination: Theology and the Origins of Race* (New Haven: Yale University Press, 2010), p. 84, from José de Acosta, *Natural and Moral History of the Indies*, trans. Frances M. López Morillas (Durham: Duke University Press, 2002), pp. 88-89, translation of *Historia Natural y Moral de las Indias* (1590).

of sacred theology" and inferred from Holy Writ, yet experience in the New World provoked new and different interpretations.[14] But it was precisely Spanish experience in the New World that provoked new interpretations, not the experience of Indigenous peoples.

Native peoples were configured on the basis of their skin color, rather than their attachments to place, an administrative strategy loaded with economic and epistemological advantages. Indigenous knowledges could not be trusted, within the horizon of Acosta's theology, because the Indians belonged to "the blind nations of the world" whose only hope was to be illuminated by the light of the Most High God. In taking this view of the Indians, Jennings argues that the Spanish adopted one of the most common hermeneutical strategies of colonial Christianity, namely, to read "as an Israelite."[15] The illumination provided by the Christian gospel absorbs the revelation of Israel's God, thereby rendering the Spanish — in the world of their own making — the New Israel in the New World. The possibility of reading "as Gentiles" was lost, as Israel was superseded by an ideology of whiteness and racial superiority, with tragic consequences for all concerned. Retrospectively we must also note that Acosta's invocation of the Most High God — or El Elyon in Hebrew — would today strike a historian of ancient Israel as heavily ironic: El Elyon was the name of an Indigenous Creator God in Canaanite religion (cf. Genesis 14:18–22).[16]

In *The Christian Imagination*, Jennings argues that racist and colonial assumptions will continue to infect the life of the Christian churches to the extent that we resist this call to read the Scripture, and to read the world, as Gentiles. Colonialist interpretation of the story of the Canaanite woman in Matthew 15:21–18, for example, tends to assume that "we are standing with Jesus looking down on the woman in her desperation, when in fact we, the Gentiles, are the woman" and "we are to be counted among the *goyim*." An inversion of reading perspective is indeed commonly adopted in postcolonial biblical criticism, although this mode of reading is perhaps yet to have significant impact in the discipline of systematic theology.[17] More impor-

---

14. Jennings, *Christian Imagination*, pp. 87-89.

15. Jennings, *Christian Imagination*, pp. 96-98, citing Acosta, *Historia Natural y Moral de las Indias,* V:1.

16. See for example the comprehensive work of Ziony Zevit, *The Religions of Israel: A Synthesis of Parallactic Approaches* (New York: Continuum, 2001).

17. Jennings, *Christian Imagination*, p. 262. See Jim Perkinson, "A Canaanite Word in the Logos of Christ," in *Postcolonialism and Scriptural Reading*, ed. Laura Donaldson (Semeia 75; Atlanta, Ga.: Scholars Press, 1996), pp. 61-85; Alan Cadwallader, *Beyond the Word of a Woman: Recovering the Bodies of the Syrophoenician Women* (Adelaide: ATF Press, 2008).

tantly, we will need to take up Jennings's challenge not so much in reading the New Testament, where the place of the Gentiles is in many respects assured, but rather, in the Hebrew Bible, where reading as Gentiles often presents a more complex set of hermeneutical issues. A major difficulty with Jennings's argument, it seems to me, is that it tends to push a biblical metanarrative of imperialism into the hands of Israel, setting the radical challenge for a post-racial Christianity over against the assumed ethnocentrism of ancient Israelite identity.[18] In rereading the Hebrew Bible as Gentiles, however, the diversity of Scripture must first be appreciated: the relationship between Israel and her foreigners is repeatedly contested between the major streams of biblical tradition.

INNER-BIBLICAL CONVERSATION

One of the most ethnocentric of biblical traditions is no doubt to be found in the book of Deuteronomy, and perhaps paradoxically for some readers, this tradition also articulates a clear welcome for strangers.[19] This puzzle is readily understood when we appreciate that the core of Deuteronomy's law code comes not from the beginnings of Israel's story (as the metanarrative of exodus, law-making and conquest suggests) but from the seventh century BCE. In Chapter Four, we will see how this theology arose after the fall of the northern kingdom of Israel to the Assyrians, and even borrows from the treaty discourse imposed by Assyrian monarchs on their vassals. The national imagination expounded in Deuteronomy could accommodate the strangers or refugees who arrived in the southern kingdom of Judah on condition that they expressed an exclusive loyalty to Yhwh. The Deuteronomistic theology found in the subsequent narratives of Joshua, Judges, Samuel, and Kings, can therefore be understood as a response to the trauma of imperial invasions — when the northern kingdom was overwhelmed by Assyria, subsequently when the Assyrians also invaded Judah at the end of the eighth century, and then a century later, when the Babylonians destroyed Jerusalem. History has taught

18. A similar kind of problem besets the otherwise radical proposals of Alain Badiou, *Saint Paul: The Foundation of Universalism*, trans. Ray Brassier (Stanford: Stanford University Press, 2003), translation of *Saint Paul: La Fondation de l'universalisme* (Paris: Presses Universitaires France, 1997); cf. Slavoj Žižek, *The Fragile Absolute, or, Why Is the Christian Legacy Worth Fighting For?* (London: Verso, 2000).

19. See especially Jon D. Levenson, "Is there a Counterpart in the Hebrew Bible to New Testament Antisemitism?" *Journal of Ecumenical Studies* 22 (1985): 242-60.

us that nationalism is one of the most common responses to military threat.[20] But it is not the only possible response.

Chapter Five describes how the Priestly tradition unfolded after the fall of Judah and later under the imperial rule of the Persian Empire. This tradition provides a new vision for religious life even when the kind of political sovereignty given prominence in Deuteronomistic literature had been relinquished.[21] The Priestly tradition adopted distinctive perspectives that were grounded more in the theology of creation and in a multinational covenant with Abraham, rather than the national traditions of Judah. One could perhaps interpret these developments as a forced separation of religion and state, but this separation is nonetheless illuminating for theology after Christendom. The Priestly paradigm may well be fruitful, I will argue, for a postcolonial theology that both renounces political sovereignty yet advocates for minority voices in the public domain.

In the Priestly tradition we find, for example, an attempt to establish the legal equity of native citizens and immigrants (notably in Exod. 12:49 and Lev. 24:22), and this attempt can still serve as a provocation for hearing the legitimate claims of strangers within our own contexts. Deuteronomy earlier provided a quite different perspective on the strangers or immigrants who arrived in Judah during the reign of Davidic kings, and this difference between Deuteronomic and Priestly texts needs to be understood before we start to evaluate the implications of this material for our own contemporary challenges — such as those discussed in Chapter Nine of this volume, "Undocumented Immigrants, Asylum Seekers, and Human Rights."

In the context of Babylonian and Persian rule, the Priestly and prophetic traditions engage with "the *goyim*" in both positive and negative ways, and we will need to examine some of the possible reasons for this ambivalence.

---

20. There are, of course, significant differences between ancient and modern versions of nationalism, but the analogies between them are sufficient for our purposes here. See further Mark G. Brett, "National Identity as Commentary and as Metacommentary," in *Historiography and Identity (Re)formulation in Second Temple Historiographical Literature*, ed. Louis Jonker (LHBOTS 534; London: Continuum, 2010), pp. 29-40.

21. Debates about the composition of the Pentateuch are becoming more rather than less complex, and here I presume only the hypotheses that distinguish between Deuteronomy and Priestly tradition (here meaning both 'P' and the Holiness School, plus an indeterminate number of additions now somewhat vaguely known as 'post-P'). According to the majority of recent accounts, these are not so much literary sources as lively traditions that unfold over time. For a recent overview, see Thomas B. Dozeman, Konrad Schmid, and Baruch J. Schwartz, eds., *The Pentateuch: International Perspectives on Current Research* (FAT 78; Tübingen: Mohr Siebeck, 2011).

In Chapter Six, I will argue that key elements of the Priestly imagination re-appear in the later portions of Isaiah, illustrating how this non-national social imaginary includes multiple traditions and genres of literature. Similarly, in Chapter Seven, the discussion of the book of Job shows how ethical concerns for the "widow, orphan and stranger" are founded in a very different way in non-covenantal theology, yet Job converges on the same ethical concern for the most marginalized in society. By investigating these various perspectives on social marginalization in Israel's Law, Prophets, and Writings, it becomes possible to appreciate the complexities and convergences of Israel's social ethics, without pressing the Bible into the mold of a single metanarrative.

The case studies in Part Two of this volume also illustrate the scope of critical deliberation in pre-modern times. On this issue again we part company with Habermas, who has tended to view metaphysics as incompatible with political argument. Far from being something written in stone, with no capacity for fresh social imagination, the Hebrew Bible presents a conversation about God and the world that is capable of embracing a diversity of perspectives on political ethics. This is not the kind of deliberation that Habermas and other secular critics expect to find in religious traditions. Indeed, in the book of Job, we find an exemplary foreigner who is well able to argue his ethics before God without needing to draw on the laws of Israel. This model of revelation draws more from experience and nature than from law and priesthood, but it endures as part of Israel's Scripture nonetheless.

ENGAGING THE PRESENT

Having established a hermeneutical framework that is, first, sensitized to the legacies of colonialism, and second, attuned to the variety of perspectives embodied in the biblical imaginaries, it becomes possible to consider how a contemporary engagement with the Bible might influence the church's engagement with public issues. Any fusion of past and present horizons must of course bring some of the decisive changes wrought by modernity into view. If we can still find inspiration in biblical literature, it will not be because ancient social imaginaries can be grafted directly on to current socio-economic arrangements; any arguments arising from religious tradition will necessarily work by way of analogy. Accordingly, it is necessary to mention briefly at this point some of the most salient features of modern social imaginaries that will impact on the public issues discussed in Part Three of this volume.

In many respects, modernity is rooted in the attacks of the Protestant Reformation on the power of Priestly hierarchies and privileged vocations. In his major work *A Secular Age*, Charles Taylor has provided a subtle account of this disenchantment, but to highlight just one aspect of his narrative, it is important to see that the Protestant belief in the priesthood of all believers *sanctified ordinary life* and promoted an egalitarian impulse that was to become characteristic of Western politics. The egalitarian principle was politically enacted firstly in resistance to the medieval hierarchies legitimated by Roman Catholicism, and it was subsequently secularized into the horizontal solidarities that we find in modern nationalisms. Accordingly, our secular nationalisms generally lack the religious foundations of the ancient and medieval worlds, which provided metaphysical sanctions to monarchs and Priestly jurisdictions. The legal systems of modern nation states are overtly human constructions, rather than derived from sacred origins. Metaphysical foundations were slowly replaced by democracies in which sovereignty was transferred from monarchs to the people (although initially not to women, and in settler colonial societies, not to Indigenous peoples), and the nation state accordingly required no firmer foundation than its constitutional arrangements and the institutions of public debate.

In several chapters of this book, however, we will need to acknowledge the fact that the nationalisms fomented in the settler colonial states of the Anglo world (notably the USA, Canada, Australia, and Aotearoa / New Zealand) did not wholly succeed in overwriting the enchanted worlds of Indigenous people. In particular, Chapter Eight investigates the question of how reading the Hebrew Bible might contribute to Christian practices of reconciliation with the First Nations, including engagement with Indigenous knowledges. If one needs a provocation from Scripture at this point, then we might perhaps find it in the wisdom of the Gentile Job, and particularly in his conviction that creation might provide its own kind of instruction or torah:

> But now ask the beasts, and they will teach you;
> the birds of the air, and they will tell you.
> Or speak to the earth, and she will teach you;
> and the fish of the sea will explain to you. (Job 12:7-8)[22]

This perspective on nature's torah has some clear analogies with the social worlds of Indigenous peoples, where, in contrast with the anthropocentric tendencies of modern politics, traditional knowledge and kinship are embedded within local webs of non-human life. Through an investigation of this

---

22. Unless otherwise stated, all translations are my own.

analogy, and a more comprehensive consideration of creation theology in the Hebrew Bible, it becomes possible to approach contemporary questions about the environment and climate change from the fresh point of view of postcolonial biblical theology.[23] I will argue that a renewed dialogue with Indigenous peoples can in fact be connected with all four of the public issues discussed in Part Three: reconciliation, migration, ecology, and economic policy.

In pursuing these issues, and in raising questions as to what postcolonial redemption might look like, it is no longer possible to take a purely anti-colonial stance. One of the distinctive features of current postcolonial theory is that it recognizes the hybridity of settler societies today and does not seek an impossible restoration of native origins, or to impose a return to preindustrial economies.[24] This kind of realism does not imply a resignation about the past, but rather, a resolute commitment to the ongoing negotiation of complex identities and ecologies in forging social transformation. Far from the relativist and fragmented postmodernism that provides no motivation for substantive conversation in public, a postcolonial redemption would seek to restore what Jennings has called "the space of communion":

> The space of communion is always ready to appear where the people of God reach down to join the land and reach out to join those around them, their near and distant neighbors. This joining involves first a radical remembering of the place, a discerning of the histories and stories of those from whom that land was the facilitator of their identity. This must be done to gather the fragments of identity that remain to learn from them (or at least from their memory) who we might become in that place . . . so that land is never simply released to capitalism and its autonomous, self-perpetuating turnings of space inside commodity form.[25]

23. Without going into details at this point, this exploration will need to absorb what theologians call panentheism (as opposed to pantheism), notably for example in Elizabeth Johnson's discussion "Bespeaking God's Solidarity with the World," in her *She Who Is: The Mystery of God in Feminist Theological Discourse* (New York: Crossroad, 1993), pp. 228-33.

24. See, e.g., Mahmood Mamdani, "Beyond Settler and Native as Political Identities: Overcoming the Political Legacy of Colonialism," in *Comparative Studies in Society and History* 43/4 (2001): 651-64; Mahmood Mamdani, *When Victims Become Killers: Colonialism, Nativism, and the Genocide in Rwanda* (Princeton: Princeton University Press, 2001); Yin C. Paradies, "Beyond Black and White: Essentialism, Hybridity and Indigeneity," *Journal of Sociology* 42 (2006): 355-67; Bill Ashcroft, *Post-Colonial Transformation* (London: Routledge, 2001).

25. Jennings, *The Christian Imagination,* pp. 286-87; Cf. Stephen D. Moore and Mayra Rivera, eds., *Planetary Loves: Spivak, Postcoloniality and Theology* (New York: Fordham University Press, 2011).

INTRODUCTION

Accordingly, Chapter Eleven of this volume addresses the relentless de-territorialization evidenced in late capitalism and poses economic questions about the nature of redemption. What sense can be made of the proposal that pre-modern economic ideas expressed in the Hebrew Bible might yet have some relevance under the current globalized conditions, short of a return to agrarian ideals? I will argue that there is a fruitful analogy to be drawn between the ancient Hebrew concepts of *shalom* and the recent theory of human flourishing which Martha Nussbaum and Amartya Sen have expounded under the heading of a "capabilities approach" to economic development. My proposal is that the traumas wrought by colonial economies, and by their subsequent reconfiguration under globalized conditions, call for an ethic of healing and reconciliation – one which acknowledges wrong-doing, imagines reparations for the earth, and seeks to establish institutions dedicated to ecological justice.[26]

Some have suggested that we need nothing less than a Copernican revolution in postcolonial and ecological ethics.[27] In addressing these complex issues, this book will show how just such a revolution took place in the unfolding of the Hebrew Bible: Israel responded to her own political traumas by reconnecting with creation and by reframing the particularities of her identity within much larger contexts of accountability. For faith communities today, this classic literature may yet speak to many of our most pressing public issues: the legacies of colonialism, the demands of asylum seekers, the challenges of climate change, and the shaping of redemptive economies. How we address these issues may well be a matter of life and death.

26. Cf. Martha C. Nussbaum, *Frontiers of Justice: Disability, Nationality, and Species Membership* (Boston: Harvard University Press, 2006); Randy S. Woodley, *Shalom and the Community of Creation: An Indigenous Vision* (Grand Rapids: Eerdmans, 2012).

27. See, e.g., Whitney Bauman, *Theology, Creation, and Environmental Ethics: From* Creatio ex Nihilo *to* Terra Nullius (London: Routledge, 2009), p. 166.

THE ETHICS OF CONVERSATION

1. Limits and Possibilities of Secular Theology

In the wake of numerous terrorist incidents in recent years, one of the leading political philosophers of our time, Jürgen Habermas, has revisited some fundamental questions concerning the nature of public discourse in democratic contexts. Seeking to overcome the polarization of worldviews that splits societies into fundamentalist and secular camps incapable of engaging with each other in reasoned debate, he has identified the need for a "post-secular" discourse within which religious and secular contributions can learn from each other and forge the solidarities that are necessary if violence is to be avoided.[1] Particularly relevant, from the point of view of our present discussion, is Habermas's conviction that fundamentalism in some parts of the world "can be construed, among other things, in terms of the long-term impact of violent colonization and failures in decolonization."[2] Colonial violence is identified here not simply as a matter of history but as an enduring legacy, and accordingly, in the next chapter we will turn our attention to the kind of justice that may facilitate healing from colonial trauma.

1. Habermas, "Religion in the Public Sphere," *European Journal of Philosophy* 14 (2006): 18. This significant essay was reprinted in a minimally revised version in Habermas, *Between Naturalism and Religion,* trans. Ciaran Cronin (Cambridge: Polity Press, 2008), pp. 114-47. See also the recent discussion in Péter Losonczi and Aakash Sing, eds., *Discovering the Post-Secular: Essays on the Habermasian Post-Secular Turn* (Vienna: Lit Verlag, 2010), and the earlier exchange in Jürgen Habermas and Joseph Ratzinger, *The Dialectics of Secularization: On Reason and Religion,* trans. B. McNeil (San Francisco: Ignatius Press, 2006).

2. Habermas, "Religion in the Public Sphere," 1. Cf. Daniel Philpott's discussion of the Truth and Reconciliation Commission in South Africa, *Just and Unjust Peace: An Ethic of Political Reconciliation* (Oxford: Oxford University Press, 2012), pp. 97-118.

Within the discipline of philosophy, the space between fundamentalist approaches to sacred texts and modern social theory has been occupied by the discourse of hermeneutics — no longer conceived in narrow terms as the business of interpreting scriptures (or the history of exegetical methods), but rather as a constitutive feature of all social life within which meanings are exchanged, uncovered or contested. In this broader sense, hermeneutics investigates the role of interpretation and communication in facilitating a broad range of matters that are not narrowly "religious." Hermeneutical theology, similarly, has immense practical potential in covering a broad range of matters, including pressing questions about the role of religions within the constitution of secular societies. In his earlier work, Habermas was famously critical of hermeneutical philosophy to the extent that it neglected social conditions behind the communication of meaning, most notably the dimensions of class and power, which in his view often extended beyond the reach of explicitly religious language. The recent exploration of "post-secular" discourse is something of an about face, which reopens questions about the relevance of religious language in public debates, or more precisely, the relevance of hermeneutical theology in democratic discourse.

The post-secular turn can be interpreted as a self-critical move on the part of liberal theorists who acknowledge that some recent versions of secular politics have had the effect of limiting freedom of religion, which was earlier conceived as a fundamental right in the construction of modernity. Habermas suggests that there is room for repentance in this connection, a need for a mutual process of learning within which neither religious nor secular parties remain quite what they were:

> [A] secularist attitude does not suffice for the expected cooperation with fellow citizens who are religious. This cognitive act of adaptation needs to be distinguished from the political virtue of mere tolerance. What is at stake is not some respectful feel for the possible existential significance of religion for some other person. What we must also expect of the secular citizens is moreover a self-reflective transcending of a secularist self-understanding of modernity.[3]

This is indeed a fresh contribution to debates about the nature of democracy, but the logic is founded on a well-established principle of modernity: every voice deserves to be heard. The irony, perhaps, is that in some contexts

---

3. Habermas, "Religion in the Public Sphere," 15.

this principle needs to be restated in liberal democracies in order to include the multiplicity of religious voices, but Habermas has consistently advocated for a procedural justice founded on "the universalist idea that every subject in his or her individuality should get the chance of an unconstrained articulation of his or her claims."[4]

The complexity and abstractness of the philosophical debates surrounding Habermas's work should not be allowed to obscure the particular context from which it emerges. This is a philosophy that addresses the legacy of Nazism in Germany — the elevation of "blood and soil" identity in the most violent form of nationalism[5] — and this context needs to be borne in mind when considering the implications of key Habermasian concepts like universality. As he once commented in an interview,

> What, then, does universalism mean? That one relativizes one's own form of existence in relation to the legitimate claims of other forms of life, that one attribute the same rights to the strangers and the others, along with all their idiosyncrasies and incomprehensibilities, that one not insist on generalization of one's own identity, that the realm of tolerance must become endlessly larger than it is today: all this is what moral universalism means today.[6]

Habermasian discourse ethics may therefore be understood as a particular form of hermeneutical methodology that seeks to ensure the participation of all voices, and it is especially designed to counter the power of individuals or groups who have disproportionate or distorting influence in political deliberations. It is primarily this concern to establish communicative ideals that motivated Habermas's early critique of the regnant version of hermeneutical philosophy, which in its analysis of tradition appeared reluctant to interrogate the exercises of power that may lie behind the composition and transmission of classic texts like the Bible.[7] As Habermas put it in his *Theory of Communicative Action*, "ideal discourse is guided by the 'unforced force' of the better

---

4. Axel Honneth, "The Other of Justice: Habermas and the Ethical Challenge of Postmodernism," in *The Cambridge Companion to Habermas*, ed. Stephen K. White (Cambridge: Cambridge University Press, 1995), p. 307.

5. See, e.g., Habermas, *Between Naturalism and Religion*, pp. 11-23.

6. Jürgen Habermas, "Interview with J. M. Ferry," *Philosophy and Social Criticism* 14 (1988): 436; Cf. David Horrell, *Solidarity and Difference: A Contemporary Reading of Paul's Ethics* (London: T & T Clark International, 2005), pp. 282-84.

7. See the analysis of the Gadamer-Habermas debate in Mark G. Brett, *Biblical Criticism in Crisis?* (Cambridge: Cambridge University Press, 1991), pp. 135-56.

argument, a freedom from all forms of coercion," even if that coercion comes in the more subtle shape of tradition.[8]

A number of critics have, however, questioned the adequacy of this regulative ideal for communicative actions to the extent that it rests on merely individualist premises. In elevating the ideal that every individual voice should be heard, every representation of a *collective* self is apparently rendered suspicious on the grounds that it is a potentially distorting formation of power. Yet the charge of individualism (which is also leveled against many theories of human rights) cannot be raised against Habermas without acknowledging that individualism has complex roots, amongst which we must include the unintended legacies of Protestant attacks on Catholic tradition. Individualist thought in the modern West has both theological and secular dimensions.

Precisely for this reason, a key question now arising — especially since the *UN Declaration on the Rights of Indigenous Peoples* (2007)[9] — is how the human rights tradition can embody collective rights, and whether these collective rights might also be defensible in theological terms. We will return to these questions, but here we simply note the irony that the liberal principle of toleration has often been intolerant towards collectivities. In so far as liberalism attempts to accommodate this problem, it is usually via the notion of multiple cultures that are allowed to flourish under universalized conditions of citizenship, constituted democratically within a nation state or via international covenants between states.[10] The sense in which the bearers of a culture might enjoy collective or corporate rights is the key problem at issue.

As minority groups know all too well, however, liberal democracies are in practice swayed decisively by the majority of a state's population, i.e., by those who carry democratic power. In Australia, for example, Aboriginal people can never dominate elections as a group. Their very right to vote in national elections did not exist until the 1960s, and the impediments to their participation in political life could only be overcome by moral persuasion of the non-indigenous majority. Similarly, commenting on the situation in Sri Lanka, Jayadeva Uyangoda once noted that "we have had the Westminster type of democracy, which allowed an ethnic community with a numerical

---

8. Habermas, *The Theory of Communicative Action*, Volume 2: *Lifeworld and System* (Boston: Beacon, 1984), pp. 66-67.

9. Significantly, Habermas seems to suggest that Indigenous cultures might need to be considered "external to egalitarian law" in Western societies like the "United States, Canada and Australia." *Between Naturalism and Religion*, pp. 304-5.

10. See Habermas's chapter on "The Equal Treatment of Cultures and the Limits of Postmodern Liberalism," *Between Naturalism and Religion*, pp. 271-311.

majority to control political power and resources."[11] One of the key questions in postcolonial politics is indeed how moral persuasion in political life is to be understood, especially when cultural minorities hold very little democratic power. Habermas is well aware of such practical difficulties, of course, but he does not see them as a challenge to the ideals of a deliberative democracy. On the contrary, his communicative ideals are reinforced precisely by examples of political exclusion, which provoke the deliberative process of "permanent reforms."[12]

In his earlier work, Habermas attempted to distinguish between universalizable *norms* of justice, on the one hand, and *values* shaped by particular cultural or religious identities on the other. He held that universalizable norms derived through public deliberation "require a break with all of the unquestioned truths of an established, concrete ethical life, in addition to distancing oneself from the contexts of life with which one's identity is inextricably interwoven."[13] This procedural break with tradition and identity was recommended, in part, as an antidote to the potentially oppressive excesses of ethnic nationalism that may be evidenced in particular contexts. Yet if we translate this procedure into the political life of settler colonial nations like the USA or Australia, it would seem that Indigenous people could only participate in the political process to the extent that they renounce the traditions and particularities that make them Indigenous. Indeed, to put this point more broadly, the universalizing assumptions of the "ideal speech situation" seem to imply that cultural and religious identities as such are not sufficiently rational for the purposes of public dialogue.[14]

In his post-secular turn, Habermas has provided an account of mutual learning that goes some distance towards addressing this kind of problem:

> [T]he liberal state has an interest in unleashing religious voices in the political public sphere, and in the political participation of religious organizations as well. It must not discourage religious persons and communities

11. Uyangoda, "Understanding Ethnicity and Nationalism," *Ecumenical Review* 47/2 (1995): 191; cf. John Chesterman and Brian Galligan, eds., *Citizens without Rights: Aborigines and Australian Citizenship* (Melbourne: Cambridge University Press, 1997).

12. Habermas, *Between Naturalism and Religion*, p. 309.

13. Habermas, *Justification and Application*, trans. C. Lenhardt (Oxford: Polity, 1990), p. 12.

14. Cf. Jeffrey Stout, *Democracy and Tradition* (Princeton: Princeton University Press, 2003), p. 81: "The practical expression of social contract theory is, unsurprisingly, a program of social control, an attempt to enforce moral restraint on discursive exchange by counting only those who want to reason on the basis of a common set of fixed rules as *reasonable*."

from also expressing themselves politically as such, for it cannot know whether secular society would not otherwise cut itself off from key resources for the creation of meaning and identity. Secular citizens or those of other religious persuasions can under certain circumstances learn something from religious contributions; this is, for example, the case if they recognize in the normative truth content of a religious utterance hidden intuitions of their own.

Religious traditions have a special power to articulate moral intuitions, especially with regard to vulnerable forms of communal life. In the event of the corresponding political debates, this potential makes religious speech a serious candidate to transporting possible truth contents, which can then be translated from the vocabulary of a particular religious community into a generally accessible language.[15]

Questions have been raised about this requirement that the truth contents of religious traditions need to be translated into "generally accessible language,"[16] but in Habermas's defense we may recall the point made above that he is envisaging an expansion of public life that explicitly does *not* insist on the generalization of a dominant identity. Nevertheless, this new proposal for post-secular public discourse does seem to envisage that the secularized citizen can perform a ready separation of truth contents from religious practices, and accordingly travel "with light metaphysical baggage."[17] One might need to forgive those critics who suggest that this freshly ecumenical version of liberal democracy still requires more argument.

If we are to contemplate the inclusion of religious voices in public deliberation on the fresh terms suggested by Habermas, then we must surely allow for a spectrum of voices — only some of whom will possess the capacity for the discursive, post-metaphysical transformations that are ostensibly the ideal in modern democracies. Yet a key problem here is that the argument threatens to collapse into a tautology: for religious traditions locked into their metaphysical strictures there appears to be little capacity for transformative engagement with others, as Habermas himself argued in his major work *The Theory of Communicative Action*.[18]

15. Habermas, "Religion in the Public Sphere," 10.
16. See, e.g., Nicholas Adams, "A Response to Heuser: Two Problems in Habermas' Recent Comments on Religion," *Political Theology* 9 (2008): 552-56; Michael Welker, "Habermas and Ratzinger on the Future of Religion," *Scottish Journal of Theology* 63 (2010): 456-73.
17. Habermas, *Between Naturalism and Religion*, p. 309.
18. Habermas, *The Theory of Communicative Action*, vol. 2, pp. 77-111.

Social scientists have described primordial social bonds in very similar terms, as for example when Clifford Geertz suggests that "Congruities of blood, speech, custom, and so on are seen to have an ineffable, and at times overpowering coerciveness in and of themselves."[19] Another comparison might be drawn with Charles Taylor's argument that the "porous" self in the enchanted worlds of pre-modern life is vulnerable to the spiritual world "as immediate reality, like stones, rivers and mountains," whereas the modern self is "buffered" and more self-reflexive — not immediately impinged on by gods and demons, and empowered to see religious construals precisely as construals, as *options* that may be adopted or rejected by a deliberating self without thereby falling into the hands of malevolent spiritual powers.[20] What this comparison with Taylor's work reveals, however, is that Habermas seems to attribute the characteristics of pre-modern metaphysics to religion *as such*, while in effect requiring that gifted philosophical translators render the opacities of religious commitment into the constructive norms of modern, public life, apparently since religious people are unlikely to possess this capacity:

> By dint of their possibly even rationally defended reference to the dogmatic authority of an inviolable core of infallible revelatory truths, religiously rooted existential convictions evade that kind of unreserved discursive deliberation to which other ethical orientations and world views, i.e., secular 'concepts of the good' expose themselves.[21]

Taylor's detailed historical narrative in *A Secular Age* illustrates how religious belief after modernity does, indeed, often expose itself to "discursive deliberation" in ways that are less clearly distinguishable from secular argument. Up until relatively modern times, disbelief in gods or spirits was extremely difficult to conceive of, whereas it is now a commonplace in Western cultures. The burden of Taylor's narrative, however, is not to rehearse the idea that science has triumphed over prejudice, but rather, to explain how the characteristic inability of earlier societies to imagine themselves outside of a particular

19. Clifford Geertz, "The Integrative Revolution: Primordial Sentiments and Civil Politics in the New States" in his influential *The Interpretation of Cultures* (New York: Basic Books, 1973), p. 259; cf. Edward Shils, "Primordial, Personal, Sacred, and Civil Ties," *British Journal of Sociology* 8 (1957): 130-45.

20. Taylor, *A Secular Age* (Cambridge, Mass.: Belknap Press, 2007), pp. 12, 3-39, and 154-55 on the "disembedding" of identities; cf. Stanley Tambiah, *Magic, Science, Religion and the Scope of Rationality* (Cambridge: Cambridge University Press, 1990), p. 134.

21. Habermas, "Religion in the Public Sphere," 9.

embeddedness (in clans and tribes or sacred structures) was turned within a few modern centuries into a matter of choosing religious identities from among a range of options.

Nevertheless, we need not conclude that there is an intractable disagreement here between Habermas and Taylor, since the substance of Habermas's point above is still valid if it is taken to be a comment on the enduring forms of fundamentalism. Taylor's argument, on the other hand, can be read primarily as an account of Western religious expressions *to the extent* that they are infused with the characteristics of modernity.

Taylor's argument is complex, and it begins long before the advent of Protestantism, but his narrative leads us to conclude that the abolition of the enchanted cosmos was especially an unintended consequence of Protestant attacks on Catholic practices of the sacred. Belief in the priesthood of all believers, for example, sanctified ordinary life and promoted an egalitarian impulse that was first enacted as resistance to priestly hierarchies and the jurisdiction of Rome, and subsequently secularized into the horizontal solidarities of modern nationalisms, within which individuals can become the bearers of inherent human rights. These horizontal solidarities were repeatedly opposed to the hierarchical structures that in pre-modern thought had been directly embedded in metaphysical reality.[22]

To risk a statement of the obvious, modern secular societies are characterized by separations between church and state that were in the first instance forged by *theological* arguments. Secular states were severed from their older religious foundations, for example, in an underlying Great Chain of Being that provides sanctions for dynasties or priestly jurisdictions. Legal arrangements are seen as human constructions, rather than as a system of laws that derive from time immemorial. And out of these complex historical processes, according to Taylor, the plasticity of modern constructivist identities were eventually born, in tandem with the new opportunities afforded by exclusive humanism. These are then the ideal circumstances, one might infer, for post-metaphysical, transformative encounters with others. It is not that hermeneutical theology as such has been superseded, but rather, that any fundamentalist attempt to relieve religion of its burden of interpretation is no longer plausible in the public realm.

Habermas's recent proposals are overtly welcoming of the historic theological contributions that have been made to the creating of secular polities. He acknowledges, for example, that the human rights tradition is in part inspired

22. Taylor, *A Secular Age*, pp. 77, 95, 104, 146, 155, 179.

by the claim in Genesis 1 that humans are made in the "image of God," which has been secularized with redemptive effects: "The translation of the human likeness to God [*Gottesebenbildlichkeit*] into the equal dignity of all humans, a dignity to be respected unconditionally, is such a saving translation," Habermas suggests.[23] The contributions of Martin Luther King Jr., who could translate the specific cadences of Baptist preaching into a generalized advocacy of civil rights, represents one of the most recent contributions to the tradition.[24]

Nonetheless, it is precisely this expectation that thick theological language must be translated into generally accessible public discourse that has attracted criticism from several theologians. To be fair to Habermas, the key problem is not so much that a rich and complex lived experience of faith has to be watered down to a thin collection of propositions; the more substantive question for the making of political and legal discourse in secular societies is how a variety of competing cultural and religious traditions might be mediated, or at least made intelligible one to the other. Without successful translation, Habermas suggests that "there is no prospect of the substantive content of religious voices being taken up in the agendas and negotiations within political bodies and in the broader political process." He specifically objects to the views of Nicholas Wolterstorff and Paul Weithman on this issue, who see no need for this requirement: "In so doing, contrary to their own claim to remain in line with the premises of the liberal argument, they violate the principle that the state shall remain neutral in the face of competing world views."[25]

While we may agree that this principle of neutrality cannot be readily dismissed in secular contexts, and similarly that public language has to be carefully shaped in order to ensure that it is broadly intelligible, it does not follow that the particularities of a worldview or tradition have to be expunged. As Wolterstorff has argued, this proposal to expunge any religious reasoning from

23. Habermas, "On the Relation between the Secular Liberal State and Religion," in *The Frankfurt School on Religion*, ed. Eduardo Mendieta (New York: Routledge, 2004), pp. 337-46, 346; Jürgen Habermas, *Between Naturalism and Religion*, p. 309.

24. Habermas, *Between Naturalism and Religion*, p. 124. Stout, *Democracy and Tradition* (81) also mentions King as exemplary of why democratic discourse should be understood as an unfolding dialectic, open to religious voices when revising what counts as "reasonable" in political practice. Both Habermas and Stout cite King in the course of providing quite different critiques of John Rawls, "The Idea of Public Reason Revisited," *University of Chicago Law Review* 64 (1997): 765-807.

25. Habermas, "Religion in the Public Sphere," p. 11, referring to Robert Audi and Nicholas Wolterstorff, *Religion in the Public Sphere: The Place of Religious Convictions in Political Debate* (New York: Rowman and Littlefield, 1997); Paul Weithman, *Religion and the Obligations of Citizenship* (Cambridge: Cambridge University Press, 2002).

public debate would make liberal democracy something less than liberal.[26] On the contrary, in order to ensure that some minority voices are actually heard, it may be necessary not to *reduce* their claims to a common discourse but to expound their perspectives in greater detail before their logic can be actually understood by a wider audience. In many cases, the force of a novel argument cannot be grasped until a good deal of background knowledge is made explicit, and therefore a greater depth of presentation in public debates may be necessary. And, of course, to satisfy the principle of neutrality, the variety of traditions that may have a stake in a particular public debate would need to be given the same level of attention until it is clear that they have at least been *understood*, especially when their view does not enjoy significant demographic power.

The requirement for a democratic state to be "neutral" — that is, obligated to consider a variety of normative traditions — was linked historically to the invention of international law in the early modern period. As Europe struggled with the theological consequences of the Wars of Religion, and encountered new kinds of conflict in the competition for colonial territories, international law could no longer be secured on the foundation of a single Christian tradition. The influential work of Hugo Grotius, for example, was scrupulous in citing a range of normative sources, and in ways that often entailed giving less priority to the authority of the Bible. This was not because Grotius was an atheist, but because his generation was facing entirely new challenges presented by religious diversity. He decided that if the separation of church and state was to be effectively implemented, then the use of the Bible as a privileged source in international legal argument is insufficient to the politically complex task at hand.[27]

Postcolonial critics will, no doubt, fault Grotius today for not giving sufficient attention or weight to *Indigenous* legal traditions in the shaping of an intercultural legal theory,[28] and that is exactly the sort of critique that Haber-

26. Nicholas Wolterstorff, "The Role of Religion in Decision and Discussion of Political Issues," in *Religion in the Public Sphere*, p. 77. Wolterstorff's position on the inclusion of religious voices has been recently reiterated by Miroslav Volf, *A Public Faith: How Followers of Christ Should Serve the Common Good* (Grand Rapids: Brazos Press, 2011), pp. 124-27.

27. Mark Samos, "Secularization in *De Iure Praedae*: from Bible Criticism to International Law," *Grotiana* 26-28 (2005-2007): 147-91.

28. See further Andrew Fitzmaurice, "Anticolonialism in Western Political Thought: The Colonial Origins of the Concept of Genocide," in *Empire, Colony, Genocide: Conquest, Occupation and Subaltern Resistance in World History*, ed. A. Dirk Moses (New York: Bergham, 2008), pp. 55-80.

masian discourse ethics would require us to make if we are to maintain a democratic process of permanent reform. The fact that the exercise of European power in modern colonial projects led to the exclusion of Indigenous voices should provoke us to ensure, to the best of our ability, that similar failures of due process do not occur.

DEMOCRACY AND POSTCOLONIAL THEOLOGY

Instead of further investigating these issues in philosophical terms, we turn now to consider the ways in which postcolonial theology might contribute to secular democratic conversation. Our starting point can be stated in simple terms: a necessary feature of any postcolonial theology will be the advocacy of practices of repentance that not only confess to the collusion of Christianity and colonialism but, as a consequence, resolutely resist new temptations to exercise mastery over others — even if that mastery is exercised by a democratic majority. The participation of formerly excluded voices requires a kind of renunciation on the part of the powerful.

In *Decolonizing God*, I explored this theological resolve by beginning with a theology of *kenosis*, or self-emptying. The German theologian Jürgen Moltmann has, for example, repeatedly argued that *kenosis* should not just be seen as a temporary anomaly in the life of Christ — God taking humble human form in the incarnation — but as *characteristic* of the Trinitarian life that makes space for the whole created order.[29] This argument locates the Christian doctrine of God within a vision of cosmic, divine communion, rather than within the metaphysical hierarchies that spawned the abuses of power in the history of Christian colonialism. Applying this vision of divine communion in the political realm, a number of authors have accordingly suggested that postcolonial theology requires a renunciation of political sovereignty — in effect a diaspora theology[30] — and that such a renunciation might be described as self-emptying or "kenotic."

---

29. Jürgen Moltmann, "God's Kenosis in the Creation and Consummation of the World," in *The Work of Love: Creation as Kenosis*, ed. John Polkinghorne (Grand Rapids: Eerdmans, 2001), pp. 137-51. The following discussion revises portions of my paper "Diaspora and Kenosis as Postcolonial Themes," in *Decolonizing the Body of Christ: An Interdisciplinary Conversation*, ed. David Joy and Joseph Duggan (London: Palgrave, 2012), pp. 127-40. See also Michael Gorman, *Inhabiting the Cruciform God: Kenosis, Justification, and Theosis in Paul's Soteriology* (Grand Rapids: Eerdmans, 2009).

30. See, e.g., Daniel Smith-Christopher, *A Biblical Theology of Exile* (Minneapolis: Fortress,

Feminist and postcolonial critics have, however, placed a question mark over kenotic theology by pointing out that it has more relevance in contexts where groups have power and resources that might be given up.[31] Promoting the *kenosis* of fragile cultures, or selves, may simply provide a new theological means to reinforce injustice and dispossession. Hence, we must conclude that a postcolonial hermeneutic cannot advocate, as a kind of abstract proposition, that the Christian self should always and everywhere be self-sacrificial.

The Mennonite theologian Alain Epp Weaver has provided an important contribution to these issues in *States of Exile: Visions of Diaspora, Witness and Return*. Weaver reexamines the influential work of John Howard Yoder, who advanced the conception of Christian identity as embodying a kind of permanent exile or diaspora, but he brings Yoder's work into conversation with the postcolonial critic Edward Said. The key question for Weaver is how this norm of perpetual exile relates to the experience of millions of Palestinians who have been driven from their traditional country, and more generally, whether the norm of perpetual exile can speak to Indigenous peoples who have been overwhelmed by colonial migrations.[32] This formulation of the problem has particular relevance in Australia, where dispossession of our First Peoples has not yet been adequately addressed in either political or theological terms. As the Aboriginal theologian George Rosendale has put it, Aboriginal and Torres Strait Islander peoples have been effectively exiled from their own country, and it is manifestly inadequate to say — as was often said in mission theology — that they need not worry about their land because their home is in heaven (the hypocrisy of the premise is exposed as soon as it is reversed: that white Australians should give up their land because their home is in heaven).[33]

2002), pp. 1-26, 189-203; cf. Daniel Boyarin and Jonathan Boyarin, "Diaspora: Generation and the Ground of Jewish Identity," in *Identities*, ed. K. Anthony Appiah and Henry Louis Gates (Chicago: University of Chicago Press, 1995), pp. 305-37; Robert Gibbs, *Correlations in Rosenzweig and Levinas* (Princeton: Princeton University Press, 1992), pp. 257-58.

31. See Sarah Coakley, "Kenosis and Subversion: On the Repression of 'Vulnerability' in Christian Feminist Writing," in *Swallowing a Fishbone?*, ed. Daphne Hampson (London: SPCK, 1996), pp. 82-111; Sze-kar Wan, "Does Diaspora Identity Imply Some Sort of Universality? An Asian-American Reading of Galatians," in *Interpreting Beyond Borders*, ed. Fernando Segovia (Sheffield: Sheffield Academic Press, 2000), pp. 107-33.

32. Alain Epp Weaver, *States of Exile: Visions of Diaspora, Witness and Return* (Scottdale: Herald Press, 2008), p. 42. Cf. Mark G. Brett, "Interpreting Ethnicity: Method, Hermeneutics, Ethics," in *Ethnicity and the Bible*, ed. Brett (BIS 19; Leiden: EJ Brill, 1996), pp. 16-21, here responding in particular to Daniel Boyarin, *A Radical Jew: Paul and the Politics of Identity* (Berkeley: University of California Press, 1994), pp. 252-59.

33. See, e.g., George Rosendale, *Spirituality for Aboriginal Christians* (Darwin: Nungalinya

Weaver brings an important corrective to attempts in "post-Christendom" theology to establish the theme of exile as the axis around which everything else turns. In questioning the idea of perpetual exile or diaspora, he argues that the concept of exile usually carries with it some underlying expectation of return or redemption.[34] The logic of return to the homeland is, for example, central to the biblical traditions of Isaiah. As it transpired, the historic return to Judah in the 5th century BCE provoked a fresh series of debates in the biblical literature of the time, particularly focused on the nature of communal identity. Isaiah took a remarkably inclusive stance over against the exclusive and nativist ideals of purity that were proposed in the books of Ezra-Nehemiah, as will be explained further in Part Two of this volume. And the tensions between ethnic exclusivism and civic inclusivism evident in the biblical literature might be seen as analogous with many post-colonial nations of the twentieth century.[35]

While minority groups will always need a measure of exclusivity simply in order to survive, Edward Said rightly cautioned against the ideal of a restored people secured by an exclusivist political ideology.[36] A self-enclosed identity has lost the possibility for making new and redemptive connections. "Every identity therefore is a construction," Said insisted, "a composite of different histories, migrations, conquests, liberations, and so on. We can deal with these either as worlds at war, or as experiences to be reconciled."[37] Understanding this call for reconciliation in political terms, Alain Epp Weaver ironically combines Said's arguments with certain elements of post-Zionist thought that attempt to bring the theme of exile *into the very idea of the state*. The outcome of this paradoxical formulation is the advocacy of an inclusive, "diasporized" state, one that attempts a politically grounded reconciliation while steering away from nationalist ideologies that reinforce a dominant culture.[38]

The idea of a diasporized state fits awkwardly within a Mennonite theolog-

---

College, 1993), p. 19; Rainbow Spirit Elders, *Rainbow Spirit Theology* (Melbourne: Harper-Collins, 1997), p. 69.

34. Weaver, *States of Exile*, p. 17. Compare the insistence on the logic of return in John Milbank, "The Midwinter Sacrifice," in *The Blackwell Companion to Postmodern Theology*, ed. Graham Ward (Oxford: Blackwell, 2001), pp. 107-30, esp. 122-27.

35. See Daniele Conversi, "Conceptualizing Nationalism," in *Ethnonationalism in the Contemporary World*, ed. Conversi (London: Routledge, 2002), p. 10; Edward Said, "Reflections on Exile," in his *Reflections on Exile and Other Literary and Cultural Essays* (London: Granta, 2000), pp. 174 and 183; Brett, *Decolonizing God* (Sheffield: Phoenix, 2008), pp. 112-31.

36. Said, "Reflections on Exile," p. 177.

37. Edward Said, *The End of the Peace Process* (New York: Pantheon, 2000), p. 142.

38. Weaver, *States of Exile*, pp. 19 and 62. Cf. Partha Chatterjee, *The Nation and Its Fragments: Colonial and Postcolonial Histories* (Princeton: Princeton University Press, 1993).

ical tradition that advocates a strict separation of church and state. In *States of Exile*, however, Weaver takes care to identify Christian political advocacy as a matter of dealing with "one abuse at a time," rather than proposing a model Christian state. Here Weaver follows John Howard Yoder, who saw such political activities for others as no more than "signs" of the Kingdom. Avoiding the extremes of otherworldliness on the one hand, and realist defenses of states' interests on the other hand, Yoder sought to keep divinely motivated, inclusive politics mindful of the world to come.[39] In seeking a middle path between complete withdrawal and systematic involvement in political life, one could find a resonance here with Stanley Hauerwas's proposals for *ad hoc* ecclesial engagements in public life, adopting social practices that enrich the complex space between the individual and the state.[40]

If one sought to apply the model of a diasporized state in the context of settler colonial societies, models of legal pluralism and shared sovereignty would need to be explored, finding ways to include the polities of the First Nations and their *collective* rights.[41] Instead of excising Indigenous polities from the ideal political community, as Habermas appears to do, his particular conception of civic universality might be reconstructed in postcolonial terms that are more deliberately polycentric, in order to promote the participation of corporate polities within civil society, and not just individualist conceptions of cosmopolitan human rights.

In the next chapter, we will see that some of the possibilities for shared sovereignties were envisaged even within some of the settler colonial expansions of the early nineteenth century, although these possibilities were largely overwhelmed in the long run by economic interests. In the twentieth century, anti-colonial movements commonly led to Indigenous governments that often ironically exhibited new kinds of exclusionary politics and nativism.[42] In contrast, postcolonial political theory and theology have been exploring the

39. Michael G. Cartwright and Peter Ochs, eds., *The Jewish-Christian Schism Revisited: John Howard Yoder* (Grand Rapids: Eerdmans, 2003), p. 164; on political "signs," see Yoder, *The Royal Priesthood* (Grand Rapids: Eerdmans, 1994), p. 204; Cf. Weaver, *States of Exile*, pp. 62 and 93.

40. Hauerwas, *After Christendom? How the Church Is to Behave If Freedom, Justice, and a Christian Nation Are Bad Ideas* (Nashville: Abingdon, 1991), pp. 16-18; cf. Luke Bretherton, *Christianity and Contemporary Politics* (Oxford: Wiley-Blackwell, 2010), pp. 190-92.

41. See, e.g., Kayleen M. Hazlehurst, ed., *Legal Pluralism and the Colonial Legacy* (Aldershot: Avebury, 1995), and the recent overview provided by Paul L. A. H. Chartrand, "Reconciling Indigenous Peoples' Sovereignty and State Sovereignty." AIATSIS Research Discussion Paper 26, September 2009, available at http://www.aiatsis.gov.au/research/discussion.html.

42. Among many other examples, see Manu Goswami, *Producing India: From Colonial Economy to National Space* (Chicago: University of Chicago Press, 2004), pp. 10, 283-85.

possibilities for dominant groups sharing power, while weaker groups find new avenues for political participation. I would characterize both of these tasks as examples of *kenosis* or redemptive self-giving, which expand the social self into fresh networks of communion.[43]

It might seem overly paradoxical to include the self-assertion of weaker groups within a defense of kenotic theology. I have in mind especially the practice of non-violent protest that respects the humanity of political opponents while challenging their disproportionate command of power, and allowing for the possibility of renewed social connection in the long run. In the case of Mahatma Gandhi's resistance to British rule in India, *ahimsa* proved to be an effective inter-religious concept that shaped non-violent political assertion. In her recent study of postcolonial ethics, Susan Abraham has emphasized the religious content in Gandhi's discourse over and against commentators who have been inclined to diminish that content. Abraham does not explicitly link *ahimsa* to *kenosis*, although a number of analogies might be suggested (including the ultimate interconnectedness of human and non-human life). She shows how *ahimsa* as a political strategy was made broadly intelligible in India through a combination of Hindu and Jain doctrines, along with Gandhi's interpretation of the Sermon on the Mount.[44] The example illustrates the potential political significance of religious discourse in a postcolonial political mode.

Gandhi's model of political participation may, however, also provoke the question of whether it is actually possible to embody *ahimsa* in the regularized machinery of a state, even when a state like India has entrenched its ideals of equality in constitutional law. From a Christian and postcolonial point of view, I want to argue that it is not actually possible.[45]

This is because the procedural demands of equal treatment are ultimately incommensurable with the inherent relationality of love. Ecclesial solidarity is animated not so much by abstract ideals of equality, but is embodied as a "skein of human relations animated by *agape*," to use Charles Taylor's phrase.[46]

---

43. Cf. Antoinette Wire, *The Corinthian Women Prophets* (Minneapolis: Fortress Press, 1990), pp. 62-71; Sarah Coakley, "Kenosis and Subversion," reprinted in her *Powers and Submissions: Spirituality, Philosophy and Gender* (Oxford: Blackwell, 2002), pp. 36-37.

44. Susan Abraham, *Identity, Ethics and Nonviolence in Postcolonial Theory: A Rahnerian Theological Assessment* (New York: Palgrave Macmillan, 2007), esp. p. 49; cf. Daniel Philpott's comments on Archbishop Tutu's invocations of *ubuntu*, in Philpott, *Just and Unjust Peace*, pp. 117-18.

45. Cf. Gayatri Chakravorti Spivak, *A Critique of Postcolonial Reason: Toward a History of the Vanishing Present* (Cambridge, Mass.: Harvard University Press, 1999), pp. 383-84.

46. Taylor, *A Secular Age*, p. 277; cf. pp. 158, 282.

The parable of the Good Samaritan illustrates the point here, in Taylor's account, since it begins not with a theory of multicultural equality but with a personal connection in a specific context. Yet the narrative nevertheless points to the practical foundations of solidarity: "The enfleshment of God extends outward, through such new links as the Samaritan makes with the Jew, into a network we call the Church."[47] Taylor's claim is breathtakingly anachronistic as an ecclesiology, but it demonstrates the point that ever-expanding networks of *agape* inevitably cross the borders of national and cultural traditions, and accordingly, networks of communion are not reducible to the regularized procedures of a state bureaucracy.

The incommensurability between church and state, then, does not so much arise from the problem of religious language and its need for translation into public discourse. Rather, the key problem is that the surprising reciprocities of kenotic communion cannot be systematized into the neutral structures of procedural justice. Ecclesial forms of sociality would be compromised if they were constrained by abstract legal norms of justice, particularly the norms of justice framed by national boundaries.[48] Nevertheless, the commitments of a postcolonial church are thoroughly political — on the one hand resolutely opposed to abuses of power, and on the other hand working with marginalized groups to find their voice.

Reflecting further on the parable of the Good Samaritan, one would also need to insist that such networks of communion cannot be reduced to the forging of faith communities to the exclusion of other social groups. There are, in fact, an overwhelming number of biblical traditions that insist on the provision of care and resources to those who are outside the religious community. The prophets, for example, are consistently critical of religiosity that obscures the needs of the poor, as is the apostle Paul.[49] These traditions envisage a constant attention to the needs of the outsider, "the widow, orphan and alien," and provide a partial analogy for a state's concerns for disadvantaged citizens, except that a church's moral vision cannot be constrained by a state's borders.

47. Taylor, *A Secular Age*, p. 739.

48. Cf. Terry Veling, "In the Name of Who? Levinas and the Other Side of Theology," *Pacifica* 12 (1999): 275-92; Michael Wyschogrod, *The Body of Faith: Judaism as Corporeal Election* (Minneapolis: Seabury-Winston, 1983), pp. 58-65.

49. See especially Walter J. Houston, *Contending for Justice: Ideologies and Theologies of Social Justice in the Old Testament* (London: T&T Clark, 2nd ed. 2008); George Gotsis and Sarah Drakopoulou-Dodd, "Economic Ideas in the Pauline Epistles of the New Testament," *History of Economics Review* 3 (2002): 13-34.

The transnational life of the church and its agencies might imply that political theology also has significant contribution at the level of international law and policy.[50] But here again there would need to be a number of qualifications. The church in each place must seek a balance between its local commitments and its "universal" concerns, and there is no procedural logic that can readily resolve the tensions between these competing sets of norms. To the extent that energy and resources are absorbed by the local "widow, orphan and alien," that is precisely the extent to which we are sacrificing the needs of strangers in other places.[51] There is a paradox here that cannot be resolved by theoretical pretenses of universal solidarity.

It cannot be assumed, with ethnocentric confidence, that we already have all the vocabulary necessary to engage in acts of solidarity with those whose circumstances and concerns remain unknown to us until the complex work of relationship building has actually been undertaken. Actually engaging with the other means that our original standards of judgment may be transformed.[52] In theological terms, relationship building might be understood in terms of the doctrine of catholicity, as Miroslav Volf has shown.[53] And an adequate doctrine of catholicity proceeds from the concreteness of actual friendships and love, context by context in kenotic communion. This is not to say that universal economic and cultural rights are inconceivable in postcolonial terms, or that international aid and development initiatives are always misconceived, but only that such projects will always need to be conditioned by local contexts of inter-cultural negotiation.[54]

These issues will be further discussed in Chapter Eleven, but we may briefly

50. See, e.g., the historical account of the churches' participation in the UN Declaration of 1948 in John Nurser, *For All Peoples and All Nations: Christian Churches and Human Rights* (Washington: Georgetown University Press, 2005).

51. Mark G. Brett, "Abraham's 'Heretical' Imperative: A Response to Jacques Derrida," in *The Meanings We Choose: Hermeneutical Ethics, Indeterminacy and the Conflict of Interpretations*, ed. Charles Cosgrove (London: T&T Clark International, 2004), pp. 167-78.

52. Charles Taylor, "The Politics of Recognition," in *Multiculturalism and "The Politics of Recognition,"* ed. Amy Gutman (Princeton: Princeton University Press, 1992), pp. 67 and 70.

53. See the reformulation of catholicity in Miroslav Volf, *Exclusion and Embrace: A Theological Exploration of Identity, Otherness, and Reconciliation* (Nashville: Abingdon, 1996), 48-55. Cf. Abraham, *Identity*, pp. 109-120, 129-34, and from an explicitly evangelical perspective, Kevin Vanhoozer, "One Rule to Rule them All?" in *Globalizing Theology: Belief and Practice in an Era of World Christianity*, ed. Craig Ott and Harold A. Netland (Grand Rapids: Baker Academic, 2006), pp. 85-126.

54. Cf. Linda Hogan, "A Different Mode of Encounter: Egalitarian Liberalism and the Christian Tradition," *Political Theology* 7/1 (2006): 59-73.

acknowledge here that the churches urgently need a more rigorous under-standing of the neo-colonial operation of global markets. In his recent book *Justice: Rights and Wrongs,* Nicholas Wolterstorff reminds us that Christian conceptions of economic rights should be seen as the inalienable gifts of God, which is to say that they cannot be traded or degraded within a market.[55] Accordingly an adequate Christian understanding of human rights — and particularly of economic, social and cultural rights — does not in fact slide into individualist liberalism, but rather provokes *agape* into an ever-widening kenotic embodiment of intercultural communion. The language of human rights is today a *lingua franca* of secular democracies, but biblical traditions have their particular contributions to make to this conversation.

Postcolonial public theology explores the meanings and practices that embody more generous "polyphonic" societies, both nationally and interna-tionally. It is precisely those generous societies that must take action against the recent manifestations of empire that threaten to turn the world into the "smooth space" of global capital, in effect converting the old face-to-face coer-cion of slavery into more subtle forms of economic compulsion. Communities of faith need to summon the courage of our kenotic convictions: repenting of unsustainable levels of consumption, shifting resources to where they are needed, and expanding our networks of communion.

CONCLUSION

In conversation with Habermas, I have suggested that it is important at this time to restate our understanding of the separation of church and state from the point of view of Christian theology. In particular, I have begun to identify some of the postcolonial theological reasoning that supports this separation. In Part Two of this volume, I will argue that even the Hebrew Bible can be read in a way that effectively supports a separation of religion and state, even though this is not the case in the classic statement of national theology in the book of Deuteronomy. To foreshadow the argument briefly, it will be suggested that the Priestly tradition of the Hebrew Bible can be seen as part of a lively debate with the Deuteronomistic tradition about how to relinquish Israel's own political sovereignty, while retaining substantive political and religious ethics vis-à-vis the poor and the stranger. It is the Priestly tradition that points the way to an

---

55. Nicholas Wolterstorff, *Justice: Rights and Wrongs* (Princeton: Princeton University Press, 2008); Cf. Brian Tierney, *The Idea of Natural Rights* (Atlanta: Scholars Press, 1997).

international conception of human rights, rather than a national conception that relies on domestic legislation.

The exploration of inner-biblical conversation will also illustrate why it would be misleading to suggest, as both Habermas and Taylor do, that critical deliberation in pre-modern times was severely burdened by the weight of metaphysics. The hermeneutical enterprise was no doubt conducted in very different terms in biblical times, but I suggest that the theological question of how to separate religion and the state was already well articulated by the Priestly tradition in a series of proposals that were distinctly different from national theology. The biblical canon preserves such differences, and far from closing down rational deliberation, its many different voices may still point to appropriate models of political discourse and action — without presuming that biblical norms require either a theocratic state, or at the very least, philosophical translation into thin secular language for democratic contexts. Before turning to the inner-biblical conversations, however, it will be necessary to investigate in more detail the character of postcolonial justice and how this understanding of justice may shape the ethics of reading the biblical literature.

At this stage, we may conclude that democracy is not best served by a thinning of public norms in search of a unified public culture, but rather, by a thickening of dialogue between religious and non-religious traditions. Theological ethics orientated towards the marginalized ("widows, orphans and aliens" in biblical discourse) can and should inform the praxis of more inclusive, postcolonial democracies.

2. Justice and Postcolonial Challenges

The previous chapter identified some of the issues at stake in recent attempts to enrich secular democratic dialogue with the inclusion of religious voices. Jürgen Habermas's model of post-secular discourse was introduced as a paradigm case of the ambivalence that besets such attempts, even at the level of theory, to reframe what might count as reasonable in public debates. We also saw that the inclusion of Indigenous voices presents an older and perhaps deeper challenge for democratic processes, and in this connection also, theology has a high profile. Any attempt to undo the complex legacies of colonialism in pursuit of restorative justice will require some detailed attention to the interweaving of Christian discourse with the historic injustices of racism, slavery and dispossession of Indigenous peoples from traditional lands.

In agreement with Habermas, I noted that a good deal of the political violence experienced in the world today can be understood in light of the failures of decolonization, and accordingly we need a careful analysis of the elements of postcolonial justice. Rather than assuming that historic injustices have no particular relevance for democracies today, I want to argue that the legacies of these injustices endure in several different ways — not just in the obvious sense that current generations are the beneficiaries of inherited wealth that was unjustly acquired. In Part Three of this volume it will be argued that current neoliberal assumptions share with the older forms of colonialism a fatal incapacity to deal with the most substantive economic and ecological challenges today.

The historic problems of colonialism have, ironically, been shaped at points by competing notions of distributive and utilitarian justice. It is necessary to understand some of these historic mutations before we proceed to any account of how biblical traditions may, or may not, inform postcolonial Christian contributions to a just political order. I will argue that although each notion of justice may have its own validity in particular contexts of application, it is the concept of restorative justice that has an overarching value and is most needed today, particularly in societies that were founded on the assumptions of settler colonialism. In providing an account of what restorative justice looks like in political practice, it will be argued in the following chapters that the biblical literature has a significant role to play in shaping restorative measures.

First, we begin by acknowledging an essential tension between theories of justice and the complexities of actual political and legal practice. In his significant recent analysis of this tension, *The Idea of Justice*, Amartya Sen deliberately sets aside philosophical theories that begin by envisaging (as Habermas does) regulative ideals and institutions for public discourse. Sen prefers instead to begin with the variety of political and economic practices that seek above all to make the world less unjust than it currently is, arguing for example, that the discourse of human rights may be strategically effective even before we solve any of the philosophical questions as to the *foundations* of human rights.[1] Following the lead of Sen and his school, we will examine in this chapter some of the competing notions of justice at work in colonial history, not in order to provide a new system of regulative theory, but rather, to explore the question of how postcolonial Christian practice might help to make the world less unjust than what we find in the current order of things. In the previous chapter I argued that Christian practices can make this kind of contribution to public life even when "networks of *agape*" or "kenotic communion" are ultimately incommensurable with the procedural justice of democratic states.

CATHOLIC COLONIALISM

In beginning to reflect on the legacies of colonial trauma, it must be confessed that the tides of empires have ebbed and flowed throughout history, and one may doubt whether a general theory of imperialism is either possible or even desirable. More relevant to the experience of Western democracies are the particular chapters of imperial expansion that began in the fifteenth century when Spanish and Portuguese monarchs divided the globe under papal oversight, initially in the papal decree *Inter Caetera* of 1493 and then in the Treaty of Tordesillas of 1494, which established a theoretical line of demar-

1. Amartya Sen, *The Idea of Justice* (London: Allen Lane, 2009).

cation through South America that was literally a global meridian running between the Arctic and Antarctic poles. The *Inter Caetera* of 1493 was focused on Spanish interests, so the Portuguese king John II felt compelled a year later to negotiate with King Ferdinand and Queen Isabella of Spain to move the global meridian some distance to the west, in order to make more room for Portuguese expansion.

In this respect, papal authority sat a small distance behind the details of the Treaty of Tordesillas, but this was a political nuance that made little difference to the underlying theological assumption of the day, namely, that the Christian church mediated the divine sovereignty of the Creator over the whole earth, and therefore Catholic monarchs could be regarded as divine viceroys wherever new worlds were "discovered." The assumption of global, papal jurisdiction was not universally accepted — not even by some Catholic jurists at the time — but the brute force of the Iberian monarchs found sufficient theological sanction in their own eyes.[2] The suffering of Indigenous people was ultimately enfolded within a theological claim of divine providence that ordained Christian rule over Indian and African peoples.

A link between blackness and slavery was long established in medieval traditions shared by Jews, Christians, and Muslims alike (encapsulated in widespread interpretations of the "curse of Ham" in Genesis 9), so the slave regimes of the New World represented not a radically new beginning in this respect but an elaboration of old racial schemes.[3] The cases of explicit Catholic resistance to Indian slavery, notably expressed by Bartolomé de las

---

2. Alasdair MacIntyre points out that Thomas Aquinas reiterated the standard medieval view that found no difficulty in principle with papal intervention, as required, in secular (temporal) affairs. *Whose Justice? Which Rationality?* (Notre Dame: University of Notre Dame Press, 1988), p. 201, citing from *Summa Theologiae* IIa-IIae, 60,6 and *Contra Errores Graecorum* ii, 32. Francisco de Vitoria (1483-1546) defended the Spanish rights to travel, to trade and to convert the local population to Christianity, but rejected papal jurisdiction over land in the New World by affirming the property rights of the Indians. See Brian Tierney, *The Idea of Natural Rights* (Atlanta: Scholars, 1997), pp. 265-71; Cf. Yvonne Sherword, "Francisco de Vitoria's More Excellent Way: How the Bible of Empire Discovered the Tricks of [the Argument from] Trade," *Biblical Interpretation* 21 (2013): 215-75.

3. David M. Goldenberg, *The Curse of Ham: Race and Slavery in Early Judaism, Christianity, and Islam* (Princeton: Princeton University Press, 2003). It should be noted here that Islamic jurists did not produce anything comparable to the elaborate racial hierarchies proposed in Christian missiology of the early colonial period. See, e.g., the discussion of the Jesuit Allessandro Valignano (1539-1606) in Willie James Jennings, *The Christian Imagination: Theology and the Origins of Race* (New Haven: Yale University Press, 2010), pp. 31-36, and the nuanced discussion of Bernard Lewis, *Race and Slavery in the Middle East* (New York: Oxford University Press, 1990).

Casas (1474–1564), were couched as a plea for more humanitarian schemes of dispossession. His critique of the theories of just war against the Indians provided no substantial questioning of the basic racial hierarchy that assigned black Africans to slavery.[4] Las Casas initially suggested, for example, that Spanish colonists might hold black slaves, rather than Indians, although he retreated from this opinion in later life when it became clear to him that African slaves had not been taken in just wars.[5] His critique of colonial violence did not amount to a complete rejection of just war theory as such, nor of the legitimacy of taking slaves in wars deemed to be just. In this respect, colonial accounts of slavery, both Christian and Islamic, extrapolated from scriptural sources but also at times from classical warrants in Aristotle, who had no difficulty in finding rational justification for wars against people who were in any case slaves "by nature."[6]

PROTESTANT COLONIALISM

Protestant colonial initiatives, on the other hand, necessarily began with different approaches to justice. They were on principle opposed both to Aristotelian philosophy and to papal authority, but arguments from Scripture and from natural law persisted nonetheless. The Puritan colonists of Massachusetts provide some early examples of Protestant invocations of Genesis in colonial discourse, and in ways that provided antecedents for the idea

4. Bartolomé de las Casas, *The Only Way to Draw All People to a Living Faith*, ed. Helen Rand (New York: Paulist, 1992). Contrast the notorious argument of Juan Ginés de Sepúlveda, *Tratado sobre las justas causas de la guerra contra los Indios* (Mexico City: Fondo de Cultura Económica, 1979), discussed in Pablo Richard, "Biblical Interpretation from the Perspective of Indigenous Cultures of Latin America (Mayas, Kunas and Quechuas)," in *Ethnicity and the Bible*, ed. Mark G. Brett (BIS 19; Leiden: Brill, 1996), pp. 298-301; Tierney, *The Idea of Natural Rights*, pp. 255-87.

5. Louis Rivera, *A Violent Evangelism: The Political and Religious Conquest of the Americas* (Louisville: Westminster John Knox, 1992), 183-95; Lawrence A. Clayton, *Bartolomé de Las Casas and the Conquest of the Americas* (Oxford: Wiley-Blackwell, 2011), pp. 135-42; cf. A. C. de C. M. Saunders' discussion of "Legal and Philosophical Justifications of the Slave Trade," *A Social History of Black Slaves in Portugal, 1441-1555* (Cambridge: Cambridge University Press, 1982), pp. 35-46. On the affirmation of Indian property rights in the late work of Las Casas, see Tierney, *The Idea of Natural Rights*, pp. 272-86.

6. Bernard Lewis, *Race and Slavery*, pp. 54-56, citing Aristotle's *Politics* 1254b20, 1255a1ff., 1255a8, 1278b23; see also Joel L. Kraemer, "The Jihad of the Falasifa," *Jerusalem Studies in Arabic and Islam* 10 (1987): 313 for the Islamic Aristotelian literature.

of "waste" lands in later international law. Robert Cushman, for example, proposed in 1622 an argument that was to become foundational in many different contexts:

> As the ancient patriarchs . . . removed from straighter places into more roomy, where the land lay idle and waste, and none used it, though there dwelt inhabitants by them (as Genesis 13:6, 11, 12 and 34:21 and 41:20), so it is lawful now to take a land which none useth, and make use of it.[7]

While Protestants from time to time cited the precedent of violent expansion in the book of Joshua, configuring themselves as a New Israel pitted against new Canaanites, it is in fact the notion of unused land that was to become more significant in legal histories from the seventeenth century onwards. The concept of "waste" land was, as we shall see, linked to concepts of distributive justice and economic opportunity as Protestant imperial competition unfolded.[8]

Secular theories of international law in the seventeenth century gave no special place to the authority of Scripture, as the Puritans had, and instead reframed the idea of just war by drawing on a broad range of classical sources in order to establish a system of natural rights, including Indigenous rights.[9] Hugo Grotius, for example, in his foundational work *The Rights of War and Peace* (1645), argued that although colonial expansion could be justified on the grounds of efficient usage of land, such expansion did not extinguish the land rights and political autonomy of native tribes. As we noted in the Introduction, Grotius did not regard the Bible as the preeminent source for international legal argument, yet he was able to argue from scriptural precedent when affirming native rights of occupation. Thus, in *De jure belli ac pacis* (chapter 4, sect. II) he writes:

---

7. Robert Cushman, *Reasons and Considerations Touching the Lawfulness of Removing out of England into the Parts of America* (1622), as quoted in Alan Heimert and Andrew Delbanco, *The Puritans in America: A Narrative Anthology* (Cambridge, Mass.: Harvard University Press, 2005), p. 44.

8. See the historical overview provided by Jane Burbank and Frederick Cooper, *Empires in World History: Power and the Politics of Difference* (Princeton: Princeton University Press, 2010), pp. 117-84.

9. Eric Wilson, *Savage Republic: De Indis of Hugo Grotius, Republicanism and Dutch Hegemony within the Early Modern World System, c.1600-1619* (Leiden: Brill, 2008), pp. 467-512; cf. Martine Julia Van Ittersum, *Profit and Principle: Hugo Grotius, Natural Rights Theories and the Rise of Dutch Power in the East Indies, 1595-1615* (Leiden: Brill, 2006).

To disturb any one in the actual and long possession of territory has in all ages been considered as repugnant to the general interests and feelings of mankind. For we find in holy writ, that when the King of the Ammonites demanded the lands situated between the rivers Arnon and Jabok, and those extending from the deserts of Arabia to the Jordan, Jephthah opposed his pretentions by proving his own possession of the same for three hundred years.[10]

The claim to traditional land rights in the biblical passage adduced by Grotius is, of course, logically opposed to the famous texts in Deuteronomy and Joshua which deny the prior inhabitants of the Promised Land any traditional rights. (Indeed, in Judges 11, the appeal to three hundred years of possession in 11:26 is supplemented by a divinely legitimated right of conquest asserted by Jephthah in 11:21, and the Ammonite possession of territory is taken to be an act of their own national deity in Judges 11:24.) The selective reading of the Jephthah narrative in *De jure belli ac pacis* seems to be one among a range of exegetical examples in which Grotius's interpretation of Scripture stands against prior hermeneutical traditions.[11]

Whatever one makes of Grotius's hermeneutical motives, however, his argument for traditional rights of occupation became a foundation stone for subsequent developments in thinking about colonial justice. Beginning from the acknowledgment of such traditional rights, there arose in international legal theory a higher standard of engagement with Indigenous peoples that envisaged the possibility of negotiation between sovereign polities. Emmerich de Vattel's *The Law of Nations* (1758), for example, holds up William Penn's treaty of 1682 with the Delaware Indians as a model which:

notwithstanding being furnished with a Charter from their sovereign, purchased of the Indians the land of which they intended to take possession. This laudable example was followed by William Penn and the colony of Quakers that he conducted to Pennsylvania.[12]

---

10. Hugo Grotius, *The Rights of War and Peace, Including the Law of Nature and of Nations*, trans. A. C. Campbell (Pontefract: B. Boothroyd, 1814), p. 295.

11. For a detailed analysis, see especially Mark Samos, "Secularization in *De Iure Praedae*: from Bible Criticism to International Law," *Grotiana* 26-28 (2005-2007): 147-91.

12. Emmerich de Vattel, *The Law of Nations; or, Principles of the Law of Nature, applied to the conduct and affairs of Nations and Sovereigns* (London: G. G. and J. Robinson, Paternoster-Row, 1797), p. 101.

The admiration for Penn expressed in secular legal theory is an interesting example of how the theological motives of the Quakers were translated by Vattel into a public language and reconfigured as a secular model of justice. This translation perhaps has some affinities with Habermas's theory of post-secular discourse, discussed in Chapter One, and in this case the Quakers themselves were in turn to build the philosophical theories of natural rights quite explicitly into their theological vision. Quaker political ethics in the early nineteenth century, for example, were influenced in part by the legal ideas of Grotius and Vattel in the campaigns against slavery and the defenses of Indigenous rights.[13]

With regard to the colonial acquisition of land, Grotius had distinguished between waste lands on the one hand, and inhabited lands on the other, providing a defense of Indigenous rights in the case of inhabited land. This became a fundamental distinction for the Aborigines Protection Society, established in Britain in 1838.[14] For example, when discussing Maori rights, we find Louis Chamerovzow making specific reference to the distinction in Grotius's *The Rights of War and Peace* along with Vattel's *The Law of Nations*, where it is proclaimed that "all men have an equal right to the things that have not yet fallen into the possession of anyone." Chamerovzow insists that New Zealand was clearly inhabited, and no presumed "right of discovery" could circumvent this fact. And again adducing Vattel's authority, he argued that if the presumed right of discovery were asserted merely by a "vain ceremony" rather than by actual settlement, such a right would have no more meaning than "the arrangement of the Popes, who divided a great part of the world between the Crowns of Castile and Portugal."[15] Chamerovzow draws the conclusion that:

13. Jonathan Dymond, *Essays on the Principles of Morality and on the Private and Political Rights and Obligations of Mankind,* 2 volumes (London: Hamilton, Adams and Co., 1829); Cf. Thomas Clarkson, *A Portraiture of Quakerism* (London: Longman, Hurst, Rees and Orme, 1806).

14. See the defence of Aboriginal sovereignty and the advocacy of treaties in the APS submission to the British parliament in Standish Motte, *Outline of a system of legislation, for securing protection to the aboriginal inhabitants of all countries colonized by Great Britain; extending to them political and social rights, ameliorating their condition, and promoting their civilization* (London: John Murray, 1840), pp. 13-14.

15. Louis A. Chamerovzow, *The New Zealand Question and the Rights of Aborigines* (London: T. C. Newby, 1848), pp. 23-25, 36-39, making use of a new translation of Vattel's work by Joseph Chitty. Emmerich de Vattel, *The Law of Nations; or, Principles of the Law of Nature, applied to the conduct and affairs of Nations and Sovereigns* (London: S. Sweet, Chancery Lane, Stevens and Sons, 1834).

If native tribes, that is, Aboriginal nations are to be shut out from the great system of inter-national polity, and declared incompetent to the exercise of sovereign power over themselves, simply because they differ from us in customs and habits, then is opened a wide field for oppression, injustice and inhumanity.[16]

This passage goes to one of the fundamental flaws in the practice of the treaty tradition as it unfolded in the nineteenth century. Chamerovzow interprets Grotius and Vattel to be saying that "'discovery' confers no *proprietary* title to any such lands as are already in occupancy, even though of a savage or heathen people"; indeed, the discovering nation can "assert no title at all." Thus, Chamerovzow explicitly denounces William Blackstone's legal fiction that had been extrapolated from feudal to colonial arrangements in order to assert that "the King is the source of all title" whether land is inhabited or not.[17] But this extrapolation was already well entrenched in its secular mutation in America, even when there was no longer a king to underwrite its law of discovery.

A SECULAR DOCTRINE OF DISCOVERY

Anglophone colonists were well aware that a medieval fiction had been inscribed in American law by Chief Justice John Marshall in the early nineteenth century, when he provided a distinction between Indian "occupancy" of land and underlying title. Behind this legal subtlety lay a secularized version of the doctrine of discovery, which Justice Marshall set out in the following terms in *Johnson v. McIntosh* (1823):

The potentates of the old world found no difficulty in convincing themselves that they made ample compensation to the inhabitants of the new, by bestowing on them civilization and Christianity. . . . But, as they were all in pursuit of nearly the same object, it was necessary, in order to avoid conflicting settlements, and consequent war with each other, to establish a principle . . . that discovery gave title to the government by whose subjects, or by whose authority, it was made, against all other European governments. . . . The exclusion of all other Europeans necessarily gave to the nation making the discovery the sole right of acquiring the soil from the

16. Chamerovzow, *Rights of Aborigines*, pp. 48-49.
17. Chamerovzow, *Rights of Aborigines*, pp. 42 and 45.

natives. . . . [The Indians] were admitted to be the rightful *occupants* of the soil . . . but their rights to complete sovereignty, as independent nations, were necessarily diminished, and their power to dispose of the soil at their own will, to whomsoever they pleased, was denied by the original fundamental principle, that discovery gave exclusive *title* to those who made it.[18]

The notion of limited sovereignty then allowed Marshall to speak of "domestic dependent nations" from whom land could be purchased, and with whom the discovering European nation could negotiate treaties.

There were hundreds of treaties negotiated before the *Johnson v. McIntosh* case in 1823, but this judgment provided a devastating legal wedge that could be wielded in all subsequent interpretations of treaties. Even James Stephen, the influential undersecretary of the Colonial Office in London from 1836 to 1847, was moved to write concerning *Johnson v. McIntosh* that the British colonial law in Canada was "far more humane" than what he found in "American Law," since in Canada the Crown had to purchase land from the Indians before it could be granted to any British subjects. Indeed, he goes on to say that

> Whatever may be the ground occupied by international jurists they never forget the policy and interests of their own Country. Their business is to give to rapacity and injustice, the most decorous veil which legal ingenuity can weave.[19]

This comment, written in 1839 by an Anglican bureaucrat, is hardly less biting than recent Indigenous studies that describe the doctrine of discovery as a bizarre feat of social imagination, imposed by sheer force and enabled by a racialized imagination living off borrowed plots from ancient Israel.[20]

18. *Johnson v. McIntosh* (1823), 21 U. S. (8 Wheaton), 572-74. There are good reasons to think that this watershed case should be regarded as invalid even in terms of procedural justice. See the detailed historical analysis in Lindsay G. Robertson, *Conquest by Law: How the Discovery of America Dispossessed Indigenous Peoples of Their Lands* (New York: Oxford University Press, 2005). The *Johnson* opinion provided a lever for forced migrations under the *Indian Removal Act* of 1830, a tragedy that Marshall himself attempted to address in *Worcester v. Georgia* (1832), but the floodgates had been opened.

19. James Stephen, memorandum to the parliamentary undersecretary, 28 July 1839. Quoted in Paul Knaplund, *James Stephen and the British Colonial System, 1813-1847* (Madison: University of Wisconsin Press, 1953), p. 89.

20. Steven T. Newcomb, *Pagans in the Promised Land: Decoding the Doctrine of Christian Discovery* (Golden: Fulcrum, 2008); Robert Miller, Jacinta Ruru, Larissa Behrendt, Tracey Lindberg, *Discovering Indigenous Lands: The Doctrine of Discovery in the English Colonies*

Despite the strenuous efforts of James Stephen as colonial undersecretary, his views seem to have had little effect beyond his period of official service. And his perception that there was a greater measure of justice in the British colonies of his day would be considered questionable by many legal commentators. The United States has recognized the internal sovereignty of Indigenous nations (as opposed to international sovereignty), and thus created separate jurisdictions in many Indian territories, whereas Canada, New Zealand and Australia have generally used parliamentary sovereignty to deny even Justice Marshall's notion of "domestic dependant nations."[21] Furthermore, Australia continues to distinguish itself in the world of former British colonies in having secured with its Indigenous nations no treaties at all. James Stephen apparently pushed for treaties in the new colony of South Australia, which was under construction in the early years of his tenure as undersecretary, and he (along with a number of other evangelical and Quaker reformers) was influential in the background of the Treaty of Waitangi in New Zealand,[22] but he was not able to implement his treaty policy either in South Australia or in the new colony of Victoria.

SOUTH AUSTRALIA AND VICTORIA IN THE 1830S

The failure to negotiate treaties in the Australian colonies has been the focus of renewed historical research in recent years, and it is a complex story of competing notions of justice that has some analogies with the American experience even though the legal outcomes were different on each continent. While it is not possible to analyze all the contributing factors, a brief look at the founding of South Australia and Victoria will be instructive as to the key issues at stake in our discussion. *The South Australian Colonization Act* of 1834 did not specifically mention treaties, but there was a change of British government in 1835,

---

(Oxford: Oxford University Press, 2010); Walter R. Echo-Hawk, "Colonialism and Law in the Postcolonial Era," in *Coming to Terms: Aboriginal Title in South Australia*, ed. Sean Berg (Kent Town: Wakefield Press, 2010), pp. 148-205; Kay Higuera Smith, Jayachitra Lalitha and L. Daniel Hawk, eds., *Evangelical Postcolonial Conversations: Global Awakenings in Theology and Practice* (Downers Grove: InterVarsity Press, 2014).

21. Kent McNeil, "Judicial Treatment of Indigenous Land Rights in the Common Law World," in *Indigenous Peoples and the Law: Comparative and Critical Perspectives*, ed. Benjamin J. Richardson, Shin Imai, and Kent McNeil (Oxford: Hart, 2009), pp. 257-58.

22. See the overview provided in Knaplund, *James Stephen*, pp. 66-94.

and in 1836 the colonial administration received Letters Patent from the king adding new strictures on the implementation of the colony's founding statute:

> PROVIDED ALWAYS that nothing in those our Letters Patent contained shall affect or be construed to affect the rights of any Aboriginal Natives of the said Province to the actual occupation or enjoyment in their own Person or in the Persons of their Descendants of any Land therein now actually occupied or enjoyed by such Natives.

The Commissioners empowered by the original statute then issued instructions in 1836 to the Resident Commissioner in South Australia itself, reiterating the terms of the king's Letters Patent:

> You will see that no lands which the natives may possess in occupation or enjoyment be offered for sale until previously ceded by the natives to yourself. You will furnish the protector of the aborigines with evidence of the faithful fulfillment of the bargain or treaties which you may effect with the aborigines for the cession of lands.[23]

This is exactly the policy that James Stephen generally promoted, as mentioned above in relation to his memorandum from three years later, condemning the judgment in *Johnson v. McIntosh*. As was the case in Canada, the land of the South Australian colony was to be ceded first by treaty before it was sold to British citizens. This had not been the practice in the earlier colony of New South Wales, which was at this stage established within a limited compass, but here was a new age of evangelical vision, fresh from the successes of the anti-slavery movement in Britain.

As history unfolded, however, this was indeed more a case of vision than practice. Not only did the South Australian administration fail to negotiate any treaties, but at the same time, the Colonial Office rejected a treaty initiative in the area that was to become the colony of Victoria. In 1835, on behalf of a private company, John Batman negotiated what he understood to be a treaty in Port Philip (the site of the later city of Melbourne), and while he was styled "the Tasmanian Penn" in the local press at the time, he was not an agent of the

---

23. Quoted in Sean Brennan, "The Disregard for Legal Protections of Aboriginal Land Rights in Early South Australia," in Berg, ed., *Coming to Terms*, pp. 90-121, 101. The *South Australia Amendment Act* of 1838 includes a provision in the same terms provided by the king in the Letters Patent of 1836. See Act 1 and 2 Victoria, Cap 60, reprinted in *Coming to Terms*, 390.

Crown and therefore not authorized to make a treaty. The complexities in this case are similar to those in *Johnson v. McIntosh*, since in the American case the leading question was also whether a private company could treat with the Indians.[24] Nevertheless, what remains unclear is why the Colonial Office in London did not press for valid treaties in Victoria and South Australia.

In attempting to answer this question, the historian James Boyce contrasts two pieces of communication in 1836 from the Secretary of State for the Colonies. The first letter, written in January to the Governor in Hobart, clearly rejects the Batman project on the grounds of established policy, noting that unlicensed settlement "exposed both natives and the new settlers to many dangers and calamities." The conclusion was that such settlement should be restrained. A second letter, written a few months later to the Governor in Sydney, adopts a quite different tone. This letter celebrates the achievements of English industry in two colonies of New South Wales and Van Diemen's Land, having in the past half century "converted unproductive waste into two great flourishing provinces." Commenting on the unauthorized settlement at Port Philip, the letter concedes that "It is perhaps inevitable that the sanguine ardor of private speculation should quicken and anticipate the more cautious movements of the Government," giving passive license to the expansion of settlements.[25] As has so often been the case in Australian history, matters of principle were overwhelmed by economic interests. The Legislative Council of New South Wales then introduced a law in July 1836 allowing persons who could afford the fees to purchase a license to use Crown land, rather than purchase a title to the land, and thus began the regime of the pastoralists or "squatters." Subsequently, an Aboriginal Protector was appointed, with no powers to protect the traditional ownership of land or other natural resources.

ECONOMIC UTILITARIANISM AND COLONIAL EXPANSION

James Stephen expressed many regrets about the situation of Australian Aboriginal people in the late 1830s, but he seems to have labored both with competing concepts of justice and with a pragmatic resignation about the power of London's officials to influence the local practice of colonial ad-

24. The complexities of the John Batman story have been discussed in Bain Attwood, *Possession: Batman's Treaty and the Matter of History* (Melbourne: Miegunyah Press, 2009); and James Boyce, *1835: The Founding of Melbourne and the Conquest of Australia* (Melbourne: Black Inc, 2011).

25. Boyce, *1835*, pp. 127-30; cf. Attwood, *Possession*, pp. 72-101.

ministration. When later given opportunity to reflect on the beginnings of the colony in Victoria, he referred only to the "small body of English adventurers" who had within roughly two decades given birth to settlements "now inhabited by half a million of free men" along with a capital city "as large and as populous as Oxford." In an address to the National Association for the Promotion of Social Science in 1858, Stephen defended the justice of colonization against its critics, not in terms of Aboriginal rights but in relation to the good government that could disprove the "dismal science" of Thomas Malthus. Malthus had presented a version of political economy in his celebrated *Essay on Population* (1798), arguing that unless population growth was restrained, it would outstrip food supplies. Malthus's prophecy, according to Stephen, was false because he had not anticipated the changes wrought by a range of political reforms and technological innovations, including the "commercial enfranchisement" brought by the abolition of slavery and colonial self-government.[26]

James Stephen passionately affirmed the value of legal reforms, and indeed he drafted the *Slavery Abolition Act* of 1833, but he also lived at a time when the early theories of capitalism were thoroughly imbued with the spirit of natural theology.[27] In Britain, Thomas Chalmers had famously forged a systematic combination of moral theory and economics, even more explicitly than Adam Smith had himself achieved in his bi-focal vision set out in *The Theory of Moral Sentiments* and *The Wealth of Nations*. International trade was promoted as a civilizing influence in accord with the will of God.[28]

---

26. James Stephen, "Colonization as a Branch of Social Economy," reprinted in Knaplund, *James Stephen and the British Colonial System*, pp. 281-98, esp. pp. 288 and 297.

27. See especially, Thomas Chalmers, *On Political Economy: In Connection with the Moral State and Moral Prospects of Society* (Glasgow: Collins, 1832); Thomas Chalmers, *On the Power, Wisdom and Goodness of God Manifested in the Adaption of External Nature to the Moral and Intellectual Constitution of Man* (Philadelphia: Carey, Lea and Blanchard, 1833); Stewart Davenport, *Friends of the Unrighteous Mammon: Northern Christians and Market Capitalism, 1815-1860* (Chicago: University of Chicago Press, 2008); Boyd Hilton, *The Age of Atonement: The Influence of Evangelicalism on Social and Economic Thought, 1785-1965* (Oxford: Oxford University Press, 1988).

28. See for example John McVickar, "Introductory Lecture to a Course on Political Economy," *Banner of the Constitution* 1/35 (1830): 273, cited in Davenport, *Unrighteous Mammon*, pp. 61 and 80-81; cf. Francis Weyland, *The Elements of Political Economy* (New York: Leavitt, Lord, 4th ed. 1854), p. 15. On the making of commercial civilization, see the overview provided by Charles Taylor, *A Secular Age* (Cambridge, MA: Belknap, 2007), pp. 159-85; Albert O. Hirshman, *The Passions and the Interests: Political Arguments for Capitalism before Its Triumph* (Princeton: Princeton University Press, 1977).

Indeed, the civilizing influence of trade was regularly combined with the civilizing influence of Christianity to provide utilitarian evidence for the justice of colonization.[29] The greatest good for the greatest number could then outweigh the regrettable suffering of the poor and of the Indigenous peoples of the colonies, while, taken as a whole, the social economy was blessed by a higher providence. Explaining in 1833 the way that providence supervened on the ardor of private interests, Thomas Chalmers wrote:

> The greatest economic good is rendered to the community, by each man being left to consult and to labour for his own particular good — or, in other words, a more prosperous result is obtained by the spontaneous play and busy competition of many thousand wills, each bent on the prosecution of its own selfishness, than by the anxious superintendance of a government, vainly attempting to medicate the fancied imperfections of nature . . . it is then that markets are best supplied; that commodities are furnished for general use, of best quality, and in greatest cheapness . . . and the most free and rapid augmentation takes place in the riches and resources of the commonwealth. Such a result . . . strongly bespeaks a higher agent, by whose transcendental wisdom it is, that all is made to conspire so harmoniously and to terminate so beneficially. . . . When we look at the effect of this universal principle, in cheapening and multiplying to the uttermost all the articles of human enjoyment, and establishing a thousand reciprocities of mutual interest in the world — we see in this the benevolence and comprehensive wisdom of God.[30]

With practical theology like this circulating among the decision makers of the Anglo-World, it becomes easy to understand how Aboriginal rights would succumb to the rights of settlers.[31]

Within a year of Chalmers's publication quoted above, the passing of the British *Poor Law Amendment Act* in 1834 represented a triumph of the new economics, which removed poverty relief from the parish system and thereby created a floating market of labor. According to Karl Polanyi's classic account of these changes,

---

29. E.g., James Stephen, "Colonization as a Branch of Social Economy," p. 284.

30. Chalmers, *On the Power, Wisdom and Goodness of God*, pp. 172-73.

31. See especially the overview provided by James Belich, *Replenishing the Earth: The Settler Revolution and the Rise of the Anglo-World, 1783-1939* (Oxford: Oxford University Press, 2009).

> To separate labor from other activities of life and to subject it to the
> laws of the market was to annihilate all organic forms of existence and
> to replace them by a different type of organization, an atomistic and
> individualistic one.[32]

If the "organic forms of existence" were undermined in England, the impact
on Indigenous polities in the colonies would be even greater.

America was commonly seen as the place where the iron grip of European
poverty could be escaped. The historian James Huston has demonstrated how
this popular conviction was enhanced by an ideal of distributive justice that
has animated American politics at least since the Revolutionary War, beginning with the agrarian vision that each person was properly rewarded with the
benefits of one's own labor. Thus, an editorial in the *New York Times* in 1857
summarized a common version of American exceptionalism by suggesting
that "the doctrine that a man has a right to be supplied with labor and wages by
the government or anybody, whether his services are needed or not, is a doctrine which took its rise in aristocratic countries in which the working classes
are in a position of degradation and dependence."[33] The colonial American
model of distributive justice was thereby opposed to government intervention
and relied instead on the private providence of labor.

The projection of egalitarianism in the colonial Anglo world was founded
on the judgment that each should be rewarded according to their labor, rather
than according to their hereditary rights, a judgment that fell ironically against
both the European aristocracy and against Indigenous peoples.[34] The older
defense of native rights in international law that distinguished between inhabited and uninhabited land was remolded to require of traditional habitation
some evidence of efficient land use. The Grotian distinction was deliberately
obscured by the repeated assertion that uncultivated land was effectively uninhabited, an agrarian ideology given license both by John Locke's theory that
it is primarily labor that creates private property and by an economic inter-

32. Polanyi, *The Great Transformation: The Political and Economic Origins of Our Time*,
2nd ed. (Boston: Beacon, 2001), p. 171; cf. pp. 106-7: "It was at the behest of these laws that
compassion was removed from the hearts, and a stoic determination to renounce human
solidarity in the name of the greatest happiness of the greatest number gained the dignity of
a secular religion."

33. Cited in James L. Huston, *Securing the Fruits of Labor: The American Concept of Wealth
Distribution, 1765-1900* (Baton Rouge: Louisiana State University Press, 1998), pp. 293-94.

34. Marilyn Lake and Henry Reynolds, *Drawing the Global Colour Line: White Men's Countries and the Question of Racial Equality* (Melbourne: Melbourne University Press, 2008).

pretation of the mandate in Genesis 1 to "fill the earth and subdue it."[35] The Australian colonies played host to a virulent strain of agrarian ideology, since they were said to be legally established on "waste and uninhabited" land, a conscious fiction repeatedly asserted by the Colonial Office and reiterated still in the *South Australian Colonization Act* of 1834, although in later years the legal expression "waste and uninhabited" was usually truncated simply to "waste" lands of the Crown — in effect, the doctrine of *terra nullius*.

It is an astonishing fact that this peculiar Australian legal history was only brought to an end by the High Court in 1992, when the *Mabo* case rediscovered a Common Law conception of native title in the islands of the Torres Strait. Yet, in unmasking the fiction of *terra nullius*, the High Court and the federal legislation that followed in the *Native Title Act* (1993) arguably reinstated the medieval fiction that the Crown owns all underlying or radical title, and therefore has an exclusive right to alienate land, reviving the doctrine of discovery from *Johnson v. McIntosh*.[36] Subsequent jurisprudence has found that native title in Australia is not really title at all, but rather a bundle of traditional rights on analogy with the medieval English rights to take game on common lands (a tradition that has precedent in "usufruct" rights in Roman law).[37] Prior to the *Mabo* case, there had since the 1970s been various state-based examples of "land rights" legislation designed to return Crown land to Aboriginal people, and in these cases the creation of Indigenous estates was accompanied by no recognition of Indigenous sovereignty. Native title, on the other hand, was

35. See especially Barbara Aneil, *John Locke and America: The Defence of English Colonialism* (Oxford: Clarendon, 1996); cf. Peter Harrison, "'Fill the Earth and Subdue It': Biblical Warrants for Colonization in Seventeenth Century England," *Journal of Religious History* 29/1 (2005): 3-24; cf. Brett, *Decolonizing God* (Sheffield: Phoenix, 2008), pp. 19-21; Whitney Bauman, *Theology, Creation, and Environmental Ethics: From* creatio ex nihilo *to* terra nullius (New York: Routledge, 2009), pp. 67-87.

36. Samantha Hepburn, "Feudal Tenure and Native Title: Revising an Enduring Fiction," *Sydney Law Review* 27/1 (2005): 49-86; Samantha Hepburn, "Disinterested Truth: Legitimation of the Doctrine of Tenure post-*Mabo*," *Melbourne University Law Review* 29 (2005): 1-38; Ulla Secher, "The Doctrine of Tenure in Australia post-*Mabo*: Replacing the 'Feudal Fiction' with the 'mere Radical Title Fiction'–Part 2," *Australian Property Law Journal* 13 (2006): 140-78.

37. See the incisive critique from the Aboriginal lawyer Noel Pearson, "Land Is Capable of Ownership," in *Honour Among Nations? Treaties and Agreements with Indigenous People*, ed. Marcia Langton et al. (Melbourne: Melbourne University Press, 2004), pp. 83-100. Similarly, on appeal to the Privy Council in London in 1888, the Canadian St Catherine's Milling case concluded that the Ojibway Indians held only usufruct rights as a "burden on the Crown." See Blake A. Watson, "The Impact of the American Doctrine of Discovery on Native Land Rights in Australia, Canada and New Zealand," *Seattle University Law Review* 34 (2011): 532-35.

seen as a burden on the Crown — traditional rights that somehow needed to be accommodated within an expanded conception of Australian law.

The question then arose of how the Crown should compensate Indigenous people for ignoring these traditional rights, and three of the High Court judges in *Mabo* proposed that since the federal Constitution had since its inception in 1901 envisaged compensation "on just terms" for the compulsory acquisition of land, then compensation for the extinguishment of native title should be made available from that date. But the prevailing opinion in *Mabo* was that native title holders should be compensated for loss of native title only after the advent of the *Racial Discrimination Act* (1975).[38] The present state of native title law, then, is that the racist history of colonial injustice cannot be addressed by the courts, and indeed, there are as yet no examples of litigation that have delivered compensation even for the loss of native title rights since 1975.

CONCLUSION

While there are many complexities that arise in any attempt to address the wrongdoing of previous generations, there are also a number of practical strategies that have demonstrated their effectiveness in postcolonial contexts.[39] Daniel Philpott's analysis of reconciliation in *Just and Unjust Peace*, for example, proposes the combination of acknowledgment, reparations, punishment, apology, forgiveness, and the establishment of just institutions.[40] Taken together, these practices constitute a political ethic of reconciliation founded on restorative justice, rather than distributive or utilitarian norms.

The norms of a welfare state can still today be stretched to cover Indigenous disadvantage, although the recent tide of neoliberal governments has

---

38. See for example *Mabo v. Queensland* [No. 2] (1992) 175 CLR 1, 111 and the discussion in Lisa Strelein, *Compromised Jurisprudence: Native Title Cases since Mabo* (Canberra: Aboriginal Studies Press, 2006), pp. 20-23. In *Tee-Hit-Ton Indians v. United States*, 348 U. S. 272, 279 (1955), the American judge Stanley Reed referred to the "great case of *Johnson v. McIntosh*" in resolving that indigenous title may be terminated "without any legally enforceable obligation to compensate the Indians." Watson, "The Impact of the American Doctrine of Discovery," p. 508.

39. See, e.g., Marcia Langton, et al., eds., *Settling with Indigenous People: Modern Treaty and Agreement-making* (Sydney: The Federation Press, 2006). Jakobus M. Vorster has provided a lucid argument that redress and reconciliation are two theological principles of redemption that can contribute to postcolonial land reforms. Vorster, "The Ethics of Land Restitution," *Journal of Religious Ethics* 34 (2006): 685-707.

40. Philpott, *Just and Unjust Peace: An Ethic of Political Reconciliation* (New York: Oxford University Press, 2012).

eroded even this stronghold of distributive justice.[41] There is even greater political resistance to acknowledging the rights of Indigenous peoples in ways that might go beyond the universal rights of citizens. Social commentators of various persuasions have, for example, attempted to invalidate the collective rights, and rights to redress, expressed in the UN *Declaration on the Rights of Indigenous Peoples* (2007). In his more recent work, Jürgen Habermas still wants to assert that "a culture as such is not a suitable candidate for the status of a legal subject," preferring to find appropriate legal subjects in cosmopolitan individuals and democratic processes. As suggested in Chapter One, the individualist tradition of human rights seems ill-equipped to deal with the complex challenges of postcolonial justice, but the human rights tradition is constantly on the move, as is any living tradition.

Habermas is a leading voice in the recent revival of cosmopolitan politics, which too often reveals its own tendency towards *terra nullius* presumptions by finding inspiration in Immanuel Kant's view that "no-one originally has any greater right than any one else to occupy any particular portion of the earth."[42] This sentiment fits neatly if ironically together with a late capitalism in which there is no longer any need to annex whole countries to enhance the efficiency of markets, but rather global flows of capital are set moving in the smooth cosmopolitan space that purports to set identity politics free from its "specifically coded territories."[43]

There is very little evidence that recent expressions of parliamentary democracy or jurisprudence have reached the level of moral imagination that

41. Samuel Fleischacker argues that it was not until the latter half of the eighteenth century that we find, beyond older Christian arguments for charity, the idea a welfare state might address poverty through redistribution. *A Short History of Distributive Justice* (Cambridge, Mass.: Harvard University Press, 2004). Similarly, Gareth Stedman Jones, *An End to Poverty? A Historical Debate* (London: Profile, 2004) argues that this welfare perspective begins with Thomas Paine's *The Rights of Man* (1792), thereby establishing a tension with the imperatives in classical economics to minimize the role of government in poverty relief.

42. Kant, "Perpetual Peace: A Philosophical Sketch," in *Kant's Political Writings*, ed. H. Reiss (Cambridge: Cambridge University Press, 1971), p. 106, cited favorably in Namsoon Kang, "Toward a Cosmopolitan Theology: Constructing Public Theology from the Future," in *Planetary Loves: Spivak, Postcoloniality and Theology*, ed. Stephen D. Moore and Mayra Rivera (New York: Fordham University Press, 2011), pp. 263-64.

43. Cf. Michael Hardt and Antonio Negri, *Empire* (Cambridge: Harvard University Press, 2000), pp. 186, 326-27; Brett, *Decolonizing God*, p. 191; cf. David Held, "Principles of Cosmopolitan Order," in *The Political Philosophy of Cosmopolitanism*, ed. Gillian Brock and Harry Brighouse (Cambridge: Cambridge University Press, 2005), pp. 10-27; and Darrel Moellendorf, "Persons' Interests, States' Duties, and Global Governance," in Brock and Brighouse, *Cosmopolitanism*, pp. 148-63.

even the Aboriginal Protection Society did in the 1830s. In the chapters that follow, we will take up the question of how a social imagination informed by a rereading of Jewish and Christian scriptures might now be embodied in redemptive practices that are more respectful of local forms of economy and belonging, integrated through restorative justice.[44] In Part Three, "Engaging the Present," the implications of this argument will be related not just to the practices of reconciliation with Indigenous peoples as these are commonly understood, but also to the environmental and economic issues that reflect the richer understanding of postcolonial justice most needed today.

44. Cf. Jennings, *The Christian Imagination*, pp. 286-87.

3. Authors, Imaginaries, and the Ethics of Interpretation

The preceding chapters have reflected on the character of public dialogue from two different starting points, first, by contemplating the possibilities for post-secular discourse in recent political theory, and secondly, by considering the competing concepts of justice at work in colonial histories. Chapter Two worked mainly by way of negative examples to raise questions about the imagination of more redemptive theological contributions to postcolonial predicaments. Our discussion has introduced, from different disciplinary perspectives, some of the challenges for political theology. The multiple dimensions of hermeneutics have so far been explored without close examination of the principles of interpretation that may govern allusions to biblical literature in any particular context, although we have already encountered a number of examples where Scripture has been cited in the course of a philosophical, theological or legal argument laden with political significance. In this chapter, we turn to consider more directly the range of ethical issues that surround the interpretation of Scripture, bearing in mind the legacies of the ideological complexes already discussed (especially slavery, racism and colonialism) that have drawn sanctions particularly from the Bible.

It must be recognized at the outset that hermeneutical discussions focused on the exegesis of Scripture have been drawn into the wider culture wars within the humanities. With the rise of postmodernism, the older norms of Enlightenment and Romantic thought — reason, history, culture, and authorship — have all been rendered suspicious by one school of thought or another. In the present intellectual environment, one way to proceed would be to adopt a thoroughly pragmatist approach to exegesis, denying perhaps that there is any important difference between the meaning of texts and their use. Or to put that in more moderate terms, wherever multiple exegetical options are arguable, one could adopt a theological pragmatism and consciously choose interpretations that best serve the "love of neighbour,"[1] or more specifically, the texts and interpretations that best suit a political ethic of reconciliation.[2]

While there is considerable value in this latter variant of pragmatist hermeneutics, it also begs the question of how, to take an example from Chapter Two, one might take a stand against the kind of Christian utilitarianism that finds on balance the benefits of colonialism outweighing its injustices (the kind of pragmatism ultimately adopted by James Stephen in reflecting on his time as Undersecretary within the Colonial Office in the 1830s). In other words, is it possible to arbitrate between competing pragmatisms? For some, the question itself would be oxymoronic, since they deny the very possibility of arbitration in rational terms. I want to resist this skepticism and attempt to answer the question by breaking it down into a series of smaller questions about different modes of interpretation and the limits and possibilities that belong to each. Most importantly, I will argue that a responsible use of Scripture in public ethics will need to attend not simply to isolated verses or individual works but to the unfolding conversation between the variety of perspectives expressed in the biblical traditions and imaginaries.

In unpacking these issues, the argument will succumb neither to relativist nor to naïvely objectivist understandings of knowledge.[3] For our present purposes, it will be more fruitful to explore the ground between these two extremes, not least because this middle space offers more opportunity for developing the practices of critical dialogue on which responsible political theology and ethics depend. This chapter will be shaped primarily by dialogue with a leading theologian, Kevin Vanhoozer, who has developed a subtle and detailed account of how the Bible might inform theology and ethics. To his credit,

---

1. See especially Charles Cosgrove's Augustinian formulation of this argument in "Towards a Postmodern *Hermeneutica Sacra*," in *The Meanings We Choose: Hermeneutical Ethics, Indeterminacy and the Conflict of Interpretations*, ed. Charles H. Cosgrove (London: T & T Clark, 2004), pp. 39-61; cf. Stephen Fowl, *Engaging Scripture* (Oxford: Blackwell, 1998), pp. 40-61; Andrew K. M. Adam, *Faithful Interpretation* (Minneapolis: Fortress, 2006).

2. This is effectively Daniel Philpott's approach to Jewish, Christian, and Islamic scriptures in *Just and Unjust Peace: An Ethic of Political Reconciliation* (New York: Oxford University Press, 2012).

3. I am expanding in this chapter on my earlier formulations of hermeneutical pluralism, which have been construed by some readers to be merely relativist in their implications. For another attempt to avoid the false polarity of relativist and objectivist epistemologies, see for example Nancy Murphy, *Beyond Liberalism and Fundamentalism: How Modern and Postmodern Philosophy Set the Theological Agenda* (Valley Forge: Trinity, 1996).

Vanhoozer has acknowledged the ways in which particular texts may reflect more than one layer of meaning without thereby sinking into indeterminate meaning, as radical critics suggest. I will argue, however, that his account is finally not adequate for public ethics, and that another approach is necessary.

MEANINGS AND IDEOLOGIES

It is not difficult to find an ironic contradiction in recent postmodern scholarship between, on the one hand, insisting that all interpretations are merely fabricated by particular readers, and on the other hand, suggesting that biblical texts really do contain ideologies that must be denounced if a scholar is to maintain a good conscience. Insofar as critics manage to clear their conscience by distancing themselves from the ideology of a biblical text, they have inadvertently reinstated a distinction between the "meaning" and "significance" of biblical texts: in this case, a meaning is discovered in the text, which is then found to be oppressive — apparently beyond any readerly volition. This hermeneutic of suspicion then permits enlightened readers to be emancipated, at least according to the lights of their own critical strategies.

Deconstructive approaches to biblical interpretation, on the other hand, go beyond this simple contradiction, as Vanhoozer has recognized, to assert that no emancipatory scheme is immune from its own contradictions or limitations. Deconstructive ethics resist any form of interpretive closure that would presume in a "totalizing" way that all the relevant evidence is in hand and that interpretation can terminate therefore with a final grasp of the truth, a mastery of the subject matter. An emphasis on the contingency of knowledge allows a critical reader to resist the regime of truth that might be asserted in any particular context, not because the fabrications of ideology have been scraped away — whether ideologies of gender, race, or class — but because justice demands an enduring recognition of otherness, alterity, and heterogeneity. In effect, interpretation is endlessly deferred, or embraced in an almost arbitrary decision of the reader.

Vanhoozer joins hands with a number of critical schools (amongst which he includes Habermasian discourse ethics) in opposing this deconstructive notion of justice with a version of critical realism. His approach seeks to provide the most persuasive critical arguments to date while being fully aware that the advent of new evidence and argument is always possible. In his major work from 1998, *Is There a Meaning in this Text?*, Vanhoozer proposes that the focus of his critical realism lies in paying attention to one particular class of "others," the biblical *authors*, whose meaning must be given priority over any significance invented by readers.[4]

Vanhoozer sounds the hermeneutical alarm by suggesting, for example, that when the biblical scholar William Robertson Smith was dismissed in 1881 from his teaching position for the "heresy" of not believing that Moses wrote the Pentateuch, this could in some respects still be justified on the grounds that "those responsible for that decision perhaps glimpsed what is now all too apparent: without authors, texts have neither authority nor determinate sense," since "without the author to serve as touchstone of the distinction between meaning and significance, every interpretation becomes just as authorized a version as another."[5] We will discuss below the more productive developments in Vanhoozer's subsequent works, but to begin with it is necessary to recognize the conflation of quite separate issues that makes these initial claims problematic.

First, although many critics would regard any distinction between "meaning" and "significance" as *passé*, there is more than one way to formulate such distinctions, and each formulation should be considered on its own merits. Some have suggested that pursuing the meaning of a text should be the focus of exegesis narrowly conceived, whereas explorations of the significance of a text would be a matter of "hermeneutics." Given the impact of ideology-orientated criticism of various kinds in biblical studies (within which the prejudices of interpreters become the focus of attention — notably their gender, race, or class), this may appear to be no longer a viable demarcation between different interpretive interests.[6] Even it were possible to bring diverse studies of history, language, tradition, literary sources, manuscript variations, genres of communication, and so on, under a single technical heading called exegesis, the very structure of some exegetical questions complicates matters, as for example, when New Testament scholars debate the extent to which the Pauline letters are implicated in imperial symbolism.[7] In many cases the emancipatory

4. Vanhoozer, *Is There a Meaning in This Text? The Bible, the Reader and the Morality of Literary Knowledge* (Grand Rapids: Zondervan, 1998), pp. 182-87, 321-32.

5. Vanhoozer, *Is There a Meaning in This Text?*, pp. 70 and 86.

6. Cf. Ben C. Ollenburger, "Old Testament Theology: A Discourse on Method," in *Biblical Theology: Problems and Perspectives*, ed. Stephen J. Kraftchick, Charles D. Meyers, and Ben C. Ollenburger (Nashville: Abingdon, 1995), pp. 81-103; Leo Perdue, "Old Testament Theology since Barth's *Epistle to the Romans*," in *Biblical Theology: Introducing the Conversation*, ed. Leo G. Perdue, Robert Morgan, and Benjamin D. Sommer (LBT; Nashville: Abingdon, 2009), pp. 55-136.

7. See the recent review essay by Stephen Moore, "Paul after Empire," in *The Colonized*

interests of interpreters underpin their research projects precisely when these projects are undertaken according to the professional norms of critical rigor and scholarly detachment. Nevertheless, I want to defend at least one version of a distinction between meaning and significance, but not on the terms promoted in Vanhoozer's earlier work.

There is, of course, more than one kind of meaning, and we can readily agree with Vanhoozer that an interest in *communicative* agency does not entail the older conviction that authorial intentions can be grasped by reaching behind linguistic acts to grasp the inner psychological experiences of authors. There is a wide range of intentions or motives that may lie behind an author's particular use of language.[8] The concept of communicative intention, or authorial discourse, requires a distinction between *what* authors might be saying in a particular setting, and *why* they are saying it. The motives behind any act are often not evident in the act itself, and accordingly, any attempt to interpret the motives behind a text is logically separable from attempts to interpret linguistic acts as such. A communicative intention is publically accessible in language, and not hidden away.[9]

Even discerning *what* is being said in a particular context is, however, often highly complex, not least because strategies of communication (*how* it is said, if you like) can vary enormously. Strategies of indirect communication such as irony, satire, humor and all kinds of elliptical rhetoric omit some assumptions or premises that must be supplied by an audience in order to grasp what is being said. Even two native speakers who share a culture can sometimes have difficulty grasping a point that is made indirectly, so it should come as no surprise that the business of understanding an author from another culture might need to progress laboriously through all the potentially relevant data

---

Apostle: Paul through Postcolonial Eyes, ed. Christopher D. Stanley (Minneapolis: Fortress, 2011), pp. 9-23.

8. A distinction between communicative intentions and motives is explicated in my two essays "Four or Five Things to Do with Texts: A Taxonomy of Interpretative Interests," in *The Bible in Three Dimensions*, ed. David J. A. Clines, Stephen E. Fowl, and Stanley E. Porter (Sheffield: JSOT Press, 1990), pp. 357-77; "Motives and Intentions in Genesis 1," *Journal of Theological Studies* 42 (1991): 1-16.

9. The concept of *communicative* intention here is essentially equivalent to what Nicholas Wolterstorff has more recently dubbed "authorial discourse," although for the sake of clarity Wolterstorff avoids using the concept of intention. See Wolterstorff, "A Response to Trevor Hart," in *Renewing Biblical Interpretation*, ed. Craig Bartholomew, Colin Greene, and Karl Möller (Grand Rapids: Zondervan, 2000), pp. 335-41; Nicholas Wolterstorff, *Divine Discourse: Philosophical Reflections on the Claim That God Speaks* (Cambridge: Cambridge University Press, 1995).

of syntax, semantics, phonology, and pragmatics (speech acts and "conversational implicatures" of various kinds[10]), linking these to situations that might be characterized by cultural, religious, economic, and political backgrounds that never find explicit expression in the text at issue. If this is not done with due diligence, one could make exegetical errors on the scale of interpreting Swift's *Modest Proposal* not as satire, but as a genuine proposal for the disposal of Irish infants.[11] Or to take a biblical example, an exegetical study that brims with observations on Hebrew grammar yet fails to illuminate the satirical features of the book of Jonah (and especially its complex critique of the idea of prophetic prediction) would not have done justice to the authorial discourse.

While Vanhoozer acknowledges that there is indeed a range of logically discrete interpretive interests that scholars bring to a text, he argues that these should be organized into a hierarchy with the higher levels of literary meaning emerging from the lower levels of data derived from language, culture, and history. He sees responsible interpretation as a moral act conceived within a "covenantal" social space, responding above all to the speech acts of authors, discerning in particular what kinds of acts they are performing, for example, in making an assertion, issuing a command, asking a question, making a promise, and so on.[12] Identifying such genres of communicative action has in biblical studies often been seen as one of the tasks of the critical method called "form criticism," but Vanhoozer prefers the philosophical language of "illocutionary force" derived from speech act theory, arguing that this approach puts a clearer emphasis on authorial agency in making use of linguistic conventions. In scholarly biblical studies, this emphasis on an author's agency has been accommodated within studies of rhetoric, which also distinguish between conventional literary forms and their peculiarities in actual use.

Unfortunately, Vanhoozer further complicates matters by envisaging an-

10. Beyond the philosophical literature on speech acts often adopted by Vanhoozer, linguists have refined a wealth of concepts for analyzing the strategies of communicative intention. See, e.g., Stephen C. Levinson, *Pragmatics* (Cambridge: Cambridge University Press, 1983); Yan Huang, *Pragmatics* (Oxford: Oxford University Press, 2007); Alan Cruse, *Meaning in Language: An Introduction to Semantics and Pragmatics* (Oxford: Oxford University Press, 2011); Siobhan Chapman, *Pragmatics* (Basingstoke: Palgrave Macmillan, 2011).

11. George Lindbeck, "Postcritical Canonical Interpretation: Three Modes of Retrieval," in *Theological Exegesis: Essays in Honor of Brevard S. Childs*, ed. Christopher Seitz and Kathryn Greene-McCreight (Grand Rapids: Eerdmans, 1990), p. 40.

12. Vanhoozer depends especially on the foundational work of John R. Searle, *Speech Acts: An Essay in the Philosophy of Language* (Cambridge: Cambridge University Press, 1969). See further Richard Briggs, *Words in Action: Speech Act Theory and Biblical Interpretation* (Edinburgh: T & T Clark, 2001).

other layer of literary meaning that emerges through the formation of the biblical canons, thereby raising questions about how all these layers of meaning are to be related.

DIVINE APPROPRIATION OF AUTHORIAL DISCOURSE IN THE CHRISTIAN CANON

Against alternative accounts of interpretation that distinguish between canonical textuality and authorial intention,[13] Vanhoozer remains focused on authors in part because of his conviction "that reality is ultimately a matter of interpersonal communication and communion, not of an impersonal (and conflictual) *différance.*"[14] When divine discourse emerges from authorial discourse within the Christian canon, the two strata of discourse should not be set in opposition to each other in the way that theories of textuality often propose, he suggests, because each stratum unfolds within a single covenantal framework that is divinely constituted.[15] The theological task of biblical interpretation is then to participate in this canonical communion in a spirit that corresponds to the nature of the sacred literature. The ultimate unity of Scripture is thereby posited by a faith that is then ethically obligated to embody this same unity in the history of biblical interpretation.

Our discussion of colonialism in Chapter Two, however, would be sufficient to demonstrate that a fundamental vision of interpersonal communion in the history of biblical interpretation is in large measure a counterfactual phenomenon. And if the interpretation of Scripture is to be conceived in covenantal terms, then it could be argued that covenantal relationships have been repeatedly and relentlessly undermined not just by the recent excesses

13. On the metaphor of textual intentions, see Mark G. Brett, *Biblical Criticism in Crisis? The Impact of the Canonical Approach on Old Testament Studies* (Cambridge: Cambridge University Press, 1991), pp. 116-48; cf. Gordon McConville, "Old Testament Laws and Canonical Intentionality," in *Canon and Biblical Interpretation*, ed. Craig G. Bartholomew et al. (Milton Keynes: Paternoster, 2006), pp. 259-81, who explores the notion of *intentio operis* in dialogue with Umberto Eco, "Overinterpreting Texts," in *Interpretation and Overinterpretation*, ed. Stefan Collini (Cambridge: Cambridge University Press, 1992), pp. 45-66.

14. Vanhoozer, *Is There a Meaning in This Text?*, pp. 160-61.

15. Vanhoozer, "Imprisoned or Free?" in Andrew K. M. Adam, Stephen E. Fowl, Kevin J. Vanhoozer, and Francis Watson, *Reading Scripture with the Church: Toward a Hermeneutic for Theological Interpretation* (Grand Rapids: Baker, 2006), p. 69, here alluding to Alister E. McGrath, *A Scientific Theology*, vol. 2 (Grand Rapids: Eerdmans, 2002), ch. 10: "Critical Realism: Engaging with a Stratified Reality."

of deconstruction or postmodernism, but by the long and deep patterns of oppressive interpretations that have scarred both medieval and colonial expressions of Christianity — Christianities that were shaped, at least in their own eyes, by the metaphysical securities of a "rule of faith." The common, if not overwhelming, experience of Indigenous and colored peoples is that Christian communion beyond the conventional solidarities of ethnicity has only been glimpsed in fragments.[16]

Vanhoozer is of course aware of this history of ideological interpretation, and his overall objective is to describe the hermeneutical conditions under which the study of Scripture might come closer to the ideal of covenantal, interpersonal communion. Especially in his more recent work, he has shifted his emphasis from philosophical to theological frameworks, but I will now seek to show why some of the specifically theological dimensions of Vanhoozer's hermeneutics potentially undermine the practices of Christian engagement in public dialogue, an unfortunate outcome for a theological program oriented around the ethics of communication.

The first major difficulty with his position is that he proposes a focus on the final or canonical form of biblical texts while at the same time insisting that *authorial* agency is foundational for the canonical task of interpretation. Despite the controversies on points of detail, the overwhelming scholarly consensus is that most books in the Hebrew Bible have more than one author, and that understanding the differences between earlier authors and later editors is often a key feature of interpretation, so the conflation of final form and authorship in Vanhoozer's program presents a logical puzzle. One way to resolve the tension, perhaps, would be to say that the focus on the canonical form really amounts to giving theological priority to the agency of the final editors, but this would then beg the question of why "interpersonal communion" with earlier biblical authors has been superseded.

Vanhoozer attempts to resolve this problem in part by recourse to the doctrine that Scripture has dual authorship — human and divine. The selection of some authors over others is seen to be a matter of divine revelation and confessional conviction.[17] That is, "the canon as a whole" is apparently the

16. See Michael O. Emerson and Christian Smith, *Divided by Faith: Evangelical Religion and the Problem of Race in America* (New York: Oxford University Press, 2000); Willie James Jennings, *The Christian Imagination: Theology and the Origins of Race* (New Haven: Yale University Press, 2010).

17. This is also the approach taken by Paul Noble, *The Canonical Approach: A Critical Reconstruction of the Hermeneutics of Brevard S. Childs* (BIS 16; Leiden: E. J. Brill, 1995), who like Vanhoozer proposes that a defense of authors is sufficient to stem the tides of relativism,

unified act of God in so far as "divine intention supervenes on the intention of the human authors" and can be regarded as "an emergent property of the Old and New Testaments."[18] It seems, however, that Vanhoozer's concept of an emergent divine discourse collapses his distinction between meaning and significance: he acknowledges that the *canonical* relationships between the variety of human discourses were not actually manifest to human authors: "God says more than the human authors know in their own timeframe,"[19] and in this respect the divine intentions or motives behind any particular text remain at least partially hidden from its authors. In a particularly revealing example, Vanhoozer confesses that the Christological significance of Old Testament texts (the construal of Israelite meanings as relating to Jesus Christ) remains largely unknown to ancient Israelite authors. This well-worn hermeneutical idea conflicts with his defense of the integrity of authorial discourse. His position on this key issue demonstrates that the authors of the Hebrew Bible do not in fact "serve as touchstone of the distinction between meaning and significance" in his wider account; rather, their discourse is reconfigured in relation to events beyond the horizon of their comprehension. Later Christian authors discover new *significance* in old Israelite meanings, and it is only this kind of emergent significance that makes theological interpretation canonical and normative.

Vanhoozer's emphasis on the unity of divine action in constituting the Christian canon may be distinguished from Nicholas Wolterstorff's more recent account of Scripture that similarly envisages the divine appropriation of diverse human discourses, yet leaves open the question "whether those scriptures should be regarded as one work or many — God's single *opus* or God's *opera omnia*."[20] In my opinion, a view of the Bible as God's *opera omnia* is both historically and theologically preferable, but whichever view is taken, one point remains: if the human discourses are believed to be authorized by

---

but then invokes divine authorship in order to plug the logical gaps in his position. See also the critique of Noble's position in William John Lyons, *Canon and Exegesis: Canonical Praxis and the Sodom Narrative* (JSOTSup 352; Sheffield: Sheffield Academic Press, 2002), pp. 85-94.

18. Vanhoozer, *Is There a Meaning in This Text?*, p. 265.

19. Vanhoozer, *Remythologizing Theology: Divine Action, Passion and Authorship* (Cambridge: Cambridge University Press, 2010), p. 478 n.25, cf. p. 480.

20. Nicholas Wolterstorff, "The Unity behind the Canon," in *One Scripture or Many? Canon from Biblical, Theological and Philosophical Perspectives*, ed. Christine Helmer and Christof Landmesser (Oxford: Oxford University Press, 2004), p. 232; cf. Anthony Thiselton, "Dialectic in Hermeneutics and Doctrine: Coherence and Polyphony," in his *The Hermeneutics of Doctrine* (Grand Rapids: Eerdmans, 2007), pp. 119-44.

divine action, this authorization is necessarily *external* to the particularities of biblical language, as Wolterstorff emphasizes in his argument that the unity of Scripture lies "behind the canon."[21]

My main objection to Vanhoozer's position can be summarized quite simply: a conviction about the divine appropriation of human discourses in the Bible may well shape theological reflection and praxis, but that is logically a quite different matter from exegesis as a publically accessible set of disciplines. Biblical exegesis as a field of study plays host to a vast range of interpretive communities. This hermeneutical plurality could be readily accommodated, indeed welcomed, by critical realists who hold theological convictions.

The problems with Vanhoozer's approach to divine discourse are exacerbated by his stress on the *embodiment* of authors over against any literary theory that implies a disembodied intertextuality (including canonical intertextuality). If a hermeneutical ethic were to require equal attention to every embodied author and the particularities of their agency, then the priority of historical criticism in biblical studies would be assured, a logical outcome that Vanhoozer resists. A key question arising here is whether the divine agency that is held to lie *behind* the canon, authorizing its polyphonic discourses, should be seen as a communicative agency in the same terms as a human author or editor. In what sense, for example, is this divine author embodied in the particular situations or contexts that inform the pragmatics of discourse? Or to put the question another way, in what way can a divine intention behind the biblical text make a substantive difference to the task of exegesis?

I would argue that a conviction about the divine authorization of Scripture has more relevance to the *significance* that readers attach to exegesis. The divine commissioning and appropriating of human discourse is not focally a matter of meaning in any linguistic sense. As, for example, the prophetic literature itself repeatedly asserts, it is quite possible to understand a discourse and then to reject its claims; the addition of the messenger formula "Thus says the Lord," for example, adds no semantic or pragmatic content to an oracle. In the jargon of speech act theory, being receptive to a prophetic oracle is not so much a matter of communication in the narrow sense of authorial discourse but of "perlocutionary effects." Vanhoozer himself makes a similar point when he says that the Holy Spirit works "in illuminating readers and effecting perlocutions," referring at this point to Calvin's similar view in the *Institutes of*

---

21. Wolterstorff, "The Unity behind the Canon." Cf. Vanhoozer, "Imprisoned," p. 68, where he says that the only justification for reading the canon as a unified work lies in the divine authorization "outside" the text.

Christian Religion (1.9.3) that the Spirit provides "efficacious confirmation of the Word."[22] This implies however that the meaning of a biblical text is in the first instance a public matter, even if religious readers might adopt the claims of the texts in different ways from others — especially through reflecting on the relationships between a range of religious texts and their significance for a community's life before God.[23] And this is a two-edged sword, since laying claim to the Holy Spirit's confirmation does not in itself absolve readers from distorted and oppressive interpretation of the Bible.

In this connection, Vanhoozer argues that the history of the Bible's reception is indeed full of ideological distortions but it does not follow that these are a part of the biblical authors' communicative intentions: "If the biblical narratives have come to be read as promoting sexism (or racism, for that matter), this should be seen as an unintended consequence of the authors' communicative action for which they ought not be held responsible."[24] But in absolving biblical authors in this way, he has exceeded the bounds of his philosophical method, because this is a matter that only detailed biblical scholarship can decide on a case-by-case basis. As noted above, for example, the extent to which the Pauline literature might be implicated in sexist or imperialist discourses is precisely the subject of recent scholarly controversies; these are not matters that can be so readily resolved by theological fiat.

Nor are they resolved by speech act theory, as Dan Stiver rightly points out: "With speech act theory's concern to show the complexity of language that we *do* understand, it has hardly dealt with the problems of ideology and power relations that go so far to undo and disturb communication."[25] This point coheres with Habermas's classic argument that hermeneutics fails to grasp systematically distorted communication, and Stiver provides Dietrich Bonhoeffer's critique of the German churches' absorption of Nazism as an example of the struggle against ideological distortions. In short, participation

22. Vanhoozer, "Imprisoned," p. 72; Vanhoozer, *Remythologizing Theology*, pp. 365-66, 374, 494; Vanhoozer, *The Drama of Doctrine: A Canonical-linguistic Approach to Christian Theology* (Louisville: Westminster John Knox, 2005), p. 182, n. 140.

23. In speaking loosely here about "a range of religious texts" both biblical and non-biblical, I am acknowledging that not even Protestants today agree on the significance of the Reformation doctrine of *sola scriptura*. See, e.g., Stanley Hauerwas and D. Stephen Long, "Interpreting the Bible as a Political Act," *Religion and Intellectual Life* 9 (1989): 139.

24. Vanhoozer, *Is There a Meaning in This Text?*, p. 255.

25. Dan R. Stiver, "Felicity and Fusion: Speech Act Theory and Hermeneutical Philosophy," in *Transcending Boundaries in Philosophy and Theology*, ed. Kevin J. Vanhoozer and Martin Warner (Aldershot: Ashgate, 2007), pp. 145-56, 148.

in redemptive communion could well entail not just a charitable understanding of theological discourse but a *critique* of that discourse where it exhibits a blindness to particular evils.

It is clear that Vanhoozer and some other theologians wish to insulate the Bible from this kind of critique because of the significance that they attach to its divine authorization, but in so doing they make a logically invalid move backwards from significance to meaning. Interpreters who hold a different view about how divine appropriation of human discourse is to be construed may not see any difficulty with examining the all-too-human dimensions of the biblical discourses, whether in their original composition or in their history of reception. Indeed, many of the prophetic and wisdom traditions quite clearly exercise a critique of royal or legal ideologies found elsewhere in the Bible itself, and a doctrinaire refusal to engage with the ideological dimensions of biblical exegesis would render many canonical texts mute.[26]

To mention one example that we will take up in more detail below, Vanhoozer refers at one point to the Hebrew Bible's own colonization story only in order to deprive it of any hermeneutical importance. He suggests that the "taking of Canaan was to be a once-for-all event" and that "in the context of the canon as a whole, it is Jesus, not Joshua, who leads his people into a new, eschatological rest (Heb. 4:1-11)."[27] This example reflects a number of unhelpful presumptions, both historical and theological, which will be further discussed in Chapter Four. Rabbinic tradition, for example, also reads the conquest as "once-for-all," and not to be replicated, but instead of engaging in a wider conversation about shared scriptures, Vanhoozer gives a supersessionist privilege to the authorial discourse of Hebrews over the authorial (and covenantal) discourses of Deuteronomy and Joshua. It is evident that his ethical respect

---

26. This inner-biblical dynamic has been a major focus of Walter Brueggemann's biblical theology, exemplified in very simple terms in his work *David's Truth in Israel's Imagination and Memory*, 2nd ed. (Minneapolis: Fortress, 2002) and more comprehensively in the traditions he labels "counter testimony" in his *Theology of the Old Testament: Testimony, Dispute, Advocacy* (Minneapolis: Fortress, 1997). Gordon McConville even includes Deuteronomy as part of inner-biblical critique of royal ideology in "Law and Monarchy in the Old Testament," in *A Royal Priesthood? A Dialogue with Oliver O'Donovan*, ed. Craig Bartholomew et al. (Carlisle: Paternoster, 2002), pp. 69-88.

27. Vanhoozer, *Is There a Meaning in This Text?*, p. 193, n. 172; see further his comments in I. Howard Marshall, with Kevin J. Vanhoozer and Stanley E. Porter, *Beyond the Bible: Moving from Scripture to Theology* (Grand Rapids: Baker Academic, 2004), pp. 85-86. For a reading of Hebrews 4 that resists supersessionist tendencies, see Gerhard von Rad, "There Remains Still a Rest for the People of God," in his *The Problem of the Hexateuch and Other Essays* (London: Oliver & Boyd, 1966), pp. 94-102.

for authors is not consistently applied even within the domain of Scripture; instead, a metanarrative of redemptive history provides an external framework for deciding which of the authorial discourses within the scriptures are to be given hermeneutical privilege. This kind of Christian hermeneutic is problematic in several respects.

Inevitably, Jewish and Christian traditions each evaluate the diversity of voices in Scripture, and they have their own distinctive ways of acknowledging biblical literature as authoritative even when it is no longer regarded as normative for ongoing religious practice.[28] But Vanhoozer has not made coherent use of his own philosophical theory; it should have prompted him to ask more searching questions about the authorial discourses in Deuteronomy and Joshua — especially about the pragmatics of their genres and settings.[29] In neglecting these issues, he has compromised the expansive interpretive dialogue required by critical realism, whether a broad conversation among historians of various persuasions, or more particularly, a conversation with Jewish scholars who share covenantal traditions with Christian faith.

While it may well be the case that the theological significance attached to Deuteronomy or Joshua will raise questions that are only resolved by hermeneutical decisions made by particular faith communities, the study of the authorial discourse in these books is a separable and more public matter.[30] To put this point another way, while theology may be a communitarian enterprise, exegesis is essentially more public. Exegesis is the sort of study that can be conducted within universities alongside the study of any other religious tradition that might be deemed worthy of scholarly interest. In this respect at least, I support Vanhoozer's attempt to reclaim a distinction between meaning and significance, and the division between Parts Two and Three of the present volume rests on this distinction. We should first understand, to the best of our ability, the discourses of the Bible and the ancient relationships between them before we discuss their significance in public dialogue today. This does not exclude the real possibility that research

28. See especially Benjamin D. Sommer, "Unity and Plurality in Jewish Canons," in *One Scripture or Many? Canon from Biblical, Theological and Philosophical Perspectives*, ed. Christine Helmer and Christof Landmesser (Oxford: Oxford University Press, 2004), pp. 108-50.

29. Contrast the more subtle treatment in Nicholas Wolterstorff, "Reading Joshua," in *Divine Evil? The Moral Character of the God of Abraham*, ed. Michael Bergmann, Michael J. Murray and Michael C. Rea (New York: Oxford University Press, 2010), discussed in Chapter Four.

30. Similarly, even if one rejects authorial discourse in favour of a theory of autonomous textuality, or of "canonical intentionality," exegesis would still be a different enterprise from construing the significance of biblical texts for particular interpretive communities. See below.

questions in biblical studies may be generated by contemporary concerns — and in this sense be orientated towards questions of "significance" — but this does not imply that the answers to those questions will be readily applicable in contemporary practice without further reflection on the differences between past and present cultures.[31]

TEXTUALITY, TRADITIONS, AND SOCIAL IMAGINARIES

Having argued that the exegesis of biblical literature is a publicly accessible enterprise, which is distinguishable from reflection on the significance biblical discourses within particular communities, it is still necessary to resist a simplistic version of the distinction between meaning and significance that recognizes no important difference between speech and writing in setting the parameters of meaning. Here we can invoke the classic defender of authorial intention, E. D. Hirsch, who introduced in his later hermeneutical work a series of qualifications in relation to particular genres of literature. When Hirsch shifted his view from an exclusive focus on authors' intentions to a limited defense of textual independence from their original context, he did not thereby turn towards a general theory of "textuality" that has been characterized by one biblical scholar in the following terms:

> It is integral to written communicative actions that their effect may be indefinitely extended in space and in time, and that the scope of this effect is largely beyond the control of the author. If the relative permanence of the written communicative action subjects it to the contingencies of an open future, then that is what is intended in the act of writing itself.[32]

What the later Hirsch proposed is not an indeterminacy of all written texts as such, but rather, a limited indeterminacy that applies especially to particular kinds of literary, legal and religious texts. In these kinds of cases, he finds that "while it is true that later aspects of verbal meaning *are* fixed by its originating moment in time, that moment has fixed only the *principles* of further

---

31. See further my essay "The Future of Old Testament Theology," in *IOSOT Congress Volume: Oslo*, ed. André Lemaire and Magne Sæbø (VTSup 80; Leiden: E. J. Brill, 2000), pp. 465-88; reprinted in Ben C. Ollenburger, ed., *Old Testament Theology: Flowering and Future* (Winona Lake: Eisenbrauns, 2004), pp. 481-94.

32. Francis Watson, *Text and Truth: Redeeming Biblical Theology* (Edinburgh: T&T Clark, 1997), pp. 118-19.

extrapolation," a point that is almost self-evident when it comes to the legal interpretation of constitutions.[33]

It is not our concern here to revisit the older theoretical arguments that advance the distinctiveness of texts over against speech.[34] Indeed, the idea that meaning might need to be extrapolated in some senses beyond "our momentary limitations of attention and knowledge," as the later Hirsch puts it, has been explored in great detail by cognitive linguists who have shown how speech acts (not just texts) have a relevance to the progress of a conversation that is not entirely foreseeable.[35] In this respect, the differences between speech and writing are more a matter of degree than kind. Beyond the moral commitment entailed by any careful understanding of a particular speech act, there are additional ethical challenges that belong precisely to genuine *conversations*. It is this additional element that exposes a fundamental weakness of speech act theory in biblical hermeneutics, even when the necessary modifications are made in order to translate speech acts to literary acts.[36]

One example of a failed conversational ethic would be the supersessionist tendency in some biblical theologies to overwrite the authorial discourses of the Hebrew Bible with New Testament perspectives, rather than preserving the alterity of the ancient voices. But the issues are additionally complicated within the Hebrew Bible itself when it turns out that we cannot in good conscience describe the agency of a single biblical author precisely because that author's discourse has been absorbed into a wider conversation that can be characterized as a tradition.

33. Hirsch, "Meaning and Significance Reinterpreted," *Critical Inquiry* 11 (1984): 204, discussed in Brett, *Biblical Criticism in Crisis?*, pp. 23-25. Cf. Grant Huscroft and Bradley W. Miller, eds., *The Challenge of Originalism: Theories of Constitutional Interpretation* (New York: Cambridge University Press, 2011).

34. In a previous study on the canonical approach to biblical studies, I examined a range of theories that established the autonomy of texts from their authors. Contrary to what some critics supposed, my overarching point was that this textual autonomy was readily defensible from quite different philosophical perspectives, not that the canonical approach required a single theory of textuality. Cf. Lyons, *Canon and Exegesis*, pp. 57-58 and 95 n.9, who notes that both James Barr and A. D. H. Mayes raised this objection against my argument in *Biblical Criticism in Crisis?*

35. Hirsch, "Meaning and Significance Reinterpreted," p. 202; cf. Dan Sperber and Dierdre Wilson, *Relevance: Communication and Cognition*, 2nd ed. (Oxford: Blackwells, 1995), esp. p. 201.

36. See Kevin Vanhoozer, "From Speech Acts to Scripture Acts: The Covenant of Discourse and the Discourse of the Covenant," in *After Pentecost: Language and Biblical Interpretation*, ed. Craig Bartholomew, Colin Greene and Karl Möller (Carlisle: Paternoster, 2001), pp. 1-49.

There are a number of views on what might count as a tradition, and at this point I just want to distinguish in a preliminary way between three possibilities. In the first instance (1), biblical scholars sometimes speak for example about a legal tradition in the sense of a particular collection of laws, such as the code found in Deuteronomy 12–26, or alternatively in Leviticus 17–26. The legal imperatives in these two codes share essentially the same illocutionary forces in speech act terms, yet their theological perspective is very different, and in each case their legal directives sit within much larger networks of law and narrative usually understood to be the Deuteronomistic and Priestly traditions respectively.

In the second sense (2), a tradition includes a range of genres, and broadly speaking, Jewish and Christian scholars agree on the basic contours of the larger Deuterononomistic and Priestly complexes even if they disagree on matters of textual detail and dating.[37] A major difficulty with Vanhoozer's use of Scripture is that he neglects this "middle term" in biblical reasoning — the tradition complexes — and moves directly from citations of particular verses to an overarching biblical metanarrative.

Yet, as mentioned in the Introduction above, Alasdair MacIntyre has also defined a living tradition as "an historically extended, socially embodied argument, and an argument precisely in part about the goods which constitute that tradition."[38] Beginning with such a definition it would be possible to envisage a continuum that extends from the trajectories of particular traditions in the second sense (2) to a more comprehensive sense (3) in which whole canons might yet be regarded as a single "biblical tradition" even though they are engaged in polyphonic debates that resist reduction to a single metanarrative or "theodrama," to use Vanhoozer's term.[39]

What I want to suggest here is that in coming to grips with the biblical worldviews (we could also say theology or religion, as long as these terms were taken to embrace all of life and not a discrete spiritual dimension), it may

37. See, e.g., the exemplary essays in Moshe Weinfeld, *The Place of the Law in the Religion of Ancient Israel* (VTSup 100; Leiden: Brill, 2004), who in his notable chapter on "Theological Currents in Pentateuchal Literature" holds perhaps the simplest view that the D and P traditions were pre-exilic contemporaries. Other scholars have proposed numerous layers to the D and P traditions, as we shall see in Part Two.

38. MacIntyre, *After Virtue* (Notre Dame: University of Notre Dame Press, 1981), p. 207.

39. See Dennis Olson, "Biblical Theology as Provisional Monologization: A Dialogue with Childs, Brueggemann and Bakhtin," *Biblical Interpretation* 6 (1998): 162-80; Carol Newsom, "Bakhtin, the Bible and Dialogic Truth," *Journal of Religion* 76 (1996): 290-306; Vanhoozer, *Remythologizing Theology*, pp. 306-37.

be more fruitful to adopt the term "social imaginary" rather than tradition in sense (2) above. In Charles Taylor's accessible definition, a social imaginary underpins "the ways people imagine their social existence, how they fit together with others, how things go on between them and their fellows, the expectations that are normally met, and the deeper normative notions and images that underlie these expectations." [40] Adapting Taylor's definition for our own purposes, I want to suggest for example that we should distinguish between Deuteronomistic and Priestly imaginaries.

An imaginary can encompass not just a range of genres of law and narrative, but I also want to argue that these and other genres belong to streams of conversation in the biblical literature that themselves have a perceptible character — in the sense of tradition (2) — precisely when the editors have not thought it appropriate to identify exactly who each author or editor might have been in the unfolding dialogue. Thus, for example, I would want to say that we can conceive of the Deuteronomistic and Priestly traditions as two different social imaginaries that lay claim to divine revelation, each proposing in conversation with the other not just a set of ideas, but a network of images, narratives and practices that provide their community with a shared sense of legitimacy and character. To view these two imaginaries as the serial contributions of particular authors does not seem to do justice to the character of their conversational dynamics, but on the other hand, in light of the distinctive features of each of these imaginaries, it is also unhelpful to conflate them into a single metanarrative. This same point could be made even more strongly in relation to the wisdom imaginary, within which the particular laws and history of Israel have no substantial role to play.

In Part Two, I will show how these three imaginaries propose quite different understandings of the divine sovereignty, and in the case of Deuteronomy and Priestly traditions, two different streams of covenantal theology. Moreover, these streams of covenant theology are in some respects contested by the prophetic and wisdom traditions of the biblical literature — which are themselves the literary expression of lively conversations rather than simply the products of individual authors. While Vanhoozer at times claims to respect "the various biblical points of view," he regularly finds it necessary to balance this respect theologically with "striving for a unified understanding (e.g., worldview)."[41]

40. See Charles Taylor, *Modern Social Imaginaries* (Durham: Duke University Press, 2004), esp. p. 23. On pre-modern imaginaries, see especially Charles Taylor, *A Secular Age* (Cambridge, MA: Belknap, 2007), pp. 25-89, 146-58. Other terms like social poetics may also be appropriate, but a close analysis of these interrelated concepts is not necessary for our purpose.
41. Vanhoozer, *Remythologizing Theology*, p. 349.

This kind of striving, as we shall see in Part Two of this volume, seems to propose a single hermeneutical frame for the national imaginary in Deuteronomy, the multi-cultural vision in Genesis, and the relative indifference to Israel's covenants in Job. The reduction of this diversity to a single worldview, I will argue, impoverishes the potential contributions of the distinctive biblical traditions to political theology today.

In sum, the overarching thesis to be explored in Parts Two and Three of this volume is that a hermeneutical fusion between ancient and modern horizons will need to engage with the broader compass of social imaginaries, and not just with authorial discourses. An exclusive focus on individual authors arguably represents a legacy of modern social thought, and it rarely fits well in the study of traditional and ancient societies. Particularly in the case of the Bible, historical individuals have embodied their testimony in collective works of literature deliberately shaped for future generations, and in this respect the scriptures are essentially dialogical and not just the serial expressions of individual authors.[42] Much of the subtle detail of these inner-biblical conversations will remain opaque to those who lack the motivation to engage with their complexity, and most theological reflection on that complexity belongs, no doubt, properly only within communities of faith.[43]

For those of us whose identities are partly constituted by dialogue with the biblical literature, however, there is also a pressing need to give an account of how our religious traditions and imaginaries can contribute to a renewed sense of the common good. If we choose to engage in this contemporary task, we will need to acknowledge that the meanings generated within ancient social imaginations are logically separable from their significance today. Any analogies between past and present will need to be forged in reflective practices, mindful that more than one worldview is in play, and in particular, that public norms cannot simply be asserted by metaphysical fiat. Nevertheless, I will show in Part Three that such analogies can indeed still shed light on contemporary political challenges.

42. See further Benjamin D. Sommer, "A Jewish Approach to Reading Scripture Theologically," in Perdue, Morgan and Sommer, *Biblical Theology*, pp. 1-53.

43. See for example Stephen E. Fowl, *Engaging Scripture* (Oxford: Blackwell, 1998).

INNER-BIBLICAL CONVERSATIONS

4. Unfolding the National Imaginary

The nations formed since the eighteenth century are in many ways quite un-like the polities known as "nations" in the Bible. The policing of sharply de-fined national borders, for example, has little precedent in the ancient world. Nevertheless, there are a number of analogies that may be drawn between modern nations and the vision of Deuteronomy, and it is no accident that the political convulsions in sixteenth-century England were partly shaped by fresh Protestant readings of that very book.[1] A number of modern revolutions were modelled on the biblical plot of exodus, law-making, and conquest. Prot-estant versions of colonialism were often intertwined with interpretation not just of Deuteronomy but also of the associated conquest narratives in Joshua. Accordingly, any attempt to bring biblical norms into the public discourse of post-colonial states will need, therefore, to address the problems posed by this hermeneutical history. The thorny question that will concern us in the long run is this: In what possible sense could the imperatives directed towards restorative justice in the political realm be drawn from Deuteronomy and Joshua?

In a significant study of the influence of the Bible in Australian history, Ann Curthoys has argued that an exodus–conquest typology "works against substantial acknowledgment and understanding of the colonial past."[2] In

---

1. Liah Greenfeld, *Nationalism: Five Roads to Modernity* (Cambridge, MA: Harvard University Press, 1992), pp. 1-87; Anthony D. Smith, *Chosen Peoples* (Oxford: Oxford University Press, 2003); Mark G. Brett, "National Identity as Commentary and as Metacommentary," in *Historiography and Identity (Re)formulation in Second Temple Historiographical Literature*, ed. Louis Jonker (LHBOTS 534; London: Continuum, 2010), pp. 29-40.

2. Ann Curthoys, "Expulsion, Exodus and Exile in White Australian Mythology," *Journal of Australian Studies* (1999): 1-18.

reaching this conclusion, Curthoys was influenced in part by a landmark essay by Edward Said in which he investigates the exclusion of Canaanites from the biblical world of ethical concern, and thereby questions the legitimacy of modern political movements inspired by the exodus.[3] My own research suggests that the exodus–conquest typology was less significant in the Australian national imagination than what has come to be called "the doctrine of discovery." This complex legal history was outlined in Chapter Two above, and it is hardly a single doctrine, but here we may note that that this notion of discovery was arguably more dependent on colonial interpretations of Genesis and Isaiah 40–66 than of Joshua.[4] A closer examination of this intellectual history, I would suggest, can provide significant resources for more rigorous debates around the political issues in settler colonial societies that today appear so intractable.[5]

My approach here is to respond to these contemporary problems first by investigating the unfolding of the national imaginary in Deuteronomy and Joshua, and then by placing this particular paradigm of theology and ethics in the wider context of the biblical literature. In many respects, this paradigm begins and ends in the traumas of war.[6] Israel's founding narrative of oppression and escape from Egypt manifestly begins with political trauma, and as is often the case in modern liberation narratives, the social vision that eventually emerges includes the making of a new nation. But the making of this "national" solidarity was slow and complex, and the extended period of Israel's existence as a network of tribes without kings is indicative of this historical reality.

3. Edward Said, "Michael Walzer's Exodus and Revolution: A Canaanite Reading," in *Blaming the Victims: Spurious Scholarship and the Palestinian Question*, ed. Edward Said and Christopher Hitchens (New York: Verso, 1988), pp. 161-78; cf. the review of subsequent literature in Nur Masalha, "Reading the Bible with the Eyes of the Canaanites: Neo-Zionism, Political Theology and the Land Traditions of the Bible," *Holy Land Studies* 8 (2009): 55-108.

4. Robert Miller, Jacinta Ruru, Larissa Behrendt, Tracey Lindberg, *Discovering Indigenous Lands: The Doctrine of Discovery in the English Colonies* (Oxford: Oxford University Press, 2010); Lindsay G. Robertson, *Conquest by Law: How the Discovery of America Dispossessed Indigenous Peoples of Their Lands* (New York: Oxford University Press, 2005); Mark G. Brett, "Feeling for Country: Reading the Old Testament in the Australian Context," *Pacifica* (2010): 137-56.

5. In the Australian context, see for example the "history wars" literature, notably, Keith Windschuttle, *The Fabrication of Aboriginal History*, Vol. 1, *Van Dieman's Land 1803-1847* (Sydney: Macleay Press, 2002); Robert Manne, ed., *Whitewash: On Keith Windschuttle's Fabrication of Aboriginal History* (Melbourne: Black Inc., 2003); Bain Attwood, *Telling the Truth about Aboriginal History* (Crow's Nest: Allen and Unwin, 2005).

6. Cf. Jacob L. Wright, "The Commemoration of Defeat and the Formation of a Nation in the Hebrew Bible," *Prooftexts* 29 (2009): 433-73.

Against surface appearances, it is historically unlikely that the national vision took shape before the arrival of monarchs in Israel. The Hebrew term most often translated "nation" (*goy*) normally includes the possession of political sovereignty in some measure — a rule by kings over their own territory — and this dimension of Israel's story was absent for some centuries. The advent of kings in Israel was beset by protracted conflict, and even if we take the narratives of Saul and David in the books of Samuel to be evidence of kingship in the tenth century BCE, no substantial unity among the tribes was achieved before the fall of the northern kingdom at the end of the eighth century BCE. Indeed, the secession of the northern tribes from Judah is represented in the biblical narrative as enacting its own kind of exodus,[7] and the Judean perspective on the north was relentlessly critical of the Samarian religion and politics.

Jerusalem experienced a dramatic rise in population following the incursion of the Assyrian empire in the north,[8] however, and the idea of political and religious centralization waxed on the southern soil. It is at this time that legal concern for immigrants and refugees (*gerim*) comes to the fore in Israel's Scripture, rather than in earlier centuries. The earlier prophetic literature certainly draws attention to the plight of the poor, widows, and orphans, but it does not focus on immigrants. It is Deuteronomy and the prophets subsequent to the seventh century who establish the standard formula for referring to marginalized persons as "widows, orphans and aliens" (cf. Jer. 7:6).

The story of the Deuteronomic national imaginary in this sense begins *in medias res* — in the middle of ancient Israel and Judah's attempts to assert their own political sovereignty. It is particularly the experience of defeat in war that marks the shift from scattered tribal polities to a more centralized state, specifically, with the loss of the northern kingdom of Israel when that territory was overwhelmed by an Assyrian invasion in 721 BCE. It is not that the traditions of Deuteronomy were first composed in the seventh century, since there are clear lines of tradition extending back into earlier legal material

7. Michael D. Oblath, "Of Pharaohs and Kings — Whence the Exodus?" *JSOT* 87 (2000): 23-42; Keith Bodner, *Jeroboam's Royal Drama* (Oxford: Oxford University Press, 2012), pp. 59-78.

8. Frank Crüsemann, *The Torah: Theology and Social History of Old Testament Law* (Edinburgh: T. & T. Clark, 1996), pp. 182-85; cf. Israel Finkelstein, "The Settlement History of Jerusalem in the Eighth and Seventh Centuries BC," *RB* 115 (2008): 499-515; Aaron A. Burke, "An Anthropological Model for the Investigation of the Archaeology of Refugees in Iron Age Judah and Its Environs," in *Interpreting Exile: Displacement and Deportation in Biblical and Modern Contexts*, ed. Brad E. Kell, Frank R. Ames, and Jacob L. Wright (SBLAIL 10; Atlanta, Ga.: SBL, 2011), pp. 41-56.

and signs of editing in this book that appear to come from later centuries.[9] But there are good reasons to think that the ideal of national solidarity, and the extraordinary separation of powers envisaged in Deuteronomy (under the overarching sovereignty of Yhwh), was most likely forged in response to the Assyrian invasion of the northern kingdom.[10] Moreover, as has long been recognized by historians, the Assyrian vassal treaties known as "covenants," which were imposed on conquered peoples, were clearly mimicked in Deuteronomy, not just in the overall structure of the book but also in the very precise detail of word choices.[11]

The national vision went into crisis at the end of the sixth century when Jerusalem was destroyed by the Babylonians in 587 BCE. The significance of Deuteronomy cannot, of course, be tied solely to the history of the seventh and early sixth centuries, but it would be important to acknowledge that this imaginary was decisively transformed after this time, and in the chapters that follow we will pursue these later developments especially in the Priestly and wisdom literature. A central question for these other traditions, as we shall see, is how to understand Yhwh's sovereignty and jurisdiction without presuming the possession a national territory.

The social vision of the "Deuteronomistic" history — including Joshua, Judges, Samuel, and Kings — reflects a classic model of nation–building: a violent territorial claim, assertions of sovereignty, and exhortations of national unity, including specific concerns for the administration of justice and religion, and special care for the socially marginalized "widow, orphan and alien." The extent to which these materials are deemed to be historically accurate is not our central concern here, nor is it necessary to determine the precise extent of editorial additions to Deuteronomy in later centuries. We will touch on these matters in passing. I will firstly describe the rise of the national imagi-

---

9. See especially Bernard M. Levinson, *Deuteronomy and the Hermeneutics of Legal Innovation* (Oxford: Oxford University Press, 1998).

10. Simo Parpola, "Assyria's Expansion in the 8th and 7th Centuries and Its Long-term Repercussions in the West," in *Symbiosis, Symbolism and the Power of the Past*, ed. William G. Dever and Seymour Gitin (Winona Lake, Ind.: Eisenbrauns, 2003), pp. 99-111; Bernard M. Levinson, "The First Constitution: Rethinking the Origins of Rule of Law and Separation of Powers in Light of Deuteronomy," *Cardozo Law Review* 27 (2006): 1853-88.

11. See especially Hans Ulrich Steymans, *Deuteronomium 28 und die* adê *zur Thronfolgeregelung Asarhaddons: Segen und Fluch im Alten Orient und in Israel* (OBO 145; Göttingen: Vandenhoeck & Ruprecht, 1995); William Morrow, "'To Set the Name' in the Deuteronomic Centralization Formula: A Case of Cultural Hybridity," *Journal of Semitic Studies* 55 (2010): 365-83.

nary, which can be readily distinguished from the alternatives provided in the Priestly and wisdom traditions, as we shall see.

ISRAELITE PEOPLEHOOD BEFORE DEUTERONOMY'S NATIONAL COVENANT

In contrast with the arrival of the Philistine colonists in the Levant, the formation of Israel as a people was not characterized by the imposition of a new culture. Archaeologists now agree that the majority of the Israelites were in some sense Indigenous, even if Yhwh religion originated outside the historic borders of Israel and Judah.[12] The Merneptah stele from Egypt first supplies the name "Israel" at the end of the thirteenth century, and this is the only record of the name "Israel" in sources outside the Bible before the ninth century, when it again appears in Assyrian records and in the Mesha inscription from Moab. What kind of Israelite identity would have endured between the thirteenth and the ninth centuries is difficult to say, not least because all the available evidence, biblical and historical, points to the persistence of Canaanite identities of various kinds. Establishing a decisive "fissure" between Israelite and Canaanite identity was indeed a central focus for Deuteronomy's project of nation building.[13]

In an astute analysis of the archaeological debates concerning this early period, Daniel Fleming has recently suggested that the arguments for Canaanite ethnicity down to mid–tenth century BCE are at least as strong as those for an Israelite ethnicity. More surprisingly, perhaps, he has raised doubts about the very idea of ethnicity in relation to this period.[14] While it is likely that

12. See, e.g., William Dever, *Who Were the Early Israelites, and Where Did They Come From?* (Grand Rapids: Eerdmans, 2003); Avraham Faust, *Israel's Ethnogenesis: Settlement, Interaction, Expansion and Resistance* (London: Equinox, 2006).

13. See William Dever, *The Lives of Ordinary People in Ancient Israel: Where Archaeology and the Bible Intersect* (Grand Rapids: Eerdmans, 2012), p. 129, for the idea of "post-Canaanite polities." On ethnic "fissure" — reducing the size of shared ancestry — see Thomas H. Eriksen, *Ethnicity and Nationalism: Anthropological Perspectives*, 3rd ed. (London: Pluto, 2010), pp. 68-69.

14. Daniel E. Fleming, *The Legacy of Israel in Judah's Bible: History, Politics and the Reinscribing of Tradition* (Cambridge, Mass.: Cambridge University Press, 2012), pp. 283-89, extrapolating in particular from Shlomo Bunimovitz and Zvi Lederman, "A Border Case: Beth-Shemesh and the Rise of Ancient Israel," in *Israel in Transition: From Late Bronze II to Iron IIa (c. 1250-850)*, Vol. I, *The Archaeology*, ed. Lester L. Grabbe (LHBOTS 491; London: T&T Clark, 2008), pp. 21-31, who analyze the evidence in terms of ethnicity.

many of Israel's neighbors called themselves Canaanite as a self-description, the social complexities on the ground are largely inaccessible to archaeological description (the Philistine evidence is much clearer), and we cannot rely on imperial Egyptian texts to decide the matter of self-description.[15] The notion of ethnicity is declared problematic by Fleming when no self-descriptions are available, and when recent anthropological theory has questioned the idea of ethnic groupings as bounded, culturally homogenous and territorially based.[16]

While it is no doubt the case that the postmodern emphasis in recent anthropological theory has been explicitly critical of earlier models of ethnicity, the newer versions of social poetics differ more in degree than in kind.[17] Cultural permeability and hybridity have long been features of ethnic theories, without any presumption that ethnic boundaries require a homogenous culture within clear territorial boundaries; the latter features are characteristic of ethnic nationalism rather than of ethnic "networks" or "associations" as Thomas Eriksen has defined them.[18] In the end, Fleming adopts the terminology of "association" and "collaborative politics," which perhaps begs the question of how one might distinguish these less centralized kinds of solidarity from the more subtle accounts of ethnic associations provided by Eriksen, among many others.

PORTRAITS OF JOSHUA'S WARFARE

Fleming takes the view that the writers who produced the conquest narratives in the book of Joshua should at least be divided into two quite different groups. Josh 8:3–29, for example, is likely to have been conceived in local northern tradition, and only subsequently drawn into the southern conquest narratives, after the fall of the northern kingdom. He suggests that parallels

15. By way of analogy, Indigenous Australians possess hundreds of traditional names for their local polities, a number of regional terms, as well as the generic Latin "Aboriginal" which arose as a result of colonial contact.

16. Fleming, *The Legacy of Israel in Judah's Bible*, pp. 252-54.

17. This is evident, for example, from a comparison of Michael Herzfeld's work, *Anthropology: Theoretical Practice in Culture and Society* (Malden, Mass.: Blackwell, 2001) with Eriksen, *Ethnicity and Nationalism*.

18. Eriksen, *Ethnicity and Nationalism*, pp. 41-45, discusses degrees of incorporation, distinguishing ethnic communities that share a territory and the highest degree of incorporation, from ethnic "associations," "networks" and "categories." See further Mark G. Brett, "Israel's Indigenous Origins: Cultural Hybridity and the Formation of Israelite Ethnicity," *Biblical Interpretation* 11 (2003): 400-412.

with Moabite and south Arabian texts imply the existence of an earlier and Indigenous tradition for claiming a new land, which should be distinguished from the Assyrian genre of covenantal vassal treaties, which were mimicked in Deuteronomy. The most significant discourse for this largely local assertion of land claims turns on the Hebrew word *cherem*, often translated as "ban" or "devotion to destruction." The use of this term in the earliest composition underlying Joshua 8 is likely to reflect a common understanding amongst the Levantine social groups at the time: the practice of *cherem* demanded the comprehensive ritual slaughter of a town's inhabitants, with the effect of binding the invaders simultaneously to the land and to the divinity who provides it, excluding all the prior inhabitants from economic relations.[19] The early *cherem* was in this sense not an imperial strategy for warfare, but a regional ideology that rendered a town "an empty vessel in which the conquering population and its god set up residence."[20]

In the earlier narrative core of Joshua 8, the character of Joshua conducts a local Yhwh war against Ai, a town that is located in other narratives within Benjaminite territory. Since Joshua 8 shares a number of significant features with the account of an intra-Israelite war against Benjamin in Judges 20–21, it may be possible to discern through these comparisons, according to Fleming's hypothesis, evidence of a merely local conflict amongst the northern groups: "By this scenario, Ai would have no larger identity or association; it is never called Canaanite or the like."[21] Instead of accepting the picture of colonial violence exercised by an invading nation, we are left instead with a relatively local conflict inspired by Joshua's divinity, Yhwh. In short, the earlier *cherem* traditions are at home in the northern tribal associations of the eighth century, and this picture of Joshua's war in the name of Yhwh should be distinguished from the character of Joshua as constructed in the seventh century. The later Joshua, by contrast, is seen as the agent of Deuteronomy's laws of conquest, implemented across all the territories of Israel and Judah. With the arrival of Deuteronomy's national vision in the seventh century, it seems that the story of Israel's arrival in the land has been reconfigured in light of the new version of Moses' law.

19. See especially Lauren A. S. Monroe, "Israelite, Moabite and Sabaean War–*ḥerem* Traditions and the Forging of National Identity: Reconsidering the Sabaean Text RES 3945 in Light of Biblical and Moabite Evidence," *VT* 57 (2007): 318-41.

20. Monroe, "Forging of National Identity," p. 326.

21. Fleming, *The Legacy of Israel in Judah's Bible*, pp. 140-41, drawing on Sara J. Milstein, "Expanding Ancient Narratives: Revision through Introduction in Biblical and Mesopotamian Texts," PhD dissertation, New York University, 2010.

Strictly speaking, this kind of historical reconstruction provides no more than plausible hypotheses for traditions that sit behind the biblical texts as we now have them, but we are compelled to engage in this kind of construction both by archaeological evidence and by seams in the biblical texts that point to the complexities of compositional history. To begin with, there is a tension in the biblical material between the authority of Joshua and the authority of Moses, and while subtle narrative analyses might illuminate this tension in some respects, the conflict between the voices in the text can hardly be accounted for by hypotheses concerning the ancient conventions of story telling or narratology.[22] The chain of command in Joshua 8:8, for example, descends directly from Yhwh to Joshua without looping through Mosaic Law, i.e., Joshua himself receives specific divine commands rather than acting on the basis of older Mosaic legislation. The fact that these divine commands to Joshua do not exactly match Deuteronomic law is one among the several reasons to distinguish the older story of the conquest of Ai from its surrounding narrative frame.

A comparison between Joshua 8 and 11 is instructive. In 11:6, Joshua is commanded directly by Yhwh only to hamstring horses and burn chariots, but by the end of the chapter, all the humans are slaughtered and animals are excluded from the ban while confidently claiming that everything was done according to the command of Moses (11:11–15).[23] Joshua 11:6 might well reflect an older narrator's point of view that sees Joshua as acting without a mediating legal tradition, but even when Mosaic authority is brought into view, this chapter does not yet see the sacrifice of animals as inevitably part of the ban. The wording of Deuteronomy 20:16 — that Israel should destroy "all that breathed" — is taken up in Joshua 11:11, 14 (cf. 10:40) without any hint that this included animals as well. The same observation may be made about the Sihon and Og narratives in Deuteronomy, where the animals are spared (2:35; 3:7). In short, even when the narrative in Joshua presumes some of the precise wording from Deuteronomy's law, the application of the law varies. It seems that we need to contemplate the editorial activity of more than one school of Deuteronomistic interpretation; for example, they differ on the question whether animals should be included in the ban.

---

22. The most impressive attempt is found in the work of L. Daniel Hawk, *Every Promise Fulfilled: Contesting Plots in Joshua* (Louisville: Westminster/John Knox, 1991).

23. Walter Brueggemann emphasizes the different voices of authority in his theological discussion of Joshua 11, *Divine Presence and Violence: Contextualizing the Book of Joshua* (Eugene: Cascade, 2009). Cf. the critique from Nicholas Wolterstorff, "Reading Joshua," in *Divine Evil? The Moral Character of the God of Abraham*, ed. Michael Bergmann, Michael J. Murray, and Michael C. Rea (Oxford: Oxford University Press 2011), pp. 236-56.

The inclusion of animals in the *cherem* ban should probably be seen as a distinct conception that belongs to a specific layer of tradition in the book of Joshua. At one level of the tradition, e.g., in 11:11–15, an "omniscient" narrator could claim faithful implementation of the Mosaic Law by assuming that "all that breathed" implied only the death of humans and not the animals. This is clearly not the case in Joshua 6–7, where the most comprehensive form of the ban is insisted on as self-evident. This is clear from the fact that the Israelite Achan is himself subjected to the ban for stealing devoted items from Ai, and his punishment includes the destruction of all his animals.

Joshua 7:24-25 describes the destruction of Achan's family and livestock in terms that reiterate the ban on Jericho in chapter 6, where the Israelites destroyed "all in the city, men and women, young and old, oxen, sheep and donkeys" (Josh. 6:21).[24] The consequences of Achan's sin can be read, more-over, as an application of Deuteronomy 13:6–15, which does not hesitate to speak of the *cherem* in verse 15 as punishment for inner-Israelite idolatry. The cairn of stones raised over Achan in Joshua 7:25–26 not only aligns with the stoning required in Deuteronomy 13:10, but suggests a link to the fate of Canaanite kings in Joshua 8:29 and 10:27, who similarly have a cairn of rocks raised upon their bodies. Taken together, Joshua 6–7 and Deuteronomy 13 seem to reflect a single understanding of the ban. Yet we are also forced to conclude that this point of view is different from the tradition that interprets the ban in Deuteronomy 20:16 to include only humans, as for example in Joshua 11:11–15 where the animals are spared without explanation.

The law in Deuteronomy 13:6–15 is sufficiently similar to the loyalty requirements in Assyrian vassal treaties, and more specifically in Esarhaddon's treaties, to warrant the dating of this text to the seventh century. Having now provided the reasons why Joshua 6–7 are closely related to this Deuteronomic law, the narratives concerning the conquest of Jericho and Ai can be understood within the same editorial horizon, as distinct from the narrower interpretation of "all that breathed" that presumably belonged to earlier tradition. If we were to construe this seventh-century ideology perhaps in light of Girard's theory of mimetic violence, one might conclude that the Deuteronomic writers have simultaneously imitated and resisted the Assyrian treaty genre, exhibiting the kind of mimetic rivalry that produces the need for "scapegoats" like Achan. Israel's divinity has taken the place of the Assyrian king as the focus of loyal love, but the exclusive demands for loyalty in Deuteronomy

24. Frank Spina, *The Faith of the Outsider: Exclusion and Inclusion in the Biblical Story* (Grand Rapids: Eerdmans, 2005), pp. 52-71.

nevertheless agree with the Assyrian models, as does the death penalty for disloyalty to the suzerain.[25]

This is not to say that the entire discourse of *cherem* in Deuteronomy was invented in the seventh century in resistance to the dominant empire of the day. Rather, as indicated above, the older local traditions concerning *cherem* war were reshaped at this time in light of the covenant genre promoted by the Assyrians. One element in this transformation of traditions, as we have seen, was the expanded national role given to Joshua, now configured as a servant of the Mosaic laws of conquest applied to a much larger jurisdiction in Levantine territory. Another element, apparently, was the application of the expanded requirements of the *cherem* in Deuteronomy 13:15 (including animals), both within the inner-Israelite ban against Achan's family in Joshua 7 and within the Jericho conquest narrative in Joshua 6:21. Or to put the overall claim here in more general terms, the articulation of a recognizably "national" imaginary in Deuteronomy and Joshua arose in response to the trauma of the imperial wars perpetrated by the Assyrian empire.

This conclusion can be reinforced from another direction by observing the difference between verses in Joshua that focus attention on particular Canaanite kings rather than peoples and ethnicities. We find references to "Jabin of Hazor, King Jobab of Madon, the king of Shimron, and the king of Achshaph" in Joshua 11:1–5, for example, before the text turns to a formulaic list of Indigenous peoples: the kings of "the Canaanites in the east and the west, the Amorites, the Hittites, the Perizzites, and the Jebusites in the hill country, and the Hivites under Hermon in the land of Mizpah." This initial focus on kings, as opposed to ethnicities, is then given a distinctive interpretation in Joshua 11:18–20a: "Joshua made war for many days with all these kings, for it was Yhwh's doing to harden their hearts so that they would come against Israel in battle." This explanation is quite irrelevant to Deuteronomy's law of conquest, and this particular text in Joshua points instead to an increasing opposition to Yhwh's sovereignty on the part of these particular kings.

The earlier traditions of Joshua are better understood as reflecting wars against particular Indigenous kings, rather than the general populace. This an-

---

25. See the overview of earlier studies in Mark G. Brett, *Decolonizing God: The Bible in the Tides of Empire* (Sheffield: Phoenix, 2008), pp. 79-93, revising my argument in "Genocide in Deuteronomy: Postcolonial Variations on Mimetic Desire," in *Seeing Signals, Reading Signs*, ed. Mark O'Brien and Howard N. Wallace (London: Continuum, 2004), pp. 76-90, particularly in conversation with Norbert Lohfink, "Opferzentralisation, Säkularisierungthese und mimetische Theorie," in *Studien zum Deuteronomium und zur deuteronomistischen Literatur III* (SBAB 20; Stuttgart: Katholisches Bibelwerk, 1995), pp. 219-60.

tagonism towards Indigenous *sovereignty* is then further evidenced in chapter 12, which presents nothing more than a catalogue of vanquished kings.[26] Such a construal of the earlier Joshua narratives (i.e., before they were edited from a Deuteronomistic perspective), fits together very well with the archaeological conclusion that the Israelites of earlier centuries were largely Indigenous. It seems that a violent intra-indigenous movement may have been associated with the arrival of Yhwh religion, with "civil wars" before fought especially with the kings of the Canaanite cities. Whether these civil wars divided the population along class lines, as has sometimes been argued, may be disputable, but the fact that Israel's story begins with a society *sans* kings is surely significant.

The narratives of Joshua chapters 2–7 and 9 (which include the "national" Deuteronomistic perspective) go to extraordinary lengths to explain why the Indigenous descendants of Rahab and the Gibeonites survive among the Israelites without their kings. The narrator in Joshua 6:25, for example, says that family of Rahab continue "until this day," indicating that the conquest events lie in the distant past. The Gibeonites purport to come from "a far country," with striking references to Deuteronomic law: they seek a covenant, and their ruse depends on the logic of Deuteronomy 20:10–18, which prohibits treaties with Indigenous people. The Gibeonites' speech in Joshua 9:5 even seems to appropriate a line from Israel's own story in Deuteronomy 29:5, with the claim that "clothes are falling apart and sandals falling to pieces."[27] In effect, the book of Joshua provides a kind of narrative jurisprudence illustrating how the statutes of Moses were interpreted in practice. The relatively complex narratives in Joshua 6 and 9 serve to explain why the conquest of Canaan was incomplete, and why the descendants of Indigenous peoples survive under the sovereignty of Yhwh, even when the Mosaic Law prohibits their existence.

Another set of textual problems arise, however, from the claims in Joshua 11:23 and 21:43–45 that "all the land" was taken. These are rhetorically excessive claims, belonging perhaps to a particular convention of story telling, and they do not fit together very well with the concern expressed in several places about "the nations who remain" (e.g., Josh. 23:4). Some scholars find the admission of an incomplete conquest to be the work of editors not from the

26. See the discussion in Lawson G. Stone, "Ethical and Apologetic Tendencies in the Redaction of the Book of Joshua," *CBQ* 53 (1991): 25-35; cf. L. Daniel Hawk, "Conquest Reconfigured: Recasting Warfare in the Redaction of Joshua," in *Writing and Reading War: Rhetoric, Gender, and Ethics in Biblical and Modern Contexts,* ed. Brad E. Kelle and Frank R. Ames (SBLSymS 42; Atlanta: SBL, 2008), pp. 145-60.

27. Hawk, "Conquest Reconfigured," p. 157.

seventh century, but from a later period — after Jerusalem had been overrun by the Babylonians. On this view, the loss of the southern kingdom required an explanation that preserved the sovereignty of Yhwh, and the reasoning is relatively clear: Israel's loyalty to Yhwh was undermined by the "nations who remained," whose gods were an enduring snare for the population of Judah even during the time that Israel's own kings ruled in Jerusalem.

Of course, a claim to have taken "all the land" may be intentional hyperbole on the part of seventh-century editors of the Joshua narrative, but it is nevertheless impossible to homogenize all the voices in Joshua — as if perhaps the same historian bent on claiming "all the land" could immediately turn, in the next breath, to a list of lands not taken.[28] This kind of tension is much better explained by the hypothesis of subsequent editors, after the trauma of Jerusalem's fall, struggling to fit new perspectives into inherited tradition.

NATIVES AND IMMIGRANTS TOGETHER IN A NORTHERN COVENANT CEREMONY?

The narrative portion in Joshua 8:30-35 presents another puzzling set of issues. It depicts Joshua inscribing the law on an altar built on Mount Ebal, but for a number of reasons this picture does not fit together very well with the seventh-century theology of conquest — not least because it envisages a peculiarly peaceful unity of "natives and immigrants." This scenario probably reflects the concerns of even later editors who are aware of the non-national Priestly tradition.[29] The reasons for this conclusion are complex, and I will discuss some of them in the next chapter, but it is worth noting here a few of the key issues at stake in the interpretation of this northern covenant ceremony.

The separable status of this unit in Joshua 8:30-35 is made clear by the ancient manuscript versions, where it is placed after Joshua 5:2 in the Qumran manuscript 4QJosh, but after Joshua 9:2 in the Greek translation of the Hebrew Bible, the Septuagint. The Massoretic text and the Septuagint nevertheless agree that this episode should precede the Gibeonite narrative in chapter 9,

---

28. *Contra* Wolterstorff, "Reading Joshua," pp. 252-54, who seems to suggest that a single historian might compose both hagiographies and more down-to-earth reports. It stretches credulity to imagine that this single historian would work with two different notions of the ban, both attributed to Mosaic law.

29. See, e.g., Rainer Albertz, "The Canonical Alignment of the Book of Joshua," in *Judah and the Judeans in the Fourth Century*, ed. Oded Lipschits, Gary N. Knoppers, and Rainer Albertz (Winona Lake, Ind.: Eisenbrauns, 2007), pp. 287-303.

which as we have seen is a narrative of native survival. The construction of an altar on Mount Ebal is especially surprising, in that it seems to contradict the law in Deuteronomy 12 that Israel can have only one legitimate altar. The "one place" for Israel's sacrifice is elsewhere clarified to be Jerusalem, so an altar built in the north is problematic. Although the narrator in 8:30–35 repeatedly defers to Mosaic Law, there is no hint that this northern altar might need a special explanation. Joshua 8:33 refers to all the people, "immigrant and native" (*ger* and *'ezrach*), participating in the ceremony on Mount Ebal, and this stands out as a glaring anachronism. To which category would the Gibeonites or Rahabites belong, for example? If they are to be considered natives, as a reader might first think, then that would make the Israelites merely immigrants or aliens (*gerim*), but this is the opposite of what is presumed in the Deuteronomic laws designed to protect the fragile "widows, orphans and aliens." In Deuteronomy's social imagination, Israelites are native citizens with power and responsibility, and they are therefore exhorted to care for the weaker aliens or immigrants.

The term *ger* has a large number of uses in the legal traditions of Exodus and Deuteronomy, with a common underlying assumption that these strangers or aliens are people who have been displaced from their country of origin for reasons such as famine or war. The word *'ezrach* ("native citizen") is not mentioned at all in the earlier legal tradition. Based on the distribution of its usage, it is evident that we are dealing here with specific vocabulary from the so-called Holiness Code in Leviticus 17–26, which is a quite distinct piece of legislation that seeks to establish the equity of immigrants and natives. Strikingly, in Leviticus 24:22 for example, we find the claim that there should be "one law" for the native and stranger. The implications of this will be discussed in the next chapter, but for the present we may simply note one biblical scholar's rather paradoxical conclusion: "the concept of אזרח [*'ezrach*] exists in the interests of elucidating the nature of Israel, precisely by pointing to the alien's integration."[30] The primary concern of Joshua 8:30–35, in spite of its narrative setting, appears to be social inclusion, and we can therefore find here perhaps the intervention of editors who are pursuing a "restorative" justice that moves beyond ethnic antagonism.

Rainer Albertz has provided a compelling account of this set of puzzles by arguing that the social vision of "native and immigrant" in Joshua 8:30–35

---

30. McConville, "'Fellow Citizens': Israel and Humanity in Leviticus," in *Reading the Law: Studies in Honour of Gordon J. Wenham*, ed. J. Gordon McConville and Karl Möller (LHBOTS 461; London: T&T Clark, 2007), pp. 10-32, 24.

has been added by editors who acknowledge the authority of all the laws of Torah by combining terminology both from Deuteronomy and from the Holiness Code in Leviticus. The focus of attention for these editors is not on the coherence of a conquest narrative from the distant past, but the alignment of such narratives with the laws of Moses taken as a canonical whole. My own view is that this is not so much a simple alignment of narrative and law, but an implied critique of ethnocentric interpretation of Mosaic Law.[31] But whatever the historical explanation might be for having natives and immigrants shoulder to shoulder on Mount Ebal (half of them facing Mount Gerizim where the Samarian temple was later built), listening to the recitation of Mosaic law, we can be reasonably sure that the "natives" of Joshua 8:30–35 are seen by the narrator here as Yahwists. These Yahwists are happy to include *gerim* in their community, even if these are only to be "hewers of wood and drawers of water," as the Gibeonites are described in Joshua 9:23 and 27.

The fact that prescriptions for an altar and ceremony on Mount Ebal are also incorporated within the very late editing of Deuteronomy 27:4–8 is suggestive. Christophe Nihan has persuasively argued that the audience of Joshua 8:30–35 is to be located at a time during the Persian period (the fifth and fourth century BCE), when northern tradition was being lent a renewed significance, not least by the temple at Gerizim.[32] In contrast with the narrowly Judean orientation of the late-seventh-century Deuteronomistic writings, Joshua 8:30–35 can be understood together with Deuteronomy 27:4–8 and a few other texts as shaping a pan-Israelite vision that had the potential to overcome the antagonism between northern and southern groups, an antagonism that was fostered in particular by Ezra and Nehemiah in the south, and by a sense that descendants of the Babylonian exiles were exclusively the people of God. The more inclusive vision grew, as we shall see below, out of the social imagination of the Holiness Code in Leviticus, whereas the core traditions of Ezra–Nehemiah remain mostly indebted to Deuteronomy, reinterpreting it for the new conditions of limited political autonomy within the Persian Empire.[33]

31. Mark G. Brett, "Natives and Immigrants in the Social Imagination of the Holiness School," in *Imagining the Other and Constructing Israelite Identity in the early Second Temple Period*, ed. Ehud Ben Zvi and Diana Edelman (LHBOTS 456; London: T & T Clark, 2014), pp. 89-104.

32. With a comprehensive review of the previous literature, see Nihan, "The Torah between Samaria and Judah: Shechem and Gerizim in Deuteronomy and Joshua," in *The Pentateuch as Torah*, ed. Gary N. Knoppers and Bernard M. Levinson (Winona Lake, Ind.: Eisenbrauns, 2007), pp. 187-223.

33. Sara Japhet, "Periodization between History and Ideology II: Chronology and Ideology

CONCLUSION

Some accounts of the nationalism in the Hebrew Bible seem to presuppose that ideologies adhere to biblical texts, almost regardless of the social contexts within which these texts are conceived or reinterpreted. There is little allowance on this essentialist model for the fact that living traditions are ongoing *debates* about the norms and content of that tradition. As Jacob L. Wright has suggested, "The construction and contestation of memories is well attested in contexts where cultural–political expressions are not monopolized by a single power and where groups can readily challenge each other on issues posed by populations within their societies and on their borders."[34]

In this chapter, I have tried to demonstrate the ironies at work even in a single biblical book like Joshua. None of the expressions of nationalism in this book amount to settler colonialism as it is now understood, although the very earliest *cherem* war traditions perhaps present a localized intra-indigenous permutation — so localized that the warring parties probably spoke dialects of the very same language.[35] The local forms of conflict reflected in these earliest *cherem* traditions are very different from the much later colonial imaginaries of the modern period, discussed in Chapter Two. Indeed, the version of national identity created in Deuteronomy was deliberately constructed in resistance to the impositions of the Assyrian empire. The fact that Jerusalem's theologians borrowed and twisted the covenant–treaty discourse from the Assyrians in a covert strategy of mimicry is something readily understood in postcolonial studies today.

In one of the ironies of biblical reception in the nineteenth-century colonial history, for example, the Maori leader Te Kooti seems to have pursed Deuteronomy's original impulse of resistance: Te Kooti configured Maori sovereignty as "Israelite" and saw himself as empowered by Mosaic authority to drive out

---

in Ezra-Nehemiah," in *Judah and the Judeans in the Persian Period,* ed. Oded Lipschits and Manfred Oeming (Winona Lake, Ind.: Eisenbrauns, 2006), pp. 491-508.

34. Quoted from a forthcoming book, *A People in Arms: War Commemoration, Nation-Building, and the Formation of the Hebrew Bible,* by kind permission of the author. For the distinctive perspectives on Canaanites in Priestly and Holiness traditions, see Baruch J. Schwartz, "Reexamining the Fate of the 'Canaanites' in the Torah Traditions," in *Sefer Moshe: The Moshe Weinfeld Jubilee Volume,* ed. Chaim Cohen, Avi Hurvitz and Shalom M. Paul (Winona Lake, Ind.: Eisenbrauns, 2004), pp. 151-70.

35. On the distinctive features of settler colonialism, see especially James Belich, *Replenishing the Earth: The Settler Revolution and the Rise of the Angloworld* (Oxford: Oxford University Press, 2009); Lorenzo Veracini, *Settler Colonialism: A Theoretical Overview* (Houndmills: Palgrave Macmillan, 2010).

the imperial British, much to the consternation of the colonial authorities at the time.[36]

Our contemporary questions about settler sovereignties, provoked especially by Edward Said, must receive more subtle treatment than he himself provided. There may well have been a historical Joshua who pointed his javelin towards Ai, but he was not likely the servant of Mosaic Law as it was conceived in Deuteronomy, and even less likely acquainted with Priestly law. Millennia later, we can hardly claim that the history of biblical interpretation bore Joshua's javelin half way round the world with Captain Cook. As we have seen, when the "doctrine of discovery" finally reached the colony of New South Wales, it was after a long and tortuous relay race run by Christian princes and secular lawyers, each with their own interests at heart. Any plausible invocation of biblical norms today would need to take account of the fate of the national imaginary after the Babylonian exile, and also of the quite different theological imagination emerging from the Priestly and wisdom writers. It is to this wider conversation that we now turn.

36. See Judith Binney, *Redemption Songs: A Life of the Nineteenth-Century Maori Leader Te Kooti Arikirangi Te Turuki* (Melbourne: Melbourne University Press, 1997), pp. 70-72, 115, 210, 219, 287, 502.

5. Sovereignty in the Priestly Tradition

In arguing for the possibility of secular theology, I have suggested that it is important for Christian theology to provide its own reasons for separating church and state. In the wake of colonialism, for example, it is necessary to relinquish any Christian claim to privilege in the public sphere. Perhaps paradoxically, I want to suggest in this chapter that some analogous issues were already explored in the unfolding of the Priestly tradition in the Hebrew Bible, particularly as this tradition struggled with the trauma of the destruction of Jerusalem in 587 BCE, the experience of forced migration, and subsequently with life in a province of the Persian Empire. It will be suggested that the Priestly theologians engaged in a lively debate around the fundamental question of how Israel might be divested of her own political sovereignty while preserving her sense of God's ultimate providence. This debate, which adopted notably different views from what we find in the national imaginary, illustrates the scope of critical deliberation in pre-modern times, precisely when that deliberation was understood in metaphysical terms as the discovery of divine revelation.[1]

The origins of the Priestly tradition are much disputed, but they may well extend back even to seventh-century Priestly sources (designated "P" in scholarly custom). If so, then the earliest P documents will have been contemporary with

---

1. For exemplary and detailed case studies of inner-biblical critique, see Bernard M. Levinson, *Deuteronomy and the Hermeneutics of Legal Innovation* (New York: Oxford University Press, 1987); Bernard M. Levinson, *Legal Revision and Religious Renewal in Ancient Israel* (Cambridge: Cambridge University Press, 2008). Levinson's studies illustrate the kind of deliberation that is largely denied by Michael Walzer, *In God's Shadow: Politics in the Hebrew Bible* (New Haven: Yale University Press, 2012), who adopts an overly narrow conception of "politics."

the form of Deuteronomy or "D" that stems from that same period.[2] A number of scholars have argued vigorously that the theological currents of D and P represent distinct ideologies or imaginaries, whether they were composed concurrently or in successive historical periods. A standard view in nineteenth-century biblical criticism assigned D to the seventh century and P to the Babylonian exile in the following century. This classic view has sometimes been condemned on the grounds that it was implicitly anti-Semitic, notably when P's theology and law was presented as a decline into legalism and priestcraft. Ironically, the leading experts on the D and P traditions today include many Jewish and Catholic scholars, and any residual Protestant disdain for P may now be regarded as irrelevant to the historical study of the Pentateuch's composition. Simplistic views of D and P as unified literary sources have been largely overwhelmed by much more complex models of composition by scribal schools who were active over long periods. Accordingly, in order to understand the extended Priestly conversation (including the so-called "post-P" developments), we will reflect in this chapter on the significance of nuances that reveal internal differences within this tradition, and in particular, the distinctive contributions of the Holiness School (now often referred to using the sigla "H").[3]

To begin with, however, it will be important to describe some of the key theological differences between D and P. In contrast with D's focus on conquest and the life of the state, the foundational themes of the Priestly tradition are creation, Abraham and the cult — the Priestly system of sacrifices and purity. For example, what is arguably the oldest summary of Israel's story in Deuteronomy points to Jacob, not Abraham, as the primary ancestor. According to this tradition, it is Jacob who sojourned in Egypt and subsequently became a "great nation": "My father was a fugitive Aramean. He went down to Egypt

2. This has been argued, for example, by the distinguished Jewish scholar, Moshe Weinfeld, *The Place of the Law in the Religion of Ancient Israel* (VTSup 100; Leiden: Brill, 2004), notably in his chapter on "Theological Currents in Pentateuchal Literature." See also Baruch H. Halpern, *From Gods to God: The Dynamics of Iron Age Cosmologies* (FAT 63; Tübingen: Mohr Siebeck, 2009), pp. 427-78.

3. See especially Israel Knohl, *The Sanctuary of Silence: The Priestly Torah and the Holiness School* (Minneapolis: Fortress, 1995); Christophe Nihan, *From Priestly Torah to Pentateuch: A Study in the Composition of the Book of Leviticus* (FAT II/25; Tübingen: Mohr Siebeck, 2007). In the discussion that follows, I will focus on the conversation between P and H, while leaving to one side the complexities that belong to the current study of the book of Numbers. An overview of these complexities is provided by Reinhard Achenbach, "Der Pentateuch, seine Theokratischen Bearbeitungen und Josua–2 Könige," in *Les Dernières Rédactions du Pentateuque, de L'Hexateuque et de L'Ennéateuque*, ed. Thomas Römer and Konrad Schmid (BETL 203; Leuven: Leuven University Press, 2007), pp. 225-53.

with meager numbers and lived there as an alien (*gur*), but there he became a great nation (*goy gadol*), mighty and populous (*rav*)" (Deut. 26:5). Some of the terminology in this verse is prominent in Genesis, yet each of the key terms in italics is turned to quite different purposes in the Priestly tradition. Notably, it is Abram in Genesis 12:2 who receives the promise from Yhwh to become a "great nation" (*goy gadol*), and in one respect this promise finds fulfilment in Jacob's great nation, referred to in Deuteronomy 26:5, but a closer reading of the Genesis narratives suggests that matters are more complex.

In one of the most popular historical hypotheses advanced in critical studies of the Pentateuch, the divine promise in Genesis 12:1-3 was taken to be part of a distinctive literary source which freely used the name "Yhwh" (the so-called "J" document following the German spelling Jhwh). Yhwh's promise in this reconstructed source was taken to reflect its time of composition, when King David and his son Solomon managed to bring a measure of unity to the separate tribes, achieving a social organization that might be described as a single nation, or in Hebrew terminology, a *goy*. Many elements in this old hypothesis have been heavily criticized in recent scholarship,[4] but the continuity of a national imaginary between Genesis 12:2 and Deuteronomy 26:5 — reflected in the phrase *goy gadol* — is striking, and not least because the Priestly account of the ancestors is so markedly different.

The Priestly tradition is at pains to emphasize that the ancestors in Genesis did not know the name of Yhwh at all, although the subtlety of the variations on the divine names is often obscured in English translations. The differences are clearer when we avoid the familiar English terms "God" and "Lord," for example in a key text that sets out the Priestly understanding of ancestral religion:

> Elohim also spoke to Moses and said to him: "I am the Yhwh. I appeared to Abraham, Isaac, and Jacob as El Shaddai, but by my name Yhwh I did not make myself known to them. I also established my covenant with them, to give them the land of Canaan, the land in which they resided as aliens. (Exod. 6:2–4)

4. Notably, see Konrad Schmid, *Genesis and the Moses Story: Israel's Dual Origins in the Hebrew Bible*, trans. James D. Nogalski (Siphrut 3; Winona Lake, Ind.: Eisenbrauns, 2010), translation of *Erzväter und Exodus: Untersuchungen zur doppelten Begründung der Ursprünge Israels in den Geschichtsbüchern des Alten Testaments* (WMANT 81; Neukirchen-Vluyn: Neukirchener, 1999); Albert de Pury, "The Jacob Story," in *A Farewell to the Yahwist? The Composition of the Pentateuch in Recent European Interpretation*, ed. Thomas B. Dozeman and Konrad Schmid (SBLSymS 34; Atlanta, Ga.: Society of Biblical Literature, 2006), pp. 51-72.

While P fully agrees with Deuteronomy's affirmation that the ancestors of the exodus generation knew the name Yhwh, the new point being made over against D is that the earlier generations of ancestors — the ancestors prior to the exodus — knew God only under the name of El Shaddai. The editors of Genesis were respectful enough to the earlier traditions to preserve many texts that referred to Yhwh, such as in Genesis 12:1-3, but P's specific contribution to this conversation has some remarkably new things to say about the character of God's promises to the ancestors.

This is made especially clear in the Priestly account of the covenant with Abraham in Genesis 17. The departure from D's national imaginary emerges in the reason supplied for the change of the ancestor's name from Abram to Abraham: he is to be the father of "many" nations, not just of the single "great nation" as suggested by the promise in Genesis 12:2. Moreover, unlike the promise from Yhwh to Abram in Genesis 12, Genesis 17:1b–6 insists that this covenant came from the mouth of El Shaddai:

> "I am El Shaddai; walk before me, and be blameless. And I will make my covenant between me and you, and will make you exceedingly numerous (*rbh*)." Then Abram fell on his face; and Elohim said to him, "As for me, this is my covenant with you: You shall be the ancestor of a multitude of nations (*goyim*). No longer shall your name be Abram, but your name shall be Abraham; for I have made you the ancestor of a multitude of nations. I will make you exceedingly fruitful; and I will make nations of you, and kings shall come from you."

The view expressed in Exodus 6:2–4, that the ancestors of Genesis knew only the divine name El Shaddai, is preserved here in Genesis 17 with complete consistency, even when the divine name Yhwh is also mentioned. The narrator in verse 1 conveys to the audience, rather than to Abram himself, that the divinity who makes this covenant is Yhwh: "When Abram was ninety-nine years old, Yhwh appeared to Abram, and said to him, "I am El Shaddai." Without any risk to later conceptions of monotheism, the Priestly theologian acknowledges a multiplicity of divine names and through them conveys a much more subtle account of divine sovereignty.

If Abraham's progeny include a multiplicity of nations, this necessarily implies for P a multiplicity of kings within the lineages of each of these *goyim*. This new multinational vision is not simply restricted to the two nations of Israel and Judah, but extends beyond these to all the descendants of Abraham. This is indicated already in Genesis 17:20–21 where we find that Abraham's son Ishmael, born to his Egyptian wife Hagar, is destined to become a nation (precisely termed a *goy gadol*) in his own right, even though he is explicitly excluded from the covenant that is to be secured with Sarah's yet unborn son, Isaac. Ishmael inherits a national promise, along with P's characteristic blessing of fecundity: "As for Ishmael, I have heard you; I will bless him and make him fruitful and exceedingly numerous; he shall be the father of twelve princes, and I will make him a great nation (*goy gadol*)." And indeed, Ishmael is immediately circumcised, taking up the symbolism of the "eternal covenant" with Abraham, which is inscribed on the flesh (17:13, 25).

How do Hagar and Ishmael then fit with the broader scope of the covenantal promises? The covenant with Abraham in Genesis 17 is clearly multilayered in its conception, and perhaps even multilayered in its history of composition. Some scholars have attempted to explain the complexity of P's vision by suggesting, for example, that although the nation descended from Ishmael belongs under the multinational covenant with Abraham's seed, only the Isaac–Jacob lineage is chosen to live in cultic relationship with Yhwh.[5] This position seems to yield the implication that all Abraham's seed belong under the covenant with El Shaddai, but a more specific covenant or cult of Yhwh is implicitly acknowledged in Genesis 17, which will belong only to Jacob–Israel. In other words, although Genesis 17 wants to emphasize Abraham's *international* descendants, the Priestly imaginary has in effect retained the vision of the "great nation" that links Abram to a united Israelite kingdom by making the national imaginary part of a much larger vision.

This is indeed an elegant solution to a difficult set of textual problems, but it begs the question of why any author or editor would want to conclude the narrative of Genesis 17 with the circumcision of Ishmael. It seems to me that we should interpret Ishmael's circumcision as a deliberate attempt on the part of a later editor to affirm the filial relationships between all of Abraham's descendants, precisely when those relationships were being challenged by a more narrowly conceived national identity. Contrary to a view that might see the chosen people as uniquely holy in ethnic terms — perhaps a single "holy nation" or "holy seed" as Ezra 9 suggests[6] — Genesis 17 insists not only that

5. See, for example, de Pury, "Pg as the Absolute Beginning," in *Les Dernières Rédactions du Pentateuque, de L'Hexateuque et de L'Ennéateuque*, ed. Thomas Römer and Konrad Schmid (BETL 203; Leuven: Leuven University Press, 2007), pp. 118-19; Albert de Pury, "Abraham: The Priestly Writer's 'Ecumenical' Ancestor," in *Rethinking the Foundations: Historiography in the Ancient World and in the Bible. Essays in Honour of John Van Seters*, ed. Stephen L. McKenzie and Thomas Römer (BZAW 239; Berlin: de Gruyter, 2000), pp. 163-81.

6. See Jean-Louis Ska, "Exode 19,3b-6 et l'identité de l'Israël postexilique," in *Studies in the*

Ishmael belongs to Abraham's seed, but in addition, that there are reasons why sons born in Abraham's household to foreigners — those "not of your seed" — should be circumcised as a sign of the broader covenant with El Shaddai (Gen. 17:12).

Before we explore the significance of this interpretation, it may be helpful to summarize some of the less controversial features of Genesis 17. First, in contrast with the national covenant, which makes blessing conditional on law observance, this Priestly covenant is essentially a divine promise. We hear of a generalized expectation that the descendants of Abraham would "walk before" El Shaddai, but the only specific requirement of this covenant is that male children be circumcised. There is no hint of the hundreds of commandments yet to emerge under the conditions of the Mosaic Law.

We should note, however, that the Priestly discourse of an "eternal covenant" (*berit 'olam*) has already appeared in Genesis in the promise to Noah, which encompasses "every living creature" (Gen. 9:10, 16). It is this radically inclusive covenant in P that encompasses also the unity of all humanity, both male and female, made in the "image of Elohim" (as P has claimed in Gen. 1:26-27). There is never any suggestion in Priestly theology that this divine image can be damaged by sin or impurity. Thus, although the essential dignity of all human beings before God is not stated in specifically covenantal language, P's universal conception of human dignity is embedded more broadly within the eternal covenant with "every living creature," and on the basis of the divine image in humankind, a universalized ethic is asserted in Genesis 9:6. In short, the Priestly theology of eternal covenants provides the outer frame for the more specifically Israelite particularity of identity.[7]

While it may be tempting to conclude that the Priestly imaginary is simply "non-national,"[8] we also need to account for P's retention of the political vocabulary of nations or *goyim*. A long-standing scholarly view distinguishes

---

Book of Exodus: Redaction – Reception – Interpretation, ed. Marc Vervenne (BETL 126; Leuven: Peeters, 1996), pp. 289-317; translated as "Exodus 19:3-6 and the Identity of Postexilic Israel" in Ska, *The Exegesis of the Pentateuch* (FAT 66; Tübingen: Mohr-Siebeck, 2009), pp. 139-64.

7. On the details and development of Priestly covenant theology, see Christophe Nihan "The Priestly Covenant, Its Reinterpretation and the Composition of 'P,'" in *The Strata of the Priestly Writings: Contemporary Debate and Future Directions*, ed. Sarah Shectman and Joel Baden (ATANT 95: Zürich: Theologischer Verlag Zürich, 2009), pp. 87-134; Joseph Blenkinsopp, "Abraham as Paradigm in the Priestly History in Genesis," *Journal of Biblical Literature* 128 (2009): 225-41.

8. Cf. Michaela Bauks's comment that "The people of Yhwh are more than a nation." "Les notions de 'peuple' et de 'terre' dans l'oeuvre sacerdotale (Pᵍ)," *Transeuphratène* 30 (2005): 19-36, 30.

in Hebrew semantics between an *'am*, a people group reflecting an ethnic solidarity of some kind, and a *goy*, a people who normally possess both territory
and monarchic sovereignty.[9] For P to describe Abraham as the father of "many
nations," and Jacob as the father of an "assembly of nations" (Gen. 35:11), is
a striking choice of words when we realize that this vision cannot readily be
aligned with the two national histories of Israel and Judah. The Priestly vision
speaks beyond this narrower horizon specifically to include the Ishmaelite
"great nation" within the seed of Abraham, and beyond Ishmael to large number of *goyim* who trace their lineage in some sense back to Abraham. How is
the boldness of this vision to be understood?

THE PRIESTLY IMAGINARY AFTER THE TRAUMA OF EXILE

For the purposes of the present discussion, we may accept the hypothesis
mentioned above that the earliest P documents were substantially formed in
the late seventh and early sixth century. But there are a number of reasons
to think that these documents were revised after the exile, when the Persian
Empire overwhelmed the Babylonians and allowed the Israelite "children of
the exile" to return from Babylon to their homeland. This later historical setting of P's story of Abraham is betrayed, for example, by the anachronistic
reference to the patriarch's home city as "Ur of Chaldeans" (Gen. 11:27-32), a
name that can only be derived from the time of the Neo-Babylonian Empire
and not from earlier centuries. Indeed, we can be reasonably sure that it was
specifically a P author who transformed the traditional association of Abraham with Haran in order to assert that the patriarch came from the same area
where the Judean exiles lived, making Haran merely a stopover on the way to
the promised land. This view has led to a renewed appreciation of the Priestly
Abraham as, in effect, a model immigrant from Babylon to Judah during the
time of Persian rule.[10]

---

9. The terminology overlaps in some cases, but the semantic fields are not identical. See,
e.g., Leonard Rost, "Die Bezeichnungen für Land und Volk im alten Testament" (1934), in *Das
kleine Credo und andere Studien zum Alten Testament* (Heidelberg: Quelle & Meyer, 1965),
pp. 76-101; Ephraim A. Speiser, "'People' and 'Nation' in Israel," *JBL* 79 (1960): 157-63; Aelred
Cody, "When Is the Chosen People called a Goy?," *VT* 14 (1964): 1-6; Ron Clements, "גוי *goy*,"
in *TDOT*, II: 426-33.

10. See Erhard Blum, *Die Komposition der Vätergeschichte* (WMANT 57; Neukirchen-
Vluyn: Neukirchener Verlag, 1984), pp. 343-44; cf. Jakob Wöhrle, "The Un-Empty Land: The
Concept of Exile and Land in P," in *The Concept of Exile in Ancient Israel and Its Historical*

Having been deprived of political sovereignty, a key question for Judeans after the exile was not just whether they could again become a unified people or 'am, but whether they could in some sense still form a single nation or goy. One might presume that the semantics are sufficiently clear for this to be a non-question: Judah (or "Yehud" in the administrative language of Aramaic) became a province of the Persian Empire, and while this province may in some sense have possessed territory, it did not possess sovereignty. The time of Israelite and Judean kings was past. There may have been something of a semantic shift in the Persian period, since in the later prophetic traditions of the day we find references to a multiplicity of goyim within the empire. Perhaps these "nations" enjoyed a relative measure of autonomy, even including local forms of kingship. Yehud, however, possessed Persian-sponsored native governors like Nehemiah, rather than kings, so our original question returns: how could Abraham as the ideal returnee from exile also be seen as in some sense the father of "many nations"?

According to Jean-Louis Ska, the editors who composed Exodus 19:3b-6 were also writing during the Persian period, and yet they were still willing to describe Israel as a single "holy nation":[11]

> [3b] Thus you shall say to the house of Jacob, and tell the Israelites: [4] You have seen what I did to the Egyptians, and how I bore you on eagles' wings and brought you to myself. [5] Now therefore, if you obey my voice and keep my covenant, you shall be my treasured possession out of all the peoples. Indeed, the whole earth is mine, [6] but you shall be for me a *kingdom of priests* and a *holy nation*. These are the words that you shall speak to the Israelites.

While it is not necessary to rehearse here all of Ska's arguments relating to the dating of Exodus 19:3-6, his conclusions are suggestive: this text, which combines elements from both the Deuteronomic and Priestly traditions, comes from a period during which "Israel must renounce the restoration of the monarchy" while at the same time asserting a distinct identity over against other social groups within the Persian Empire.[12] Ska proposes a chronological

---

Contexts, ed. Ehud Ben Zvi and Christophe Levin (BZAW 404; Berlin: de Gruyter, 2010), pp. 189-206, 192-93; Blenkinsopp, "Abraham as Paradigm."

11. This reference to a single "holy nation" overlaps with the "great nation" discourse of Genesis 12:2 and 46:3, the latter text proposing that Jacob can become a "great nation" in Egypt (as does Deut. 26:5). Ska proposes that the "great nation" discourse in Genesis is also a product of Persian period editing, but this point is not necessary to my argument here. *Exegesis of the Pentateuch*, pp. 46-66.

12. Ska, *Exegesis of the Pentateuch*, p. 141.

scheme which sees Exodus 19:3-6 written *after* what he calls "the optimistic preaching of the post-exilic prophets who took a positive view of Israel's relations with the nations" but *before* suspicion against the nations hardened to the extent that we find in Ezra-Nehemiah.[13] In Ezra-Nehemiah, the national imaginary was reinterpreted not as a legal obligation to destroy Canaanites but as a call for the Israelites to maintain a clear separateness from other groups or *goyim*. In this tradition, the nation was reborn with a vocation of holiness construed in ethnic terms.

Some of Ska's chronological hypotheses are open to question, not least his dating of Exodus 19:3-6, but his basic insight is compelling: at the beginning of the Persian period, Israel was exploring a range of options for articulating religious and cultural autonomy, provoked especially by the traumatic loss of political sovereignty. One line of tradition has drawn the Priestly language of holiness into the heart of the national imaginary in Ezra-Nehemiah, calling for a separation from foreign impurities even in cases where Israelites had intermarried with the so-called "peoples of the lands" (e.g., Neh. 9:2; 10:29; Ezra 9:1-3).[14] Where Deuteronomy's law called for slaughter of Canaanites, Ezra-Nehemiah called for divorce, but nevertheless, the clear boundaries of a holy nation were to be maintained.

This is an illuminating account of how a community might survive the trauma of exile and revitalize itself by returning to national, cultural roots. What it does not explain, however, is the multinational rhetoric of the Priestly tradition.[15] As we have seen, the Priestly imagination has situated Abraham's many *goyim* within an "ecumenical" scheme, with concentric circles constructed in hierarchical terms: in the outermost circle, which encompasses the entire created order, the name of the Creator is Elohim. Yet this Elohim has also been made known to the circle of Abraham's seed under the name El

---

13. Ska, "Identity of Postexilic Israel," p. 141. See the use of "separate" (*bdl* in the *hiphil* stem) in Ezra 8:24; 9:1; 10:8, 11, 16; Nehemiah 9:2; 10:29; 13:3. Many scholars find an easing of the social boundaries in Ezra 6:21, but this text almost certainly comes from a later layer of Ezra-Nehemiah traditions, as we will show below.

14. See further Rainer Albertz, "Purity Strategies and Political Interests in the Policy of Nehemiah," in *Confronting the Past: Archaeological and Historical Essays on Ancient Israel in Honor of William G. Dever*, ed. Seymour Gitin, J. Edward Wright, and J. P. Dessel (Winona Lake, Ind.: Eisenbrauns, 2006), pp. 199-206.

15. On the internationalism of P's Abraham, see Albert de Pury, "Abraham: The Priestly Writer's 'Ecumenical' Ancestor"; Konrad Schmid, "Judean Identity and Ecumenicity: The Political Theology of the Priestly Document," in *Judah and Judeans in the Achaemenid Period: Negotiating Identity in an International Context*, ed. Oded Lipschits, Gary N. Knoppers, and Manfred Oeming (Winona Lake: Eisenbrauns, 2011), pp. 3-26.

Shaddai, and more specifically to the seed of Jacob-Israel as Yhwh.[16] Among others, Thomas Römer has aptly described this universalizing scheme as a kind of "inclusive" monotheism": in spite of the very specific requirements of holiness given to Israel, "all people of the earth venerate the same god, irrespective of whether they address him as Elohim, El, or El Shaddai."[17] Why would this scheme, along with its multinational discourse, have come to fruition in the Persian period?

A number of biblical scholars have recently converged on the conclusion that the Priestly theologians are mimicking the Persian imperial religion.[18] The multinational visions of Genesis 17:4 and 35:11 can in this light be read as imperial mimicry, and indeed, the inclusive monotheism expressed by P is strikingly analogous to the Persian inclusive monotheism, within which Ahura-mazda was seen as the creator of the world and the giver of lands.[19] Persian rhetoric configured their empire as a network of nations, and their monarchs as "king of countries."[20] Some commentators have suggested that this imperial rhetoric has been absorbed by the Priestly writers in a process of ideological accommodation, but it seems more likely to me that what we find in the biblical texts is a strategy of "sly civility," to use a concept derived from postcolonial studies.[21] In spite of appearances, P's ecumenical tone does not

---

16. The identification of these three "circles" may be traced back to Gerhard von Rad, *Die Priesterschrift im Hexateuch. Literarisch untersucht und theologisch gewertet* (Stuttgart: Kohlhammer, 1934), p. 167.

17. Thomas Römer, "The Exodus Narrative," in *Strata of the Priestly Writings*, p. 162; cf. Christophe Nihan, *From Priestly Torah*, p. 386.

18. de Pury, "Pg as Absolute Beginning," pp. 123-26; cf. Mark G. Brett, "Permutations of Sovereignty in the Priestly Tradition," *Vetus Testamentum* 63 (2013): 383-92.

19. Gregor Ahn, *Religiöse Herrscherlegitimation im Achämenidschen Iran: Die Voraussetzungen und die Strukturen ihrer Argumentation* (Acta Iranica 31; Leiden: Brill, 1992), pp. 255-85; Eckart Otto, "The Holiness Code in Diachrony and Synchrony," in *The Strata of the Priestly Writings*, ed. Shectman and Baden, p. 137; Römer, "The Exodus Narrative," pp. 162-63, 169. Another clue to the Priestly social imagination may be provided by the use of a closely related phrase "assembly of great nations" in Jeremiah 50:9, describing the military capacity of the Persian Empire.

20. Ahn, *Religiöse Herrscherlegitimation*, pp. 258-71; cf. Pierre Briant, *From Cyrus to Alexander: A History of the Persian Empire* (Winona Lake, Ind.: Eisenbrauns, 2002), 173-78; Jakob Wöhrle, "Abraham amidst the Nations: The Priestly Concept of Covenant and the Persian Imperial Ideology," in *Covenant in the Persian Period*, ed. Richard J. Bautch and Gary N. Knoppers (Winona Lake, Ind.: Eisenbrauns, 2015), pp. 23-39.

21. See the foundational work in Homi Bhabha, *The Location of Culture* (London: Routledge, 1994) and the application in Anselm C. Hagedorn, "Local Law in an Imperial Context: The Role of Torah in the (Imagined) Persian Period," in *The Pentateuch as Torah: New Models*

express a "gentleman's agreement" with the empire, but a transformation of political discourse that subtly contests the ultimate grounds of sovereignty.[22] Yhwh's jurisdiction is retained, even if God may be known by other names, but this jurisdiction no longer needs a national conquest narrative to support it. Abraham is in this respect not so much the father of an "empire" as a divinely constituted counter-empire. Israel's dignity and Yhwh's sovereignty are preserved, even when experience might suggest otherwise.

LAND TENURE IN ABRAHAM'S EMPIRE

This understanding of an Abrahamic counter-empire can be further illustrated in relation to the principal expression of political sovereignty: the ownership of land. From the Priestly point of view, the possession of land is envisaged as a benefit for all of Abraham's descendants, regardless of whether they belong to the elect or to the non-elect, i.e., whether they worship God under the name of Yhwh or not. Radical title is owned by God, and the land is, in effect, leased to each generation as a "holding" (*'achuzzah*), with conditions that bind all those who live in the land, regardless of their ethnic identity.[23] This theology of "leasehold" tenure is taken to extremes in the Holiness Code, where it is even claimed that because Yhwh is the ultimate landowner, Israelites can only ever be tenants in the land. From this legal perspective, if Yhwh owns the radical title to land, then in contrast with Deuteronomy's assumptions, all Israelites are to be understood as *gerim*, i.e., as immigrants or sojourners, not just a marginalized category of non-natives (Lev. 25:23).

The first clue to this theology of land may be found in Genesis 17:8, where the divine promises relating to land would seem to descend without discrimination on all of Abraham's seed: "And I will give to you, and to your seed after you, the

---

for Understanding Its Promulgation and Acceptance, ed. Gary N. Knoppers and Bernard M. Levinson (Winona Lake, Ind.: Eisenbrauns, 2007), pp. 57-76; Mark G. Brett, *Decolonizing God: The Bible in the Tides of Empire* (Sheffield: Phoenix, 2008), pp. 112-131.

22. De Pury refers to this accommodation as a "gentlemen's agreement," in "Pg as Absolute Beginning," p. 125; contrast Brett, "Permutations of Sovereignty," pp. 388-89.

23. See especially Michaela Bauks, "Die Begriffe מורשה und אחזה) in Pg. Überlegungen zur landkonzeption der Priestergrundschrift," *ZAW* 116 (2004): 171-88; Manfred Köckert, "Das Land in der priesterlichen Komposition des Pentateuch," in *Von Gott reden: Beiträge zur Theologie und Exegese des Alten Testaments. Festschrift für Siegfried Wagner,* ed. Dieter Viewege and Ernst-Joachim Waschke (Neukirchen-Vluyn: Neukirchener Verlag, 1995), pp. 147-62; Philippe Guillaume, *Land and Calendar: The Priestly Document from Genesis 1 to Joshua 18* (LHBOTS 391; New York: T&T Clark, 2009), pp. 102-22; Konrad Schmid, *Genesis and the Moses Story,* pp. 244-45.

land of your sojourning, all the land of Canaan, for a perpetual holding; and I will be their Elohim."[24] This text is somewhat ambiguous, since the reference to Canaan might be interpreted as a merely national boundary, rather than conveying an expansive force with the reference to "*all* the land of Canaan." The suggestion that the blessing of land is dispersed even beyond the boundaries of Canaan, and certainly beyond the narrowed borders of the province of Yehud in the Persian period, can be found in the description of the dwelling places of Esau's clans as "their holdings" (Gen. 36:43), a text that takes up P's key terminology for the use of land, '*achuzzah*.[25] Why, we may ask, have the Priestly authors departed from the older conceptions of land title within the national imaginary and concerned themselves also with the landholdings of Esau's clans, the Edomites, and indeed, with the land and kings of Ishmael's clans?

In the context of the early Persian period, the Priestly tradition has apparently reformulated the particularity of Israel's identity in ways that promoted peaceful relations both inside and outside of the province of Yehud — whether with the people who remained in Judah during the Babylonian exile,[26] or with people groups who were living close by as neighbours. P's "ecumenical" tone may also be related to the historical likelihood that Abraham's tomb was venerated by Judeans, Arabs and Edomites, and its location in Hebron implies that it lay outside of Yehud, in Idumea.[27] The peripheral location of this ancestral tomb, outside the borders of Yehud, effectively undermines the potential function of this site as a national symbol, and instead provides for a more complex layering of filial relationships.

24. See de Pury, "Abraham," pp. 172-75; Albert de Pury, "Der priesterschriftliche Umgang mit der Jakobsgeschichte," in *Schriftauslegung in der Schrift. Festschrift für Odil Hannes Steck*, ed. Rainer G. Kratz, Thomas Krüger and Konrad Schmid (BZAW 300; Berlin: de Gruyter, 2000), pp. 52-54.

25. Köckert, "Das Land in der priesterlichen Komposition," p. 155; Nihan, *From Priestly Torah*, p. 68.

26. Wöhrle, "The Un-Empty Land," pp. 189-206; Jakob Wöhrle, *Fremdlinge im eigenen Land: Zur Entstehung und Intention der priesterlichen Passagen der Vätergeschichte* (FRLANT 246; Göttingen: Vandenhoeck & Ruprecht, 2012), pp. 189-92, 217-21. Similarly, Nihan argues that P promotes the "cohabitation between returning exiles and non-exiles." *From Priestly Torah*, p. 387.

27. Schmid, "Judean Identity and Ecumenicity: The Political Theology of the Priestly Document," in *Judah and Judeans in the Achaemenid Period: Negotiating Identity in an International Context*, ed. Oded Lipschits, Gary N. Knoppers, and Manfred Oeming (Winona Lake: Eisenbrauns, 2011), pp. 3-26, 26; following Ernst A. Knauf, "Grenzen der Toleranz in der Priesterschaft," *BK* 58 (2003): 224-27; Albert de Pury, "Le tombeau des Abrahamides d'Hébron et sa fonction au début de l'époque perse," *Transeuphratene* 30 (2005): 183-84.

In his recent analysis of these issues, Jakob Wöhrle has attempted to bring greater precision to P's picture of peaceful co-existence by arguing that the descent of land rights among Abraham's seed actually envisages their dispersal to neighboring territories, rather than a hybrid mixing of land holdings within Yehud itself. The evidence he cites from Genesis 13:6, 11–12 and 36:6–8 suggests an arrangement within which the descendants of Lot and Esau disperse to their own lands on the borders of Canaan not as a result of divine command, but simply on the grounds of quotidian necessity: "their possessions were so great that they could not live together" (13:6 and 36:7). They respectfully acknowledge their separate territories, while explicitly maintaining the bonds of kinship, e.g., when Jacob and Esau together bury their father Isaac in Genesis 35:29.[28]

As for the picture of Abraham as the ideal *golah* immigrant, Wöhrle suggests that:

> According to P, the existence of the people who already lived in the land before the ancestors came to it is not presented as being a temporary fact which has to be overcome. The land is given to the ancestors not instead of the people of the land, but in *addition* to these people.[29]

The settlers of Yehud are seen politically as a mixed body, rather than a single sovereign nation. The ancestors are described as *gerim*, for example in Genesis 17:8 and 28:4, not just because the land to which they returned was already inhabited, but because "the situation after the exile when the returnees were strangers in their own land is described as being a fact which characterizes the life in this land all along."[30] The sojourner status in the Priestly imaginary is not just a transitional arrangement but an enduring form of life before God. And thus for the communities living in imperial Persian domains, a theological tension between citizenship and sojourning will be maintained.[31] The Priestly narrative and the laws of the Holiness Code therefore agree that in a theological sense all the seed of Abraham are *gerim*, whether they live inside the borders of Yehud or not.[32]

---

28. Wöhrle, *Fremdlinge im eigenen Land*, pp. 202-207.

29. Wöhrle, "The Un-Empty Land," p. 204; so also Römer, "The Exodus Narrative," p. 165; Nihan, *From Priestly Torah*, p. 67.

30. Wöhrle, "The Un-Empty Land," p. 202.

31. Nihan, *From Priestly Torah*, 66-67; following Köckert, "Das Land in der priesterlichen Komposition," p. 155.

32. Cf. Römer, "The Exodus Narrative," p. 164. H is, however, not indifferent to whether people live in or outside the land, and Leviticus 26 deals precisely with this issue. Leviticus

A further implication of this political imagination is that those who remained in the land during the Babylonian exile are thereby placed on an equal theological footing with the immigrants from the Persian period. Since only a small proportion of Israel's traditional land lay within the boundaries of Yehud,[33] we must infer that many of these settlers would have come from lineage groups whose traditional lands lay outside the new provincial boundaries of the period. The potential conflicts around establishing legitimate connection with inherited land is, from the Priestly perspective, to be resolved in theological terms by this universalizing claim that all the descendants of Abraham are in the dependent economic position of immigrants.

This understanding may also throw light on the promise to Jacob in Genesis 35:11, where again the term "great nation" is avoided, as it was in the promise to Abraham. Instead of fathering "many" nations, Jacob is to be the ancestor of an "assembly" of nations, q^ehal goyim — using the term qahal which is normally associated with the cultic congregation. But the phrase q^ehal goyim is also strikingly similar to one used in Jeremiah 50:9, where the Persian Empire is described as "an assembly of great nations." It seems that the descendants of Jacob will lay claim to the higher sovereignty promised to Abraham, yet the possibility of cultic unity amongst a mixed group of people is also at least implicitly envisaged. The seed of Abraham may indeed be dispersed in the way that Wöhrle suggests, but the descendants of Jacob were themselves something of a mixed multitude. This possibility is made more explicit in the writings of the Holiness School.

NATIVES AND IMMIGRANTS IN THE SOCIAL IMAGINATION OF THE HOLINESS SCHOOL

I have suggested that the books of Ezra-Nehemiah reflect the unfolding of the national imaginary in the context of the Persian administration of Judah after

---

26:40-45 confidently envisages restoration after the exile, with no fundamental break of covenant relationship, as Nihan points out in "The Priestly Covenant," pp. 109-112.

33. John W. Wright, "Remapping Yehud: The Borders of Yehud and the Genealogies of Chronicles," in Lipschits and Oeming, eds., *Judah and the Judeans in the Persian Period*, pp. 67-89; Oded Lipschits, "Demographic Changes in Judah between the Seventh and the Fifth Centuries BCE," in *Judah and the Judeans in the Neo-Babylonian Period*, ed. Oded Lipschits and Joseph Blenkinsopp (Winona Lake, Ind.: Eisenbrauns, 2003), pp. 323-77; Lipschits, "Achaemenid Imperial Policy, Settlement Processes in Palestine, and the Status of Jerusalem in the Middle of the Fifth Century BCE," in Lipschits and Oeming, eds., *Judah and the Judeans in the Persian Period*, pp. 19-52.

the exile. In this context the old legal traditions have a new significance in bringing social order to a community that must come to terms with life within a province of a foreign empire. A measure of legal autonomy was apparently provided to Yehud, and native governors therefore had the opportunity to mediate between the claims of the empire and the claims of native law or to-rah. But what was the content of this law? Nehemiah 8 provides one way into this complex issue, and it throws significant light on the mixed nature of the population at the time.

Unfortunately, the events described in this narrative do not entirely co-here with any of the laws of the Pentateuch as we now have them. Nor can we readily determine the exact historical setting for these events, not least because the chapter envisages both Ezra and Nehemiah being present, when other texts suggest that their tours of duty were quite separate. Apparently the authors of Nehemiah 8 wish to emphasize in some symbolic way that Ezra, who is described as being both a priest and a scribe, is unified in purpose with Nehemiah the native governor. Nehemiah 8:1 suggests that when the people assemble as a *qahal* and request a reading of the Torah of Moses, Ezra begins to read on the "first day of the seventh month." On the second day, he initiates the Festival of Booths, which according to the Holiness Code should not take place until the fifteenth day of the month (Lev. 23:34). Conspicuously absent from the narrative is any reference to the Day of Atonement, or Day of Pur-gation, a very surprising oversight given that this ritual is designed precisely to purify the whole community. While a modern reader might be tempted to dismiss this as a mere peccadillo, the discrepancy provides a window on deeper social issues.

It is possible that the original authors of Nehemiah 8 were unaware of the Day of Atonement ritual, but it is much more likely that they were simply not using the liturgical calendar in the Holiness Code. Deuteronomy's festival calendar, found in chapter 16, refers to a Feast of Booths (or Sukkot) in the seventh month without specifying the day on which it commences and without mentioning the Day of Atonement at all. Accordingly, it may be that Nehe-miah 8 presumes Deuteronomy's calendar rather than the one in Leviticus 23. Nehemiah 8:15 makes reference to palm leaves, and this terminology is indeed found in Leviticus 23:40 and not in Deuteronomy's calendar, but this overlap simply heightens the peculiarities of Nehemiah's interpretation of the available liturgical calendars, perhaps suggesting that a version of the Holiness calendar was indeed in existence at the time. Instead of highlighting the participation of strangers (*gerim*) as envisaged in the Sukkot law even in Deuteronomy 16:14 (cf. 31:12), Nehemiah's narrative prefers to emphasize that the "seed of Israel" was separated from all foreigners (Neh. 9:2). My suggestion here is that these peculiarities be seen as further indication that Ezra-Nehemiah is to be situated mainly within the national imaginary.[34]

It is possible that the H editors only added the Day of Atonement to their liturgical calendar after the time of Nehemiah, as has been argued by Christophe Nihan, in which case Nehemiah could hardly be held responsible for overlooking all the requirements in H's calendar. Interestingly, the calendar in Leviticus 23:42 refers only to the cultic obligations of the 'ezrach, or native citizen, but in a striking addition to chapter 16, the H editors have transferred the principle of "equality before the law" from Leviticus 24:22 to the requirements for the Day of Atonement or Purgation.[35]

> This shall be a statute to you forever: In the seventh month, on the tenth day of the month, you shall deny yourselves, and shall do no work, neither the native nor the alien (*ger*) who resides among you. For on this day atonement shall be made for you, to cleanse you; from all your sins you shall be clean before Yhwh. (Lev. 16:29-30)

The *gerim* apparently have a role to play in maintaining the purity of the land, and at the very least, their presence in the community is no impediment to the performance of purity obligations. This suggests not just that the calendrical innovation of having the Day of Atonement in the seventh month arose "post Nehemiah" as Nihan argues, but in addition, that the explicit inclusion of the strangers (*gerim*) in the Day of Atonement ritual arose *in response to* Nehemiah's more exclusivist account of Israel's identity.

H's inclusiveness is striking in its contrast with the sharp distinction proposed in Ezra 9:1–2 between the returnees from the *golah* and the "peoples of the lands":

34. Jacob L. Wright has linked both the reading of the law in Nehemiah 8 and the debt release in Nehemiah 5 to the seventh-year reading of torah during Sukkot which is required in Deut. 31:9-13. His argument points again to the primary influence of D on the Ezra-Nehemiah traditions, with the notable exception of the pro-priestly responses in the later Ezra 1-6 material. The striking contrasts between the Sukkot celebration in Ezra 3 and the Sukkot in Nehemiah 8 are well described by Wright, "Writing the Restoration: Compositional Agenda and the Role of Ezra in Neh 8," *JHS* 7 (2007): 19-29. There are indeed a number of good arguments for dating most of the material in Ezra 1-6 to the late Persian period, or even early Hellenistic times. See, e.g., Hugh Williamson's classic account of the issues in "The Composition of Ezra 1-6," *JTS* 34/1 (1983): 1-30; reprinted in H. G. M. Williamson, *Studies in Persian Period Historiography* (FAT 38; Tübingen: Mohr Siebeck, 2004), pp. 244-70, esp. 269.

35. Nihan, *From Priestly Torah*, pp. 569-70, 613.

After these things had been done, the officials approached me and said, "The people of Israel, the priests, and the Levites have not separated themselves from the peoples of the lands with their abominations, from the Canaanites, the Hittites, the Perizzites, the Jebusites, the Ammonites, the Moabites, the Egyptians, and the Amorites. For they have taken some of their daughters as wives for themselves and for their sons. Thus the holy seed has mixed itself with the peoples of the lands, and in this faithlessness the officials and leaders have led the way."

Ezra 9:1-2 seems to presuppose the older *cherem* law in Deuteronomy that subjected these people to the ban, but under these new circumstances, the ban is construed as an obligation on the part of the "children of the exile" to divorce foreign women.

The Holiness School, on the other hand, proposes that the pollutions generated by strangers could be dealt with by appropriate purification. It is polluting practices, rather than persons, who are the source of the offense. H establishes a set of general conditions for all who live in the land, with the effect that Israelites and the prior occupants of Canaan are bound by essentially the same ethical code, lest the land "vomit" them out.[36] It is precisely the polluting practices of the Canaanites that are the key issue for H, rather than their ethnicity as such:

"Do not defile yourselves in any of these ways, for by all these practices the nations [*goyim*] I am casting out before you have defiled themselves. Thus the land became defiled; and I punished it for its iniquity, and the land vomited out its inhabitants." (Lev. 18:24-25)

In perhaps the most striking contrast with the Ezra-Nehemiah tradition, the Holiness Code does not see marriage to a foreigner as inherently defiling. Leviticus 21:14 imposes the requirement for endogamous marriage only on the high priest and not on the laity. Jacob Milgrom therefore concludes that "The Priestly sources (H and P), on the contrary, express neither opposition to nor prohibition of intermarriage. Endogamy is not a prerequisite for holiness."[37]

This distinction between persons and practices is also clearly evidenced in the Holiness School's law governing the Passover. In Exodus 12:43–49, we

---

36. See Baruch J. Schwartz, "Reexamining the Fate of the 'Canaanites' in the Torah Traditions," in *Sefer Moshe: The Moshe Weinfeld Jubilee Volume*, ed. Chaim Cohen, Avi Hurvitz and Shalom M. Paul (Winona Lake: Eisenbrauns, 2004), pp. 151-70.

37. Jacob Milgrom, *Leviticus 17-22* (AB 3A; New York: Doubleday, 2000), pp. 1584-85.

find that the *gerim* who wish to join in the ritual need only have their males circumcised.[38] The presumption that these strangers may be uncircumcised indicates that the law is not just addressing strangers from another tribe within the Abrahamic kinship systems. Exodus 12:49 concludes by stating the principle of equity that is derived from the Holiness Code: "you shall have one law for the stranger and for the native," wording that corresponds to Leviticus 24:22 with minor variations in legal terminology. Even circumcision can therefore be seen as a mechanism of social inclusion and the inclusion of foreigners managed without compromise to core religious identity.

The idea that there should be "one law for the stranger and native" is both distinctive to the Holiness School, and somewhat problematic since the Holiness Code also asserts that Israelites can only ever be, in a theological sense, "strangers" (*gerim*). In comparison, when referring to the citizens of Judah, Deuteronomy prefers the term "brother" and makes no reference to the "native" (*'ezrach*) at all.[39] The question that emerges, then, is why has the Holiness Code adopted this term *'ezrach*, and endowed it with such legal significance, while at the same time asserting that no Israelite could really claim to be an *'ezrach* anyway?

One clue is found in the late prophetic literature. As part of Ezekiel's vision for the allocation of land after the return from exile, we read:

> You shall allot it as an inheritance for yourselves and for the immigrants (*gerim*) who reside among you and have begotten children among you. They shall be regarded as natives (*'ezrach*) among the children of Israel; with you they shall be allotted an inheritance among the tribes of Israel. (Ezek. 47:22)

Gordon McConville's suggestion is apt, if slightly paradoxical: "the concept of אזרח [*'ezrach*] exists in the interests of elucidating the nature of Israel, pre-

---

38. A number of scholars have now converged on the conclusion that Exodus 12:43-49 belongs to H, e.g., Nihan, *From Priestly Torah*, pp. 566-67; Saul Olyan, *Rites and Rank: Hierarchy in Biblical Representations of* Cult (Princeton: Princeton University Press, 2000), pp. 69-70; Jakob Wöhrle, "The Integrative Function of the Law of Circumcision," in *The Foreigner and the Law: Perspectives from the Hebrew Bible and the Ancient Near East*, ed. Reinhard Achenbach, Rainer Albertz, and Jakob Wöhrle (BZABR 16; Wiesbaden: Harrassowitz, 2011), pp. 71-87, 81-84.

39. While the linguistic evidence for the meaning of *'ezrach* is relatively meagre, there is no real dispute that it can be rendered as "one arising from the land" or "native." See Christoph Bultmann, *Der Fremde im antiken Juda: Eine Untersuchung zum sozialen Typenbegriff 'ger' und seinem Bedeutungswandel in der alttestamentlichen Gesetzgebung* (FRLANT 153; Göttingen: Vandenhoeck & Ruprecht, 1992), p. 204; Jan Joosten, *People and Land in the Holiness Code: An Exegetical Study of the Ideational Framework of the Law in Leviticus 17-26* (VTSup 67; Leiden: Brill, 1996), p. 35.

cisely by pointing to the alien's integration."[40] It seems that in Ezekiel 47:22, as well as in the Holiness School material, there is a presumption that the "children of the exile" are in fact natives or citizens, even if they have been born in Babylon. But the over-riding point being made at the intersection of Ezekiel and H is that this privileged *'ezrach* status should not be invoked in order to deny the land rights of others who live within Israel, particularly when they have raised children within the community.

The contrast with the imperatives in Ezra-Nehemiah could hardly be more clear: where the national tradition proposes the expulsion of foreign women and children, the call to holiness in H is conceived quite differently. Specifically with regard to land rights in Yehud, Ezekiel affirms the principle of equality before the law, without imposing a religious test that might first need to be applied before the legitimacy of a land claim could be established.

This is not to say that strangers had no responsibility for maintaining the sanctity of the land, since we do find a number of stringent regulations in the Holiness Code that bind all those who live in the land (e.g., Lev. 20:2-5). But the full range of divine obligations that bind Israelites are not actually imposed on all the population in the same way, so some room is left for the negotiation of identities. As we have seen above, the *gerim* were not compelled to participate in the Passover celebrations, but if they wished to do so then their males must be circumcised. The *ger* therefore had choices in relation to the cult that the Israelites did not enjoy.[41] The Holiness School was imagining ways in which permeable social boundaries need not undermine the core identity and vocation of Israel.

We may conclude, then, that the Priestly tradition constitutes a remarkable case of healing following the traumatic loss of political sovereignty. Displacing the national imaginary in favor of a counter-imperial imaginary, it exchanges political hegemony for a divinely-given identity that is free to engage with strangers in the same social space. In Part Three of this volume I will show how this imaginary still offers significant analogies for modern circumstances where the Christian church claims no privilege in the public domain, yet continues to contribute to public life in the confidence of God's ultimate providence. In the present chapter I have attempted to show that this approach to politics was already advanced by Priestly theologians in the Hebrew Bible, in opposition to the more sectarian community envisaged by Ezra-Nehemiah.

---

40. McConville, "'Fellow Citizens': Israel and Humanity in Leviticus," in *Reading the Law: Studies in Honour of Gordon J. Wenham*, ed. J. Gordon McConville and Karl Möller (LHBOTS 461; London: T&T Clark, 2007), pp. 10-32, 24.

41. See further, Joosten, *People and Land*, pp. 63-73.

6. Isaiah, Holiness, and Justice

In presenting the possibility of public theology in secular societies, the argument of this book has arrived at a somewhat ironic conclusion: the Priestly imaginary offers a model of political life that is more relevant today than the national tradition which tends to oscillate in the Hebrew Bible between models of theocracy or, in the case of Ezra-Nehemiah, communitarian withdrawal. In this chapter, we will explore the wider significance of the Priestly political imaginary by suggesting that the book of Isaiah has more in common with this Priestly vision. Once again, my proposal might initially be seen as counterintuitive, not least because Isaiah's conception of justice is at some points directly opposed to cultic practices, the core business for priests. Nevertheless, I will show how the book of Isaiah moves from a critique of Judah's kings in Isaiah 1–39 to a conception of divine empire in Isaiah 40–66 that is substantially aligned with the Priestly conception of sovereignty as I have described it. And as in the case of the Priestly imaginary, the final stage in the composition of Isaiah presents a social vision of healing from the trauma of exile, which is shaped by "counter-imperial" symbolism, rather than by a return to the national imaginary such as we find in Ezra-Nehemiah.

The figure of Isaiah from the eighth century BCE establishes the priority of justice in the most dramatic terms, criticizing both cultic and royal institutions. However, prophecy in the Hebrew Bible tends to present social critique in poetic discourse, rather engage in the rather more practical tasks of maintaining cults or governments. The prophetic poetry of Isaiah is nevertheless political in the broadest sense, and at the centre of this tradition we find visions of justice, grounded in the reality of God. In relation to religion, the implication is clear:

What need have I for the abundance of your sacrifices? says Yhwh. I have had enough of burnt offerings. . . . Learn to do good, seek justice (*mishpat*), provide guidance for the oppressed, defend the rights of the orphan; plead the case of the widow. (Isa. 1:11, 17)

Much of the language here is derived from the legal sphere, but the scope of the poetry extends beyond the institutional location of the courts — precisely because the courts may fail in their duty:

> Woe to those who establish iniquitous statutes,
>   and write oppressive documents,
> to subvert the case of the poor
>   and to rob the needy among my people of
>   their justice (*mishpat*),
> that widows may be their spoil,
>   and orphans their plunder! (Isa. 10:1-2)

The *mishpat* of the poor is here an inherent right that "belongs" to the vulnerable,[1] yet it has to be defended vigorously, precisely when legal systems and the Crown do not actually deliver justice.

Isaiah's call for social activism, it should be said, is focused primarily on justice in the domestic economy; it is not envisaged, for example, that Jerusalem's kings would take up arms in the service of international causes. Michael Walzer captures this peculiarity of the prophetic literature when he observes that "there are virtually no prophetic descriptions of Israel as nation-in-arms and no expressions of admiration for warrior or diplomat kings."[2] Pictures of violent judgment do indeed permeate the book of Isaiah, but it is God alone who prevails, even when it is foreign kings from Assyria and Babylon who are the agents of divine intervention. According to Isaiah, the central vocation of kings is radical trust in Yhwh, not the exercise of Israel's own military capacity. Ahaz and Hezekiah are accordingly urged not to trust in their own weapons and warhorses, nor to seek coalitions with other kings in defending

---

1. Gerhard Liedke suggests that in a number of cases *mishpat* is "something that 'belongs' to the poor, etc." including Isaiah 10:2 along with Exodus 23:6; Deuteronomy 10:18; 24:17; 27:19; Jeremiah 5:28; Psalm 140:12; and Job 36:6. Liedke, "שפט to judge," in *Theological Lexicon of the Old Testament*, Vol. 3, ed. Ernst Jenni and Claus Westermann, trans. Mark E. Biddle (Peabody, Mass.: Hendrickson, 1997), pp. 1392-99, here at p. 1395.

2. Michael Walzer, *In God's Shadow: Politics in the Hebrew Bible* (New Haven: Yale University Press, 2012), p. 100.

their common interests. As in the days of the exodus, when the people were told to be still (Exod. 14:13), these kings in Jerusalem were urged by the prophet simply to be quiet (Isa. 7:4).

According to the earlier traditions of Isaiah, kings and commoners alike failed in their accountability to Yhwh, and for this reason Jerusalem was destroyed by the Babylonian armies. The events at this time were so dreadful, it seems, that the book does not report them at all. Instead of the outpouring of traumatized responses that we find in the book of Lamentations, the book of Isaiah moves from the threats of judgment in the earlier chapters to promises of restoration in chapters 40–55, and the narrative bridge provided in Isaiah 36–39 is actually borrowed from the books of Kings. There is an "abyss" between Isaiah 39 and 40, as Walter Brueggemann puts it.[3] After a final allusion to the coming Babylonian threat, the story of Judah's kings ceases with Hezekiah's peculiar comfort that he himself will be spared the horrors to come (Isa. 39:8 = 2 Kings 20:19). The subsequent narrative in 2 Kings about Manasseh's sin and the fall of Jerusalem find no place in Isaiah. Instead, the book suddenly moves at the beginning of chapter 40 to address an audience for whom judgment has already passed:

> Comfort, comfort my people, says your God.
> Speak to the heart of Jerusalem, and proclaim to her
> that she has fulfilled her service, that her iniquity is expiated,
> for she has received from the hand of Yhwh
> double for all her sins.

Unlike the books of Kings, where accusations of sin are directed predominately at the cultic crimes of the monarchs in Israel and Judah, the sins mentioned in Isaiah are primarily injustices committed against the marginalized — the widow and orphan in the domestic economy. The question of why Jerusalem has received a double measure of punishment is left hanging in chapter 40 — although according to Isaiah 61:7, a double measure of shame deserves a double measure of compensation, as we shall see below.

It is strikingly evident that the pictures of Judah's redemption in Isaiah 40–66 do not have a native king restoring justice in Zion-Jerusalem. On the contrary, the only explicit references to a "messiah" are to Cyrus, the Persian king who presided over the fall of Babylon and over the restoration of the

---

3. Walter Brueggemann, "Unity and Dynamic in the Isaiah Tradition," *Journal for the Study of the Old Testament* 29 (1984): 89-107, 95-96.

Judean population (Isa. 44:28; 45:1). Judean kings are conspicuous by their absence in Isaiah 40–66, and in Isaiah 55:1-5 we even find that the promises formerly made to the line of David are devolved to the whole community:

> Hey, everyone who thirsts, come to the waters;
>> and those who have no money, come, buy and eat!
> Come, buy – without money, without price – wine and milk.
> Why do you spend money on that which is not bread,
>> and your labor on that which does not satisfy?
> Heed me, and eat what is good,
>> let your soul delight in rich food.
> Incline your ear, and come to me;
>> listen, so that your soul may be revived.
> I will make with you an enduring covenant,
>> my loyal love, promised to David.
> See, I made him a witness to the peoples,
>> a leader and commander for the peoples.
> See, you shall call nations that you did not know,
>> and nations that you did not know you shall run to you,
> because of Yhwh your God, the Holy One of Israel,
>> for he has glorified you.

This passage inverts expectations at several levels: the royal covenant is democratized, the monetary economy is suspended, and instead of the image of judgment in Isaiah 1:7 where foreigners devour the arable land,[4] here in the divine counter-empire there is eating and drinking alongside foreigners who no longer pose a threat. Land and food resources are firmly under Yhwh's control, rather than subject to the armies of Assyria or Babylon.

From Isaiah 40 onwards, the invitation to the nations is repeatedly shaped by imperial symbolism, although the primary addressee is Yhwh's "servant" who is now the "seed of Abraham" rather than a Judean king:

> But you, Israel, my servant,
>> Jacob, whom I have chosen,

4. Andrew T. Abernethy persuasively argues that the invading foreigners envisaged in Isaiah 1–39 are in the first instance Assyrians, but that Isaiah counters the Assyrian ideology that envisages their king as sovereign over land and food resources. See Abernethy, "Eating, Assyrian Imperialism and God's Kingdom in Isaiah," in *Isaiah and Imperial Context: The Book of Isaiah in the Times of Empire*, ed. Abernethy et al. (Eugene, Ore.: Pickwick, 2013), pp. 38-53.

> the seed of Abraham my friend,
> you whom I took from the ends of the earth,
>   and called from its far reaches,
> to whom I said, "You are my servant,
>   I have chosen you and not rejected you." (Isa. 41:8–9)

On the one hand, there is a universal offer of salvation to the nations, notably in 45:20–25, and the nations are to enjoy Yhwh's justice and torah (42:1–4; 51:4–6). On the other hand, some of the *goyim* come to Israel in chains (45:14) and foreign kings lick the dust of Israel's feet (49:23). The submission of the *goyim* therefore comes either by way of violence or by way of assimilation to Yhwh's justice, dual options commonly provided by imperial rule. Oppressors may either be bathed in blood (49:26) or join peacefully in the project of restoring Zion (49:22–23). While commentators have often been more attracted by the inclusive dimensions of this so-called universalism, the repeated theme of judgment cannot be ignored.

Harry Orlinsky argued that what has often been seen as universalism in Isaiah is better understood as a "nationalist-universalist" vision,[5] but this could be identified more straightforwardly as "imperialism." Some scholars have not hesitated to use the latter term even in relation to Isaiah 2:2–4, where the nations stream up to Jerusalem in an eager quest for justice and reconciliation.[6] Participation in an imperial civilization can often be presented as an opportunity for liberation and justice, but opposition to this vision of life can at the same time be dealt with harshly. Accordingly, what we find in the later oracles of Isaiah is a universal rule "which will mean salvation for Israel but submission for the other nations."[7]

With imperial expansiveness, the submission of foreign kings is described

---

5. Orlinski, "Nationalism-Universalism and Internationalism in Ancient Israel," in *Translating and Understanding the Old Testament: Essays in Honor of Herbert Gordon May*, ed. Harry T. Frank and William L. Reed (Nashville: Abingdon, 1970), pp. 206-36.

6. J. J. M. Roberts, "The End of War in the Zion Tradition: The Imperialistic Background of an Old Testament Vision of Worldwide Peace," in *Character Ethics and the Old Testament*, ed. M. Daniel Carroll R. and Jacqueline E. Lapsley (London: Westminster John Knox, 2007), pp. 119-28; cf. Irmtraud Fischer, "World Peace and Holy War — Two Sides of the Same Theological Concept: YHWH as Sole Divine Power. A Canonical-Intertextual Reading of Isaiah 2:1-5, Joel 4:9-21 and Micah 4:1-5," in *Isaiah's Vision of Peace in Biblical and Modern International Relations*, ed. Raymond Cohen and Raymond Westbrook (New York: Palgrave Macmillan, 2008), pp. 151-65.

7. R. Norman Whybray, *Isaiah 40-66* (NCB; London: Marshall, Morgan & Scott, 1975), pp. 72.

in relatively peaceful terms in chapters 60–62: "Nations shall come to your light, and kings to the brightness of your dawn" (60:3). A clear hierarchy is then established in this ideal society, which sets the holy people (cf. 62:12) who are given sacred labor over against those who are given profane labor:

> Strangers (*zarim*) shall stand and feed your flocks,
>> foreigners (*bene nekar*) shall till your land
>>> and dress your vines;
>> but you shall be called priests of Yhwh,
>>> you shall be named ministers (*mesharete*) of our God;
>> you shall enjoy the wealth of the nations,
>>> and in their riches you shall glory. (61:5-6)

This vision of strangers as agricultural workers effectively reverses the picture of judgment in Isaiah 1:7 where the strangers (*zarim*) devour the arable land.

The stratification of society envisaged in Isaiah 60–62 is deconstructed, however, in the first and last portions of so-called "Third Isaiah," found in Isaiah 56:1–8 and 66:18–24. These portions, often termed "bookends," were probably added at the latest stages of the book's composition in order to create the chiastic structure that has been discerned in the final eleven chapters, with chapters 60–62 at the center:[8]

56:1–8 *Foreigners in sacred service*
  56:9–59:8 Yhwh's challenges concerning the Jerusalem community's life
    59:9–15a Prayers for Yhwh's forgiveness and restoration
      59:15b–21 Vision of Yhwh acting in judgment
        60:1–61:4 Vision of Jerusalem restored
          61:5–6 *Foreigners in secular service*
        61:7–62:12 Vision of Jerusalem restored
      63:1–6 Vision of Yhwh acting in judgment
    63:7–64:11 Prayers for Yhwh's forgiveness and restoration
  65:1–66:17 Yhwh's challenges concerning the Jerusalem community's life
66:18–24 *Foreigners in sacred service*

---

8. Isaiah 56:6 interestingly deconstructs the hierarchy in 61:5-6 by proposing that some foreigners (*bene nekar*) will "minister" to Yhwh, using the same root *shrt* as in 61:6. Note that if the "bookends" in 56:1-8 and 66:18-24 were the final additions to Third Isaiah, as Claus Westermann and others have suggested, then this chiasm would not have been evident at earlier stages of the book's composition. Claus Westermann, *Isaiah 40-66*, trans. David Stalker (OTL; London: SCM, 1969), p. 307.

If the foreigners are at this late stage invited even to enter the cult, then this is indeed a surprisingly extreme form of assimilation, which is not explicitly contemplated in the central social vision in chapters 60–62.

The extent to which foreigners might be assimilated seems to have been a matter of ongoing debate in the Persian period. From the perspective of Ezra–Nehemiah traditions, the "children of the exile (*golah*)" were exclusively identified as the "holy seed" and consequently all the Judeans who remained behind in the land after the fall of Jerusalem were cut off from the lineage and considered outsiders.[9] If this is the case, then some of the "foreigners" who are eventually invited to join the cult in Isaiah 56:1–8 and 66:18–24 are historically likely to have been descendants of Jacob–Israel but not "children of the exile." In the discussion that follows, I will lay out the case for reading Isaiah 56–66 in these terms — as chapters that, in effect, interpret the Priestly covenant with Abraham as a theology that can reconcile diverse social factions.

LAYING CLAIM TO ABRAHAM

Indications of intra-Israelite conflict between *golah* and remainee groups are evident in the occasional references to Abraham both in Isaiah and in Ezekiel. In Isaiah 63:16, the complaint that "Abraham does not know us" raises a difficult question about how to understand the social dynamics of this conflict: which group is speaking in the first person in this text, and in what historical context? In the case of Ezekiel 33:24, it is clear that the remaining community has laid claim to Abraham: "Mortal, the inhabitants of these waste places in the land of Israel keep saying, 'Abraham was only one person (*'echad*), yet he possessed the land; but we are many; the land is surely given us to possess'" (cf. Ezek. 11:15). But the prophet goes on to condemn their logic in no uncertain terms. One line of interpretation suggests that those who remained in Ezekiel 33:24 presume Abraham to be an Indigenous figure, and that their claim on him would be undermined if Abraham were originally understood to be an immigrant from Mesopotamia.[10] But this interpretation seems to underesti-

9. For this interpretation of "foreigners" in the Persian period see especially Sara Japhet, *From the Rivers of Babylon to the Highlands of Judah* (Winona Lake, Ind.: Eisenbrauns, 2006), pp. 96-116; Katherine Southwood, *Ethnicity and the Mixed Marriage Crisis in Ezra 9-10: An Anthropological Approach* (OTM; Oxford: Oxford University Press, 2012), pp. 191-211, "Hybridity and Return Migration."

10. Thomas Römer, "Abraham Traditions in the Hebrew Bible," in *The Book of Genesis:*

mate the significance of Abraham being only "one" person, a description that relates more directly to a lonely immigrant experience than to an autoch-thonous figure who would necessarily possess numerous kinship alliances. Whether or not Abraham was seen by some groups as an immigrant figure, Ezekiel 33:24 makes clear that he was claimed by the remainees.

Isaiah 51:1–3 throws up similar problems as to whether Abraham was origi-nally seen as an Indigenous figure. Zion is here urged to take courage from the story of Abraham — "the rock from which you were hewn" — who, although he was only "one" (again *'echad*, as in Ezek. 33:24), was blessed by Yhwh with fecundity. If "Zion" refers here to a small and struggling community in Jerusa-lem who never went into exile, then these verses may represent the voice of the remainees. But the Zion in Isa 51:1–3 might equally be referring to the small, struggling *golah* community who returned to Judah after the rise of the Persian Empire. If the interpretation of these verses is to be constrained by the wider context of Second Isaiah (chapters 40–55), then it is evident that Abraham has been framed by an exilic identity already in Isaiah 41 where the seed of Abra-ham are described as "you whom I took from the ends of the earth" (41:8-9). Whether this exilic picture of Abraham should be extrapolated into Isaiah 56–66 is a key question that is at issue in the last eleven chapters of the book.

The complaint in Isaiah 63:16 raises the question whether the *golah* com-munity has claimed Abraham *exclusively* for themselves and denied kinship connections with the remainees who give voice to this complaint.

> For you are our father,
> though Abraham does not know us
> and Israel does not acknowledge us. (63:16)

The verse is located within the larger prayer in 63:7–64:11, which evidently comes from Yahwists who feel rejected both by God and by their wider com-munity. If this text is read through the lens of the later exclusivist perspectives in Ezra–Nehemiah, then we might find already here in 63:16 some evidence that Abraham has indeed been claimed exclusively by the *golah* community, and consequently, the identity of Israel has been narrowed to "the children of the exile" (cf. Neh. 9:7, which identifies Abraham as an immigrant from Ur of Chaldeans, as suggested also by the Priestly author in Genesis, as we have seen). The voice that speaks in Isaiah 63:7–64:11 responds to this sense of being

---

Composition, Reception, and Interpretation, ed. Craig A. Evans, Joel N. Lohr, and David L. Petersen (VTSup 152; Leiden: E. J. Brill, 2012), pp. 163, 178.

disowned, having experienced the withholding of divine compassion (63:15 and 64:11), yet still laying claim to Yhwh as father (63:16 and 64:7).

How are we to understand these conflicting claims to Abraham? On the one hand, the ancestor's seed could be seen as holy in a narrowly ethnic sense, which is the option taken up in the Ezra–Nehemiah traditions with their particular construal of the national vision.[11] It has often been assumed that Ezra's reference to a "holy seed" in 9:1-3 is Priestly language, and similarly, that references to the "seed of Abraham" in Isaiah must be taken in this exclusivist sense. However, building on my argument about the Priestly imaginary, my view is that Isaiah 56–66 can be read as substantially overlapping with the theology and ethics of the Holiness School (H). Ezra and Nehemiah do not advance the imperial imaginary that is shared by the Priestly tradition and Isaiah 56–66. The core traditions of Ezra–Nehemiah refuse to contemplate H's vision of "one law" for natives and strangers alike, while the bookends in Isaiah 56 and 66 push H's inclusivism to even more extreme conclusions. In the next section I will suggest that these extreme conclusions in the late editing of Isaiah were built on ecumenical possibilities outlined already in the elusive poetry of Isaiah 61 — poetry which itself implicitly alludes to the Abraham covenant.

THE SOCIAL VISION OF ISAIAH 61

The flow of the poetry in Isaiah 61:5-9 is more difficult than it first appears, particularly if we are concerned to identify the parties to the "eternal covenant" that the passage envisages. In verses 8-9, the specific terminology of *berit 'olam* and "seed" seem to be adopted from the Abraham covenant:

> [5] Strangers shall stand and feed your flocks,
>   foreigners shall till your land and dress your vines;
> [6] but you shall be called priests of Yhwh,
>   you shall be named ministers of our God;
> you shall consume the wealth of the nations,
>   and in their riches you shall glory.
> [7] Instead of your shame [there will be] a double compensation,

---

11. See especially Sara Japhet, "Periodization between History and Ideology II: Chronology and Ideology in Ezra-Nehemiah," in *Judah and Judeans in the Persian Period*, ed. Oded Lipschits and Manfred Oeming (Winona Lake, Ind.: Eisenbrauns, 2006), pp. 491-508.

and [instead of] dishonour they will rejoice
in their portion,[12]
therefore in their land a double compensation they shall possess;
eternal joy shall be theirs.
[8] For I Yhwh love justice (*mishpat*),
I hate robbery and wrongdoing;
I will faithfully give them their rightful compensation,
and I will cut an eternal covenant (*berit 'olam*) with them.
[9] And their seed will be known among the nations
and their descendants amidst the peoples;
All who see them will know them,
that they are the seed whom Yhwh has blessed.

One of the major difficulties in this passage is that initially the addressees ("you" in the second person plural) are clearly the Israelites who perform sacred service, whereas the people referred to in the third person are the strangers who perform secular service. With very few exceptions, commentators have assumed that these parties are switched in verse 7. But if this is the case, why are Abraham's promises being reiterated here in verses 8–9 as if for the first time?

For Isaiah, the Abrahamic blessing of land and descendants is now a matter of divine justice, which is signalled not only in 61:8 in the reference to *mishpat*, but already in 61:1 in its use of word *deror*, "liberty" or "release." The reference to liberty appears to be an allusion to proclamation made at the beginning of a Jubilee year, according to legislation in the Holiness Code (Lev. 25:10), which allows people to return to their traditional lands.[13] Some scholars have found in Isaiah 61:1–9 an attempt to legitimate the land claims of the *golah* returnees, over against those who had remained in the land during the Babylonian exile.[14] But as I have argued in the previous chapter, the ethics of the Holiness

12. The translation of v. 7a follows Jan L. Koole, *Isaiah: Part III*, trans. Anthony P. Runia (HCOT; Leuven: Peeters, 2001), p. 284.

13. For a more detailed discussion of Isaiah 61, see further Mark G. Brett, "Unequal Terms: A Postcolonial Approach to Isaiah 61," in *Biblical Interpretation and Method: Essays in Honour of Professor John Barton*, ed. Katharine J. Dell and Paul M. Joyce (Oxford: Oxford University Press, 2013), pp. 243-56.

14. See the overview of recent discussions in John Bergsma, "The Jubilee: A Post-exilic Priestly Attempt to Reclaim Lands?" *Biblica* 84 (2003): 225-46; Bergsma, *The Jubilee from Leviticus to Qumran: A History of Interpretation* (VTSup 115; Leiden: Brill, 2007). It is notable that Nehemiah 5 makes no attempt to relate debt problems to the Jubilee, although it might well be assuming the *shemittah* debt release of Deuteronomy 15 (as is Jer. 34:12-20).

School do not move in this exclusivist direction. H develops the "ecumenical" dimensions of the Priestly covenant with Abraham in order to assert that even in relation to worship it is possible for non-Israelites to join in cultic celebrations under certain conditions, notably the requirement of circumcision that is stipulated in Exodus 12:43–49. The possibilities for inclusion would be even clearer in the case of non-*golah* groups who claimed descent from Abraham and whose males would therefore already be circumcised.

Contrary to the view that divine justice in Isaiah 40–66 is entirely ethnocentric and "will mean salvation for Israel but submission for the other nations," it is possible to interpret Isaiah 61:1–9 as proclaiming the redemption of *golah* families to their ancestral country *and* the inclusion of the remainees as part of this divine imperial order, a social vision that we find already in the Priestly material in Genesis.[15] The paradoxical poetry in chapter 61 is apparently designed to provoke a "double-take" on the part of the reader; the allusion to an Abrahamic-sounding new covenant puts us in mind of the ideal *golah* immigrant who engages with the "people of the land" on just terms. The force of the poetry, even if one retreats to the Priestly understanding of Abraham's election, yields a complex vision of reconciliation that combines the inclusive and imperial visions of Isaiah 40–66 with the Priestly discourse of an eternal covenant.

The apparently awkward reference to judgment in Isaiah 61:2 does not conflict with this interpretation: "to proclaim the year of Yhwh's favour and the day of vengeance (*naqam*) of our God" might be taken, at first glance, as a word of judgment against foreigners. But here again, the Holiness Code may throw light on the poetry: if we can detect here in the "day of *naqam*" an allusion to the *naqam* of Leviticus 26:25, which directs judgment *against Israel* for the sake of the covenant, then Isaiah 61 is asserting that the divine landowner will exercise sovereignty in relation to land justice, and that this claim can cut both ways. This troubling assertion stands in continuity with the earlier Isaiah tradition where, for example, Isaiah 5:7 condemns Judeans themselves for the misappropriation of land:

> For the vineyard of Yhwh of hosts
>   is the house of Israel,
> and the people of Judah
>   are his pleasant planting;

15. Cf. also Römer's suggestion that Isaiah 51 seems designed to "overcome the conflict between the inhabitants of the land and the exiles"; v. 3 comforts Zion and v. 11 the exiles. Römer, "Abraham Traditions," p. 167.

> he looked for justice (*mishpat*),
>> but behold: bloodshed (*mispach*);
> for righteousness (*tsedeqah*),
>> but behold: a cry (*tse'aqah*)!

The *deror* in 61:1 is clearly an expression of sovereignty: this declaration, releasing people from debt servitude and restoring traditional land, is exclusively the preserve of monarchs in the ancient Near East,[16] so the ambiguity about who is making the declaration in Isaiah 61:1–9 is highly relevant. We might have expected that Cyrus, having been designated the "messiah" in Isaiah 44:28–45:1 would again be the one anointed to proclaim the release in Isaiah 61. Yet, as in Leviticus 25, it seems here that it is only Yhwh who ultimately has the power to declare liberty, so the authority of Cyrus is thereby relativized (cf. Isa. 41:21; 43:15; 44:6 where Yhwh is clearly identified as Israel's "king"). Isaiah and H are in agreement: contrary to imagination of the Achaemenid administration, it is Yhwh's empire that has jurisdiction in Yehud.

So instead of seeing prophetic and priestly groups pitted against each other in Isaiah 56–66, we should rather see a range of prophetic and priestly groups each expressing in their own ways the sovereignty of Yhwh over against the pretensions of Persian power. Ironically, the articulation of this resistance has actually mimicked imperial symbolism, a mimetic dynamic that is commonly found both in modern colonial history as well as in the ancient unfolding of biblical theology in the tides of successive empires. Having illuminated the complexity of the poetry in Isaiah 61, and its allusions to the Holiness Code, we can turn now to Isaiah 56 where some similar issues emerge with a confronting clarity.

SABBATH HOLINESS IN ISAIAH 56

Isaiah 56:1–8 adopts some specific terminology from the Holiness School's Sabbath law in order to make a surprisingly new point.[17] Exodus 31:13–14 speaks of

---

16. See the detailed discussion in Moshe Weinfeld, *Social Justice in Ancient Israel and in the Ancient Near East* (Jerusalem: Magnes, 1995). The Hebrew terminology corresponds to the Akkadian *andurarum*, meaning literally "return to the mother." Cf. Bergsma, *The Jubilee*, pp. 20-26.

17. See especially Saul Olyan, "Exodus 31:12-17: The Sabbath according to H, the Sabbath according to P and H," *JBL* 124 (2005): 201-9; cf. Christophe Nihan, *From Priestly Torah to Pentateuch: A Study in the Composition of the Book of Leviticus* (FAT II/25; Tübingen: Mohr Siebeck, 2007), p. 568, who reaffirms the position that all of Exodus 31:12-17 is H.

Sabbath observance as the "sign" of a covenant, much as the Priestly covenants with Noah and Abraham each have their own distinctive signs:

> You yourself are to speak to the Israelites: 'You shall observe my Sabbaths [cf. Isa. 56:4] for this is a sign between me and you throughout your generations, given in order that you may know that I, Yhwh, sanctify you. You shall observe the Sabbath [cf. Isa. 56:6] because it is holy for you; everyone who profanes it shall be put to death; whoever does any work on it shall be cut off from among his people [cf. Isa. 56:5].

The distinctive plural formulation "observe my Sabbaths," found in Exodus 31:13 and Isaiah 56:4, appears also in Leviticus 19:3, 30 and 26:2 within the Holiness Code itself.[18] The formula likely refers not just to the weekly observance but to the Sabbath year and the "Sabbath of Sabbath years" in the Jubilee.

What appears in the discourse of the H statutory law in Exodus 31:14 as a very severe ruling (the "cutting off" formula) is here in Isaiah 56:1–8 given an unexpectedly positive twist: *anyone* who observes the Sabbaths can be assimilated to Yhwh's people:

> [3] The foreigner who has joined himself to Yhwh must not say,
> "Yhwh will surely cut me off from his people,"
> and the eunuch must not say, "I am a dry tree."
> [4] For thus says Yhwh:
> "To the eunuchs who observe my Sabbaths,
> who choose the things that please me
> and hold fast my covenant,
> [5] I shall give them, in my house and within my walls,
> a memorial and a name (*yad weshem*)
> better than sons and daughters;
> I shall give them an everlasting name
> which will not be cut off.
> [6] And the foreigners who join themselves to Yhwh,
> to minister to him, to love the name of Yhwh,
> and to be his servants,
> all who observe the Sabbath, and do not profane it,
> and hold fast my covenant —

---

18. For this point, see already Jon D. Levenson, "The Temple and the World," *Journal of Religion* 64 (1984): 275-98.

[7] these I will bring to my holy mountain,
and make them joyful in my house of prayer;
their burnt-offerings and their sacrifices
will be accepted on my altar;
for my house shall be called a house of prayer for all peoples.

Interpretation of this passage has often focussed on the fact that the oracle appears to overturn the older legal traditions that excluded eunuchs and foreigners from participation in the cult. Closer attention to the peculiar phrase "memorial and name" (*yad weshem*) in 56:5 reveals it to be terminology that is derived from ancestral mortuary cults. It is terminology that relates quite specifically to land claims secured by the presence of ancestors buried in traditional land and marked by a memorial stone (*yad*).[19] In this respect, the passage belongs to the discourse of land claims just as surely as Isaiah 57:13 does: "But whoever seeks refuge in me shall inherit the land, and possess my holy mountain."

The suggestion in Isaiah 56 that foreigners might be denied legitimate rights in land is made quite explicit in the case of Nehemiah 2:20. In this context, Nehemiah makes his nativist claim over against foreign opponents:

The God of Heaven will give us success; we his servants shall arise and build; but you have no portion, or right (*tsedaqah*), or memorial (*zikkaron*) in Jerusalem.[20]

This exclusivist declaration from Nehemiah is "nativist" in the sense that it lays claim to an authentic Indigenous tradition, which excludes alternatives that are perceived to be syncretistic.[21] And the claim is asserted precisely through demonstrating proper connection with the dead, as revealed in Nehemiah 2:5, where Nehemiah seeks permission from the Persian king to go "to the city in Judah where my fathers are buried." Nehemiah thereby claims that the dead are his own.

The late editing of Isaiah opposes this nativist discourse not just by defending the land rights of non-*golah* "foreigners" descended from Abraham (a

19. Dwight van Winkle, "The Meaning of *yad wašem* in Isaiah LVI 5," *VT* 47 (1997): 378-85; Francesca Stavrakopoulou, *Land of Our Fathers: The Roles of Ancestor Veneration in Biblical Land Claims* (LHBOTS 473; London: T & T Clark, 2010), p. 124. The preservation of a "name," we may note in passing, is related to land holdings also in Num. 26:53-62; 27:3-4 and Ruth 4:10, although in these cases without clear links to mortuary cults.

20. Translation from Stavrakopoulou, *Land of Our Fathers*, p. 127.

21. Mark G. Brett, *Decolonizing God: The Bible in the Tides of Empire* (Sheffield: Sheffield Phoenix Press, 2008), pp. 112-31, esp. 129-31.

view found already in P), but in addition, by offering the possibility of cultic inclusion even to foreigners who have no genealogical connections with Abraham. This is also thinkable for H, and therefore I have concluded that both H and Isaiah provide a conception of holiness that is based on behaviour rather than kinship. Isaiah 56 also appears to be making a new and more specific point about eunuchs. In the context of the Persian period this most likely relates to eunuch administrators, whose reproductive capacity was cut off by virtue of their employment in imperial courts. It is not just that their honor or "name" beyond death is assured, but more specifically, that their devotion to the empire is here transferred specifically to Yhwh's rule. In effect, the restored temple in Jerusalem supersedes the king's palace as the centre of sovereignty.[22]

JUSTICE — HUMAN AND DIVINE

While I have so far emphasized the common ground between the Holiness School and Isaiah 56–66 in relation to their underlying social imagination, it must be acknowledged that their conceptions of justice do diverge in some respects. The combination of *mishpat* and *tsedaqah* ("justice" and "righteousness" in most English translations) appears a dozen times in the Isaiah tradition, but it is not to be found in Priestly literature, and this is not merely a semantic observation. The Priestly tradition tends to look to the past — to the inherited laws of Moses — as the primary source of social order, whereas Isaiah is more orientated to the future. Whether pronouncing judgment or envisioning a utopian redemption, the prophet's conception of justice is not limited to statutory law. Even in the dramatic vision of Isaiah 2:1–4, where swords are beaten into plowshares and the nations stream in to Jerusalem, the torah that provides reconciliation for the *goyim* on Mt. Zion is not simply the Torah of Moses revealed on Mt. Sinai:[23]

The word that Isaiah son of Amoz saw concerning Judah and Jerusalem:

> In the final days the mountain of Yhwh's house
> shall be established as the highest of the mountains,
> and shall be raised above the hills;

22. Jacob Wright and Michael Chan, "King and Eunuch: Isaiah 56:1-8 in Light of Honorific Royal Burial Practices," *JBL* 31 (2012): 99-119.

23. Baruch J. Schwartz, "Torah from Zion: Isaiah's Temple Vision (Isaiah 2.1-4)," in *Sanctity of Time and Space in Tradition and Modernity*, ed. Alberdina Houtman, Marcel Poorthuis and Joshua J. Schwartz (Leiden: Brill, 1998), pp. 12-26.

and all the nations shall stream to it.
　　Many peoples shall come and say,
"Come, let us go up to the mountain of the Yhwh,
　　to the house of the God of Jacob;
that he may show us his ways
　　and that we may walk in his paths."
For out of Zion shall go forth instruction (*torah*),
　　And the word of Yhwh from Jerusalem.
He will judge between the nations,
　　and shall decide for many peoples;
they shall beat their swords into plowshares,
　　and their spears into pruning hooks;
nation (*goy*) shall not lift up sword against nation (*goy*),
　　neither shall they learn war any more.

In the Holiness Code, on the other hand, *mishpat* regularly stands in parallel with *chuqah* ("statute" or "regulation").[24] Translations usually render this as a parallel between "judgments" and "statutes," but we may note that these *mishpatim* are not far removed from statutory *chuqot*. Similarly, H's requirement that there be one law (*mishpat*) that protects both native and immigrant in Leviticus 24:22 and Exodus 12:49 is best understood as a single regime of statutes. Only in Leviticus 19:15 and 35 does *mishpat* carry the connotation of a judicial "judgment," since in both these cases the possibility of rendering an *unfair* judgment is acknowledged. Thus, Leviticus 19:15 warns that "You shall not render an unfair judgment (*mishpat*); do not favor the poor or show deference to the rich. With righteousness (*tsedeq*) you will judge (*tishpot*) your kin." What is envisaged here is everyday legal practice conducted at the highest standards of human integrity, not a divine intervention.

There is a particular irony in the fact that the declaration of liberty (*deror*) in Leviticus 25 falls precisely within statutory law, governing regular behavior without the need of a monarch's arbitrary agency. In the ancient Near Eastern examples of such declarations, as we have noted, this redemptive initiative of the king is not regularized in law; it is seen as an exception to the quotidian patterns of debt and alienation from traditional land. In Isaiah 61, this sense of a gracious sovereign prerogative returns, without attributing the *deror* to the agency of a Judean king or to an established statute. Instead, it arises directly as a charismatic calling to an unidentified speaker who announces the arrival of God to mend the world:

24. E.g., Lev. 18:4, 5, 26; 19:37; 20:22; 25:18; 26:15, 43, 46.

> The spirit of the sovereign Yhwh is upon me,
> because Yhwh has anointed me.
> He has sent me as a herald to the humble,
> to bind up the broken of heart,
> to proclaim release (*deror*) to the captives,
> and to the imprisoned, liberation.

The servants of Yhwh are called to their own tasks and integrity, but the final task of mending the world belongs to God.

This necessary combination of divine and human agency is expressed with characteristic poetic density in Isaiah 56:1, where the wordplay in the Hebrew text is often neglected in English translations. Rolf Rendtorff has made a good case for seeing this verse as balancing the quite different conceptions of justice in the whole of the Isaiah tradition.[25]

> Thus says Yhwh: "Maintain *mishpat* and do *tsedaqah*,
> because my salvation is near,
> and my *tsedaqah* is to be revealed.

The combination of *mishpat* and *tsedaqah* is characteristic of the prophetic literature, as already mentioned, rather than the statutory laws of Moses. It was Judah's failure to do true justice in this comprehensive sense that, according to Isaiah 1–39, brought judgment. At the beginning of Third Isaiah, the call to justice points towards Yhwh's own salvation and justice. Human and divine practice mirror each other.

Notwithstanding their different genres and traditions of discourse, and perhaps their epistemological orientations, we have found substantial agreements between Isaiah 40–66 and the Holiness School. Instead of turning to the Mosaic past for authority, Isaiah interweaves visions of the future, but the two streams of tradition share a social imagination of Yhwh's imperial jurisdiction. Or better, they share a counter-imperial imaginary that contests the authority of all other empires. Isaiah 56–66 looks ultimately to divine initiative for the consummation of a just society, but within that society the human practice of justice remains fundamental, including the protection of natives and strangers alike.

---

25. Rolf Rendtorff, *Canon and Theology: Overtures to an Old Testament Theology*, trans. Margaret Kohl (OBT; Minneapolis: Fortress, 1993), pp. 181-89.

7. Alternatives to the National Tradition in Job

In previous chapters I set out some of the biblical foundations for a secular theology, first by examining the rise and decline of the national imaginary, and second, by examining the counter-imperial alternatives presented in the Priestly tradition and in Isaiah 40–48. In each case we have examined the ways in which strangers are to be treated, whether as marginal characters deserving of charity (within the national imaginary), or as subjects whose rights should in principle be indistinguishable from those of the native citizen (within the counter-imperial alternatives). The latter approach most likely arose in contexts where political sovereignty had been traumatically lost, but a divine jurisdiction lived on within a renewed social imagination. This new imaginary, shared fundamentally between the Priestly tradition and Isaiah, pointed more towards the possibilities for reconciliation than towards confrontational postures or theocratic states. It remains now to consider the politics of the book of Job, which quite explicitly reflects on the experience of trauma. Although framed within a different intellectual tradition, I want to suggest that the character of Job inhabits social space that was opened up by Priestly theology. Indeed, this wise foreigner raises significant questions about divine power and justice that are left hanging in Priestly texts.

The book of Job locates its theological alternatives at some distance from the legal, prophetic, and national traditions of Israel by depicting a conversation that is shaped around a foreign exponent of skeptical wisdom, the character of Job himself, a man who is said, even by Yhwh, to be extraordinarily just (Job 1:8). This book was written in Hebrew, and no doubt for an Israelite audience, yet it is a thought experiment that contemplates not only the existence of wise and righteous foreigners, but also the possibility that they have substantial contributions to make to the life of a society — even if they live entirely out-side the confines of Israel's story and law. We may wonder, as Martin Buber did, writing shortly after the traumas of Nazism, whether Job is also in some sense representative of many people who have suffered unjustly, including the children of the exiles born in Babylon.[1] The apparently "apolitical" character of Job's poetry may be something that belongs to the surface of this literary thought experiment, rather than to the social setting where it was first read.[2]

This character Job is given a literary license to challenge the thinking of his very traditional friends. As already suggested, none of the participants in this conversation advance the traditional cause of covenantal theology, no doubt in part because Job is a non-Israelite and therefore beyond the scope of the Moses or David traditions. In theory, however, his position is quite conceivable within the terms of the Priestly creation theologies articulated in Genesis 1 (where all humans share the image of God regardless of their ethnicity) and in Genesis 9 (the covenant with Noah, which extends to all living things regardless of their species). Ostensibly at least, there does not appear to be any explicit references to these Priestly texts in Job, but creation theology is nonetheless fundamental to the book, and it underlies the skeptical questions about the nature of divine justice that Job presses on all who will listen. The strength of his cause is enhanced by Job's own integrity, which significantly, is measured in relation to the very standards that are familiar in the laws of Israel, even though foreigners are not bound by these laws.

Notably in chapter 31 Job asserts that he has defended the rights of slaves, widows, orphans and aliens, all on the basis of an ethic drawn from creation rather than from Israel's law.[3] In this speech, he describes his ethical account-ability before "El," using the traditional Canaanite name for the creator god (and the name associated in the Priestly tradition with the ancestors before Moses, the ancestor who first learned the name Yhwh):

> If I have rejected the rights (*mishpat*) of my male or female slaves,
> when they brought a complaint against me,
> what then should I do when El arises?

---

1. Martin Buber, *The Prophetic Faith*, trans. Carlyle Witton-Davies (New York: Macmillan, 1949), p. 189.

2. *Contra* Michael Walzer, who suggests that "The apolitical character of later wisdom may have a historical cause – imperial conquest and exile – but there is no evidence that the author of Job made this cause his subject." *In God's Shadow: Politics in the Hebrew Bible* (New Haven: Yale University Press, 2012), p. 163.

3. For example, in Deuteronomy 14:28-29; 16:11-14; 24:19-22.

When he investigates, how shall I respond?
Did not He who made me in the belly make them,
  and form me in the one womb?
If I have withheld anything that the poor desired,
  or brought resignation to the eyes of the widow,
eaten my morsel alone, and the orphan has not eaten from it . . .
then let my shoulder blade fall from my shoulder,
  and let my arm be broken from its socket . . .
No sojourner spent the night outside;
  I have opened my doors in their path. (Job 31:13-17, 22, 32)

Here is a character who is apparently law-observant without need of a law. He dares to bring a case against El, first by protesting his own innocence, and secondly, in extrapolating out from his own circumstances, by accusing God of failing to create an orderly universe within which justice is distributed fairly to all parties. Thus, in 12:4 we learn that Job has become a laughingstock to his neighbours, even though he is just and blameless. This personal experience is then generalized in 12:17-19 into a claim that various figures in authority, whether kings, judges or priests — figures who may be expected to possess wisdom — can be brought undone by God's rule. Accordingly, in Job's view of the world, there is no clear correlation between the possession of wisdom and divine blessings. Indeed, violent criminals[4] and those who provoke God can rest secure in their tents (12:6). The tragedy of Job's case fits a familiar pattern in human history: he is accountable to a sovereign power who appears to act without regard for justice.

In the wider context of Job 12, the poetry goes to questions of epistemology: how does Job know what he does, when his conversation partners do not? First, he claims that his wisdom in not inferior to theirs (verses 2-3), and then comes a stinging rhetorical question: "And who does not know such things as these?" (12:3b). Who is not aware of this lack of correlation in the order of things? The friends' poverty of knowledge is almost self-evident, he suggests, and they could do with some instruction from nature on this point:

But ask the wild beast, and she will instruct you;
  the birds of the air, and they will declare to you;

---

4. The translation "violent criminals" follows Jürgen Ebach's rendering of *shodedim* in 12:6 as "Gewalttäter," in Ebach, *Streiten mit Gott. Hiob*, Part 1: *Hiob 1–20* (Neukirchen-Vluyn: Neukirchener Verlag, 1996), p. 106.

> speak to the earth, and she will instruct you;
> and the fish of the sea will relate to you.
>
> Who among all these does not know
> that the hand of Yhwh has done this?
>
> In his hand is the life of every living thing
> and the spirit of all human flesh. (12:7–10)

This passage is dense with allusions to the creation narratives in Genesis and to Isaiah, as I will demonstrate below. But to begin with, the choice of the verb form w^{e}toreka (literally, "and she will instruct you"), is striking. This wording, repeated in verses 7 and 8, is related to the familiar noun for law and instruction in the legal tradition: "torah." The semantic play is too significant to pass over.

The rhetorical effect of the speech is to deflate the arrogance of Job's friends while, at the same time, implicitly laying a further challenge to those who would make exclusive claims about the revelatory value of Mosaic Law. The legal literature, like the more optimistic genres of wisdom in the book of Proverbs, envisages a moral order in which everyone receives their just deserts, but this consensus is in Job 12 being contested.[5] The laws of kings, judges, and priests might have their own validity within their own jurisdictions, but the testimony of nature points to moral dissonances beyond their grasp. In effect, Job seems to be implying that the natural world has its own kind of torah, and it conflicts with the Torah of Moses; the content of this instruction denies the very order that the other authorities presume.[6] Such a sharp opposition between the book of nature and the books of Moses cannot be found in the mainstream traditions, and Job's speech sets up an extraordinary theological

5. This skepticism stands in contrast with Psalm 19, where we find an eirenic parallel between the speech of the cosmos and the laws of Yhwh, without setting the two genres in opposition. See also Psalm 119:90-91 where the justice (mishpat) of the cosmos is asserted. Jon D. Levenson, "The Sources of the Torah: Psalm 119 and the Modes of Revelation in Second Temple Judaism," in Ancient Israelite Religion: Essays in Honor of Frank Moore Cross, ed. Patrick D. Miller, Paul D. Hanson, and Sean D. McBride (Philadelphia: Fortress, 1987), pp. 559-74.

6. Contra David J. A. Clines, Job 1-20 (WBC 17; Dallas: Word, 1989), pp. 292-93, who follows Robert Gordis in seeing 12:7-12 as a quotation or parody of the friends' instruction to Job, the passage makes good sense as a retort to the friends. Francis Andersen notes that "so far none of the friends has suggested that Job might learn wisdom from the animals," an astute observation that undermines the approach taken by Gordis and Clines. Andersen, Job: An Introduction and Commentary (TOTC; Downers Grove: Intervarsity, 1976), p. 161.

tension to which the poet will return later. At this point in the dialogues, however, we perhaps need to assume that only an extraordinarily righteous foreigner could dare to entertain such heterodoxy and get away with it.

A number of scholars have observed that the phrase "the hand of Yhwh has done this" (12:9) is apparently borrowed from Isaiah 41:20 — which rounds off a prophetic oracle that celebrates Yhwh's redemptive provision of water resources (Isa. 41:17–20). Instead of accepting the prophetic proclamation, Job appeals to the animals and the earth:

> Who among all these does not know
> that the hand of Yhwh has done this?

Robert Gordis notes the oddity that Job does not otherwise address the divinity with Israel's peculiar name for God "Yhwh," and concludes that this simply reflects the "unconscious usage of a Hebrew poet who includes a reminiscence of a phrase from Deutero-Isaiah (41:20)."[7] But an unconscious usage is unlikely for a number of reasons, especially when there is more than one allusion in Job to Isaiah, as we shall see. Both Isaiah 41 and Job 12 are concerned with the divine ordering of creation, but they point to different conclusions: in the case of Deutero-Isaiah, Yhwh's hand in creation is redemptive, but Job is suggesting the opposite — that the animals bear witness also to the shadow side of being in God's "hand" (cf. Job 10:3, 7-8; 13:21). As he says elsewhere, using another "El" compound in referring to the divinity, "Have pity on me, have pity on me, O you my friends, for the *hand of Eloah* has touched me!" (19:21).

In making his skeptical points, Job also appears to invoke the vocabulary of the creation and flood narratives of Genesis:

> In his hand is the life of every living thing,
> and the spirit of all human flesh. (Job 12:10)

The expression "all flesh" (*kol basar*) is one of the dominant phrases throughout Genesis 6–9, and Job makes this point immediately after appealing to the animals; he invokes their testimony that they are in the hands of God whether for good or for ill, regardless of their personal virtues, whether in the creation or in the flood. The fact that the phrase is qualified here in 12:10 to read "all

---

7. Robert Gordis, *The Book of Job* (New York: Jewish Theological Seminary of America, 1978), p. 138. The connection with Isaiah 41:20 was earlier noted by Artur Weiser, *Das Buch Hiob* (ATD 13; Göttingen: Vandenhoeck & Ruprecht, 1951), p. 91.

human flesh" seems to suggest that human flesh is subject to the same ambiguity. Humans are part of the larger category of "living things," and inevitably a part of "all flesh," as is made manifest in the covenant with Noah and all living things in Genesis 9. The Priestly covenant there covers both human and non-human creatures, and in this respect it has a much larger scope than the claim in Genesis 1 that all humans are made in the image of God (using the divine name Elohim, as we saw in Chapter Five).

The ambiguity of creation/flood imagery is then given a political application as Job 12 progresses, where we find that creation theology can also be related to the national condition:

> He makes nations great, then destroys them;
> he enlarges nations, then leads them away,
> diverting understanding in the leaders of the people of the land,
> he makes them wander in wasteland (*tohu*), without a path.
>
> (12:23–24)

Nations wax and wane, Job suggests, with no apparent correlation between the possession of wisdom and the measure of divine blessings. The word *tohu* is the same word that is used in Genesis 1:2 to describe the disorder before creation begins, and in Jeremiah 4:23 to describe the undoing of creation as a result of sin. More importantly, it is also used in Isaiah 40:17 and 23 to describe the undoing of nations, as it is here in Job 12:24, and the implications of this connection with Isaiah 40 will be discussed further below.

In the rhetoric of Job 12, the friends are brought "down to earth"; their limited wisdom is inferior even to what the animals can teach. Yet the complexity of the book of Job does not stop at this point. Whatever truth Job might be asserting in his satirical self-defense in chapter 12, he does not have the last word on the matter. What he takes to be nature's witness to a disordered waxing and waning of fortune, whether individual or national, turns out to be itself only a half-truth. Behind the confidence of optimistic wisdom, which is dismissed by Job as superficial, there is nevertheless a deeper order that is claimed in the divine speeches in Job 38–41, where once again God appears under the name Yhwh. For those who can contemplate the more radical demands in these divine speeches later in the book, there may yet be a second order of faith lying beyond the "first naiveté" that finds only moral order in the world.[8] Job's

---

8. The expressions "first naiveté" and "second naiveté" were coined by Paul Ricoeur, but the discussion here does not turn on the exegesis of Ricoeur's philosophy of interpretation.

speech about the wisdom of animals in 12:7–10 is, in effect, "double-voiced" by Yhwh in chapters 38–41, who undercuts Job by suggesting another look at what animals teach.[9] As David Clines suggests, "It is a deep irony — on the poet's part, not Job's — that in the end it will be to the book of nature that God will direct Job's attention."[10]

The first naiveté is present not only in the mouths of Job's friends, but more generally in the optimistic wisdom of the book of Proverbs. Proverbs 6:6–11 even suggests that wisdom is so readily accessible that it can be learned from a single species — the ways (*derekim*) of the ant, who stores resources for winter without needing instruction from a "chief, officer or ruler." The lessons that can be learned from this acephalous society in the natural world is then translated by Proverbs 6 into their utility for human wisdom: "go to the ant: study its ways and be wise." The skeptical wisdom of Job, on the other hand, denies that the *derekim* of a seasonal economy can be mastered by just getting busy like ants. Job's position is perhaps closer to Proverbs 30:18–19 that contemplates a more complex scenario in which animals might indeed possess their own *derekim*, but these ways may not be readily reduced to human wisdom: "the way (*derek*) of the eagle in the heavens" is said to be beyond knowledge. Yhwh's speeches in Job 38–41 then push Job in this same direction: "Is it by your discernment that the hawk soars? ... Does the eagle mount at your command?" (Job 39:26–27).

In Yhwh's speeches, Job is confronted by a litany of questions that are apparently impossible to answer, similar in genre to the Buddhist koan:

> Where is the way (*derek*) to the dwelling of light,
> and where is the place of darkness? (38:19)

> What is the way to the place where the light is distributed,
> or where the east wind is scattered upon the earth? (38:24)

The opening list of rhetorical questions in Job 38 implies that beyond the limitations of human wisdom lies a hidden order of creation that is governed by divine commands and statutes. The use of legal language of "statute" and "command" is highly significant:

9. For the classic introduction to the idea of double voicing, see Mikhail Bakhtin, *Problems of Dostoevsky's Poetics*, trans. Caryl Emerson (Minneapolis: University of Minnesota Press, 1984), pp. 185-203; cf. the discussion of hidden polemic as "active double voicing" in Gary Saul Morsen and Caryl Emerson, *Mikhail Bakhtin: Creation of a Prosaics* (Stanford: Stanford University Press, 1990), pp. 154-59.

10. Clines, *Job 1-20*, p. 293.

> Where were you when I laid the foundation of the earth?
>> Tell me, if you have understanding.
> Who determined its measurements — surely you know! . . .
>> Or who shut in the sea with doors
> when it burst out from the womb? —
>> when I made a cloud its garment,
> and thick darkness its swaddling band,
>> and I prescribed my statute (*choq*), and set bars and doors,
> and said, 'Thus far shall you come, and no farther,
>> and here shall your proud waves be stopped'?
> Have you commanded the morning since your days began,
>> and caused the dawn to know its place? (38:4–5a, 8–12a)

In the context of the book of Job, these are deconstructive questions, which no human can answer in the affirmative. Yet when wisdom is personified in Proverbs 8, it is precisely the affirmative response that we find:

> When he established the heavens, I was there,
>> when he inscribed a circle on the face of the deep,
> when he made firm the skies above,
>> when he established the fountains of the deep,
> when he assigned to the sea its statute (*choq*),
>> so that the waters might not transgress his command,
> when he inscribed[11] the foundations of the earth. (Prov. 8:27–29)

The correlation between the questions posed in Job 38 and the answers in Proverbs 8 is striking. And there is a further correlation between Proverbs 8 and Job 28 in the agreement between these two chapters that, although God is the one who makes the statutes that shape the created order, it is still the case that wisdom herself is separate from God and needs to be discerned in the workings of creation. There is however an implication in Job 28:25-27 that it is only God, in the very act of creating, who has discovered the full extent and character of wisdom.[12]

---

11. The infinitive translated as "inscribe" in verses 27 and 29 is related to the noun *choq*, here translated as "statute." Cf. the *choq* for the cosmic elements in Psalm 148:6 and in Jeremiah 31:35-36; cf. Jeremiah 33:25.

12. Pierre J. P. Van Hecke, "Searching for and Exploring Wisdom," in *Job 28: Cognition in Context*, ed. Ellen Van Wolde (BIS 64; Leiden: Brill, 2003), pp. 139-62, 158-59; Jürgen van Oorschot, "Hiob 28: Die verborgene Weisheit und die Furcht Gottes also Überwindung einer

When he gave to the wind its weight,
    and the waters he regulated by measure;
when he made a decree (*choq*) for the rain,
    and a way (*derek*) for the thunderbolt's voice;
then he saw it and declared it;
    he established it, and searched its character. (28:25–27)

This reading of Proverbs 8 and Job 28 then implies, as Norman Habel has rightly suggested, that "it is Earth that God surveys and probes, not the recesses of the divine mind. . . . Wisdom is not outside of Earth but in Earth."[13]

Yet these points of contact also serve to highlight the tension between two quite different views: while Job 38 presumes that deep wisdom is beyond human grasp, Proverbs 8:15–21 confidently asserts that the kind of wisdom personified in 8:27–29 can indeed be profitably pursued by kings and by others who seek to establish their wealth on just foundations. It is precisely this tension that makes Job 12 difficult to interpret, since on the one hand, there is an ironic agreement between Job 12:17–19 and the divine speeches of Job 38–41 that deep wisdom *cannot* be domesticated by kings and other leaders. On the other hand, Job 12:8 seems to suggest that consulting the earth can indeed be a source of wisdom, as Proverbs 8:16-21 asserts, and at least in this respect God's discovery of wisdom in the earth can be imitated. How are these complexities to be understood?

Clearly, the canon preserves more than one kind of wisdom, and the book of Job does not present its theology in a simple way, free from rhetorical tensions and irony. The poetic allusions extend not only into the complexity of Job's unfolding dialogue with his friends, but also into the Joban poet's arguments with the other streams of Israelite religion and theology. When the character of Job urges his friends in 12:7–10 to consider the wisdom of the birds of the air, animals of the earth and fish of the sea, he is speaking perhaps satirically and even in anger. Yet it is precisely from creation that Job has learned his ethics; his care for widow, orphan, and alien has no other foundation. And what the Yhwh speeches in Job 38–41 disclose is that there

Generalisierten הקמה," in *The Book of Job*, ed. Willem A. M. Beuken (BETL 114; Leuven: Leuven University Press and Peeters, 1994), pp. 183-201, 187.

13. Norman Habel, "The Implications of God Discovering Wisdom in Earth," In *Job 28: Cognition in Context*, ed. Ellen van Wolde (BIS 64; Leiden: Brill, 2003), pp. 281-98, 294; so also Katherine Dell, "Plumbing the Depths of Earth: Job 28 and Deep Ecology," in *The Earth Story in Wisdom Traditions*, ed. Norman C. Habel and Shirley Wurst (Earth Bible 3; Sheffield: Sheffield Academic Press, 2001), p. 124.

is indeed a greater truth in Job's self-defense than Job himself perhaps realizes at the time. Job calls on the non-human creatures as, in effect, witnesses for the defense. He imagines that their testimony can deflate the hubris of all-too-human wisdom by providing instruction to his friends on the disorder of divine rule. But his anthropocentric attempt to call nature as a witness ironically backfires when God calls the same witness for cross-examination. Job inadvertently bears witness to another inconvenient truth, which is that the divine order in creation may not be reducible to utilitarian wisdom. If it can be contemplated at all, this kind of wisdom cannot be domesticated or mastered by mortal minds. Job asserts more than he can know, and this brings us back to some of the fundamental questions in the wisdom tradition concerning epistemology and revelation.

The translation of the opening words in Job 12:8, "speak to the earth," raises interesting questions of interpretation. The verb *sich* is ambiguous between "complain," "meditate," "study" and "speak," and although some commentators seem to think that this ambiguity is easily resolved, a careful reader would be justified in being slower to eliminate the semantic polysemy in this context. Antonine De Guglielmo, for example, claimed that "the context obviously rules out the meaning *to complain* and certainly demands that we take the verb to mean *to speak*, or perhaps 'speak musingly.'"[14] If context is the primary guide, then "speak to the earth" in this verse would need to imply the peculiar kind of speech that always remains open to instruction or conversation. Rather than denoting mere self-expression, this kind of speaking might be more a case of "meditating," as it is for the Psalmist who says "I reach out for your commandments, which I love, and I will meditate (*sich*) on your statutes" (Ps. 119:48), and "I will meditate (*sich*) on your precepts, and have regard for your ways" (119:15). To "speak" (*sich*) the laws of Israel and the instruction of the earth, we may conclude, is to study or meditate on them.

In short, Job's speech in chapter 12 is pointing to the possibility of "natural theology," although as we have noted above, this affirmation comes in the moment of a heated dialogue that is still unfolding. The poet puts into Job's mouth a truth that cannot be fully grasped at this point in the dialogues. When we arrive at 38:2, God charges Job with "speaking without knowledge," yet when Yhwh finally summarizes the whole debate, the verdict on Job's friends is that "You have not spoken firmly established truths (*nᵉkonah*) about me, as my servant Job has" (Job 42:7-8). This is an intriguing choice of words in Hebrew,

---

14. Antonine De Guglielmo, "Job 12:7-9 and the Knowability of God," *Catholic Biblical Quarterly* 6 (1944): 478-79.

which might throw some light on the ostensibly contradictory conclusion that Job has spoken both rightly and "without knowledge." Perhaps this contradiction can be relieved somewhat by appreciating that Job sometimes draws the wrong conclusions from the right premises. If it is indeed the case that something is to be learned from the world of non-human animals, perhaps their instruction is more difficult than even Job would like to hear.

The failure in Job's own logic is shaped into a divine question in 38:2, and then reiterated in 40:8. In the larger context of chapters 38–41, there is no question whether animals possess wisdom; that truth is well established in the divine speeches. Job was therefore right to suggest in 12:7–9 that the animals of earth, sea and sky can provide instruction, but he was apparently wrong about the *content* of their instruction. And hence the divine questions:

> Who is this that darkens counsel (*'etsah*),
> > speaking without knowledge? (38:2)

> Will you indeed annul my justice (*mishpat*)?
> > Will you condemn me in order to justify yourself? (40:8)

The more specific formulation in 40:8 suggests that Job had drawn the wrong conclusions about divine justice, and on this issue it is evident that the Joban poet is taking up a much wider conversation with the other streams of Israelite religion and theology. And this brings us back to Martin Buber's suggestion that Job's experience might in some sense be prototypical for a wider, social experience of unjust suffering, rather than being an exceptional individual predicament.

The possibility of reading the divine questions in Job 38:2 and 40:8 in light of Israel's *national* fortunes is, for example, suggested by the parallel with the wording of Isaiah 40:13–14:

> Who has weighed the spirit of Yhwh?
> > And what man could tell him his counsel (*'etsah*)?
> Whom did he consult, who guided,
> > who taught him the path of justice (*mishpat*)?
> Who taught him knowledge,
> > or showed him the way (*derek*) of understanding?

In the context of the exhortation to the exiles in Isaiah 40, it is emphasized that no human could aspire to do these things. This is the very same chapter of Isaiah that suggests that although divine justice (*mishpat*) is beyond merely political wisdom, yet it can still be found in God's cosmic ordering.[15] The forming and deforming — creation and uncreation — of nations is said to be hidden in divine counsel.

In Isaiah, these claims are part of a divine response to a doubt articulated by Jacob-Israel, which could have come from the lips of Job:

> Why do you say, O Jacob, and speak, O Israel,
> "My way is hidden from Yhwh,
>> and my just cause (*mishpat*) is disregarded by my God"?
>>>> (Isa. 40:27)

The personal in Job is the political in Isaiah, we might conclude. And the divine response in both books is essentially the same: however difficult it may be for individuals and nations to conceive, the answer lies in the mystery of creation:

> Have you not known?
>> Have you not heard?
> Has it not been told you from the beginning?
>> Have you not understood from the foundations of the earth?
> It is he who sits above the circle of the earth,
>> with its inhabitants like grasshoppers;
> who stretches out the heavens like a curtain,
>> and spreads them like a tent to live in;
> who puts rulers to naught,
>> and reduces the judges of the earth to nothing (*tohu*) . . .

> Have you not known?
>> Have you not heard?
> God of eternity, Yhwh,
>> Creator of the ends of the earth,

---

15. On the relevance of Second Isaiah, see further Samuel Terrien, "Quelques Remarques sur les affinités de Job avec le Deutéro-Esaïe," in *Volume du Congrès: Genève, 1965* (VTSup 15; Leiden: Brill, 1966), pp. 295-310; J. Gerald Janzen, "On the Moral Nature of God's Power: Yahweh and the Sea in Job and Deutero-Isaiah," *CBQ* 56 (1994): 458-78; cf. Leo Perdue, *The Sword and the Stylus: An Introduction to Wisdom in the Age of Empires* (Grand Rapids: Eerdmans, 2008), pp. 117-51.

> he does not faint or grow weary;
>> his understanding is unsearchable. (Isa. 40:21–23, 28)

Considered in the larger context of Second Isaiah, this passage claims a consistency in divine dealings with nature and nations. Despite appearances to the contrary, the prophet asserts, God does not fall asleep on the job. But the appearances are not entirely deceiving either, at least when viewed from a human point of view. The opening word of Second Isaiah in Isaiah 40:2 makes clear that Jerusalem has "received from the hand of Yhwh *double* for all her sins" (cf. "the hand of Yhwh" in Job 12:9). Whatever the sins of Jerusalem might have been, the punishment is proclaimed by the prophet to be disproportionate. So the doubt that is voiced in Isa. 40:27 contains its own grain of truth: "My way is hidden from Yhwh, and my just cause is disregarded by my God." Isaiah's exhortation meets this complaint half way: it is not that justice has been hidden or disregarded entirely, but rather, that the injustices of Jacob-Israel outlined in Isaiah 1–39 have been disproportionately judged, and the hubris of those nations who conquered Israel and Judah will itself be addressed in time. The restoration of Jerusalem belongs to the second order of prophetic faith, one might say, beyond the "first naiveté" of the old Zion theology, which presumed that Jerusalem was impregnable.

The second order of faith in the wisdom tradition, however, derives no comfort from prophetic visions of Jerusalem's redemption. When Yhwh speaks into Job's storm, the only comfort on offer seems to lie in the divine assertion that there is indeed a cosmic order. But the catch is that this order is not easily turned to human advantage, even in human wisdom. This harder truth is made clear, for example, in the images of wild animals exercising their freedom (39:5–12) and in the fearsome Leviathan who can deflate every human presumption of dominion (41:1–34). Leviathan is a beast that brooks no "covenant" of servitude (41:4), nor is it available for commercial exploitation (41:6). Interestingly, the Joban poet also wants to insist that this kind of deep ecology comes from the mouth of Yhwh. Even if the character Job does not generally know the name of Yhwh (the exceptional usage in 12:9 is often emended to El or Eloah), the reader of the book of Job is in no doubt that El is indeed another name for Yhwh. The reader can conclude that there is only one Creator, who establishes an order upon which an ethic can be built, quite outside Israel's law. Non-Israelites are therefore depicted as capable of relationship with the Creator, of being taught by creation, and of acquiring a legitimate ethic from creation. The Creator is revealed, at least to Israelite readers, to be none other than Yhwh, regardless of whether this particular name of God is known or not.

CONSEQUENCES

The Judeans and Samarians of the Persian period inherited Ezekiel's insight that children should not suffer the sins of earlier generations (Ezekiel 18), and the same conviction shaped the reformulation of Israel's history in the books of Chronicles.[16] The children of the exile were therefore, by implication, in a similar position to Job: they had suffered disproportionately. At the same time, the Priestly imaginary had begun to suggest some equivalence between natives and strangers under the rule of God, including the possibility that the strangers' name for the Creator might be different from Israel's divine name. Yet ultimately these names pointed to the same God, whether named "El" as for the ancestors in Genesis and in Job, or "Yhwh" for the Israelite generations following Moses. The book of Job took this conversation a step further by imagining the moral universe of a righteous stranger from the East, who eventually earned the direct address of Yhwh.

I have argued that Job 12 aligns ironically with the divine speeches in chapters 38–41 in undermining the view that nature is simply subservient to human desire or rule. The Joban critique of this anthropocentric view is presented as a conversation internal to wisdom circles (ironically adopting Deuteronomy's legal vocabulary), but the ramifications provide a kind of bridge to the other biblical traditions. Against the surface meaning of Genesis 1:26–28, Job avoids the suggestion that non-human creation can be ruled and subdued by the one species made in the image of Elohim. Rather, Job emphasizes the other aspect of the Priestly narratives that represent all living creatures and "all flesh" as blessed with a divinely given spirit of life, and covered by Noah's covenant. While Job's own speech in 26:12–13 alludes to the violent themes of the creation myths in the surrounding cultures, the emphasis in the divine speeches of Job 38–41 is that the fearsome beasts like Behemoth and Leviathan are not slain by God but are simply a part of the created order that humans cannot finally control.[17] In this respect, the Joban poet again seems to suggest that the created order cannot be domesticated by merely human will, not even the will of an imperial king.

While the Priestly writers do not attack anthropocentrism in the way that

16. Sara Japhet, "Theodicy in Ezra-Nehemiah and Chronicles," in *Theodicy in the World of the Bible*, ed. Antii Laato and Johannes C. de Moor (Leiden: Brill, 2004), pp. 429-69.

17. J. Gerald Janzen emphasizes that the theme of Yhwh's cosmic ordering in Second Isaiah contrasts notably with the instability and violence evident not only in the Babylonian creation story Enuma Elish but also in Psalms 74, 89 and 93. Job 26:12-13 can be added to this list of biblical texts that allude to violence in creation. Janzen, "The Moral Nature of God's Power," p. 473.

the divine speeches of Job 38–41 do, nevertheless, there is perhaps more common ground between the Joban poet and Priestly tradition than has previously been acknowledged. The Priestly tradition recoils from the politics of the national imaginary, and this is the grain of truth in Michael Walzer's conclusion that Job is "apolitical." But this does not prevent the book from providing the kind of social critique that we might otherwise associate only with the prophetic tradition:

> Why are times of judgment not kept by Shaddai,
>   and why do those who know him not see his days?
> The wicked remove boundary stones;
>   they seize flocks and pasture them.
> They lead away the donkey of the orphan;
>   they take the widow's ox for a pledge.
> They thrust the needy off the way;
>   the poor of the earth all hide themselves.
> Like wild asses of the wilderness,
>   they go out to their toil,
> the wasteland yields food for them,
>   and for their children.
> They reap fodder in a field
>   and glean in the vineyard of the wicked.
> They lodge overnight naked, without clothing,
>   and have no covering in the cold.
> They are wet with mountain rains,
>   and cling to the rock for want of shelter. (Job 24:1–8)

Here the book of Job agrees with the prophets that the poor are not necessarily poor because they are lazy (so also Proverbs 6:6–11, which urges the sluggard to consider the industry of the ant), but rather, because the powerful have acted oppressively. And this is precisely why Job brings his case against God — who appears under the name of Shaddai, the ancestral divine name from the Priestly tradition.

If we explore the non-Israelite ways of naming the Creator in the Hebrew Bible, histories of Israelite religion soon lead us to the Canaanite name for the Creator, El. Appropriating a Canaanite divine name seems to have presented no special difficulties for Job or for the Priestly tradition. The conviction of biblical wisdom that the created order is governed by "laws of nature" was in the modern period poured into the foundations of Western science, regrettably with the result that Indigenous knowledges were usually dismissed as irrelevant to the scientific enterprise of the day. In this respect, the paths of science and colonial theology ran in parallel, and therefore the business of reconciliation with Indigenous peoples is not simply a theological problem.

More recently, there has been an increasing awareness that local Indigenous knowledges have a significant contribution to make to understanding the biodiversity that is key to future practices of sustainable life on earth.[18] As we "meditate on the earth" today, bioregion by bioregion across the globe, we can expect that scientific culture and Indigenous cultures will both be transformed in the demanding dialogue ahead. Theology will not be leading this new conversation, but it can still contribute to the cultural changes that will be required. For communities of faith, reading "the book of nature" alongside the book of Job would be a good way to begin, not least when the environmental sins of the current generation are being passed on to our children.

While there are many other biblical traditions that might shape our discussion in Part Three of this book, we are sufficiently informed by the similarities and differences between the law, prophets and wisdom to turn now to some of the key public issues that concern a secular theology today. The book of Job, in particular, provides significant resources for beginning to think about the issues of reconciliation, asylum seekers, and climate change, the topics to which the following chapters are devoted.

18. See for example Fikret Berkes, *Sacred Ecology: Traditional Ecological Knowledge and Resource Management*, 2nd ed. (New York: Routledge, 2008); Serena Heckler, ed., *Landscape, Process and Power: Re-evaluating Traditional Environmental Knowledge* (New York: Berghan Books, 2009).

ENGAGING THE PRESENT

8. Reconciliation and National Sovereignties

Large-scale political violence is part of living memory in many parts of the world, and the prospect of finding legal solutions to such violence is often extremely limited. Discourses and practices of reconciliation have emerged where the number of offenders is overwhelmingly large, legal institutions have historically been distorted, or where the political consequences of judicial responses may carry new kinds of risk. In some cases, such as in South Africa, East Timor, and the Solomon Islands, the historic presence of the Christian religion has allowed an explicitly theological leadership to inform the processes of reconciliation.[1] Particularities of history and culture make comparisons difficult, and in some contexts, such as Israel-Palestine, nothing less than an inter-religious dialogue would be productive.[2] The present chapter is directed more towards the legacies of settler colonialism in the Anglo world, where former colonies have separated themselves from the British Crown and reconstituted themselves as secular multicultural societies, yet where the majority of the population continues to identify as Christian.

In settler colonial states like the USA, Canada, Australia, and New Zealand, the issues have been complicated by the number of years since overt political violence has taken place, and subsequently, by the much more subtle ways in which colonial ideology has continued to shape public life. Precisely

1. From a participant's point of view, see the discussion in Samuel T. Ata, "Towards Peace and Reconciliation: Some Churches' Response with Specific Reference to the Post-Civil War in Solomon Islands," PhD Thesis (Melbourne: Melbourne College of Divinity, 2013).

2. See the valuable international collection of case studies in Susan Allen Nan, Zachariah Cherian Mampily, and Andrea Bartoli, eds., *Peacemaking: From Practice to Theory*, 2 vols. (Santa Barbara, Calif.: Praeger, 2011).

this complexity, however, demands a close analysis of the implications of religious history for the task of reconciliation with Indigenous peoples — not least where white Christianity has failed to understand its own past. Beyond a merely existential revision of self-understanding, we will examine the particular kinds of actions that might be taken by the Christian churches, and the ways in which these actions must be distinguished from the policies of a secular state.

The position of the churches is precarious once it is acknowledged that much ecclesial property arose historically through grants of the Crown. Even the churches who refused Crown grants as a matter of principle are the beneficiaries of historic dispossession. A pressing question that arises here is what it would mean for current generations to "confess the iniquity of their ancestors" (Lev. 26:40). Instead of simply blaming governments for their lack of moral vision, many churches have made their own efforts at reconciliation, making apologies and allocating resources for ministry among Indigenous peoples. These efforts have, however, been hampered by theological tensions in some quarters, not least by the kind of individualist Christianity that is all too readily woven into liberal politics and tempered only by non-government models of charity.[3]

It is not difficult to find reasons why reconciliation might be regarded as a hollow discourse in the public domain, and lacking in practical effect. Even Patrick Dodson, the Aboriginal leader (and former Catholic priest) who chaired the Council for Aboriginal Reconciliation in Australia 1991–1997, resigned from this post when he found that "any notion of reconciled peoples is a farcical concept"[4] in the context of coercive and assimilationist policies advanced by the federal government at the time. He was responding, in particular, to the so-called Northern Territory Emergency Response, an intervention heralded as "practical reconciliation" by Liberal Party politicians.

Daniel Philpott's theory of reconciliation in *Just and Unjust Peace* proposes a combination of acknowledgment, reparations, punishment, apology, forgiveness, and the establishment of just institutions.[5] Taken together, these

3. See, for example, David Marr, *The High Price of Heaven* (St. Leonards: Allen & Unwin, 1999), pp. 27-30.

4. Patrick Dodson, "Can Australia Afford Not to Be Reconciled?" keynote address, National Indigenous Policy and Dialogue Conference, November 19, 2010.

5. Philpott, *Just and Unjust Peace: An Ethic of Political Reconciliation* (New York: Oxford University Press, 2012). Specifically addressing the Australian context, cf. Peter Lewis, *Acting in Solidarity? The Church's Journey with the Indigenous Peoples of Australia* (Melbourne: Uniting Academic Press, 2010), pp. 135-38.

practices would constitute a strong political ethic, but more often than not these practices have been de-linked from each other. Philpott's argument does not bode well for the future of relationships with Indigenous peoples in settler colonial states where punishment of previous generations is not possible, where the very idea of reparations is politically divisive, and even apologies by governments have been found wanting.[6]

In Australia, a national enquiry into the history of removing Indigenous children from their families culminated with the *Bringing Them Home* report (1997), which proposed a broad range of initiatives for healing the intergenerational trauma that is still all too evident in Aboriginal and Torres Strait Islander lives.[7] Among other things, the report recommended apologies from state parliaments, police forces, churches and from the federal Government. While the other agencies complied, the Prime Minister at the time, John Howard, famously refused. It was said that apologies were merely symbolic and therefore lacking in practical significance, although behind the scenes, there were also questions about what legal obligations might be triggered by a formal apology from a federal government.

Prime Minister Howard also dismissed proposals for a treaty with Aboriginal people on the grounds that "a nation cannot make a treaty with itself."[8] As a piece of political rhetoric, this sentiment appealed to liberal political philosophy, but it was nonsense as a historical claim. Australia remains the only nation within the so-called "common law" tradition not to have secured treaties with its First Nations. The USA, Canada, and New Zealand have all done so. Movements seeking a treaty process in Australia have ebbed and flowed since the 1980s, and many Indigenous leaders have promoted aspirations for a treaty as an expression of the justice that rightly belongs to any adequate understanding of reconciliation and healing.[9] In developing political practices of reconciliation, a treaty can provide the foundation for acknowledgment of past wrongs, principles for reparations, and the infra-

6. See the detailed analysis in Melissa Nobles, *The Politics of Official Apologies* (Cambridge: Cambridge University Press, 2008).

7. Human Rights and Equal Opportunity Commission, *Bringing Them Home: Report of the National Inquiry into the Separation of Aboriginal and Torres Strait Islander Children from Their Families* (Sydney: HREOC, 1997).

8. Quoted in Mark McKenna, "A History for Our Time? The Idea of the People in Australian Democracy," *History Compass* 1 (2003): 1-15, 5.

9. See especially Irene Moores, ed., *Voices of Aboriginal Australia: Past, Present, Future* (Melbourne: Butterfly Books, Springwood, 1995); Michelle Grattan, ed., *Essays on Australian Reconciliation* (Melbourne: Bookman, 2000).

structure for just institutions. This has at least been the case in New Zealand if not in the USA.

The *Bringing Them Home* report also recommended that government agencies should adopt a broad conception of therapeutic healing that includes spiritual and cultural renewal. In her philosophical discussion of political reconciliation, Susan Dwyer suggests that the adoption of the therapeutic language of healing might be seen as "merely a ruse to disguise the fact that a 'purer' type of justice cannot be realized."[10] But writing in response to the *Bringing Them Home* report, the Aboriginal and Torres Strait Islander Social Justice Commissioner, Tom Calma, claimed that health was indeed a matter of justice, and for example, that increasing Indigenous communal agency can be linked with positive outcomes in public health. As many studies have shown, a perception of agency is a major factor in the social determinants of health, with concrete implications for policy and governance. At the same time, Calma suggested that it is important to recognize the role of spirituality in Aboriginal and Torres Strait Islander health: "Spirituality is largely outside the dominant paradigm of policy makers and funding bodies in Australia, yet it is an intrinsic part of healing."[11]

The links between healing, spirituality and justice have been asserted by many religious and political leaders. My initial concern here is to identify some of the ways in which these themes sit between sacred and secular discourse. Then we will turn our attention to the ways in which biblical traditions might continue to inform the church's advocacy and practice of reconciliation in the public realm. A number of studies have focused understandably on New Testament contributions to restorative justice,[12] but perhaps against expectations, I want to stress the possible relevance of traditions from the Hebrew Bible that can inform the discussion.

---

10. Susan Dwyer, "Reconciliation for Realists," *Ethics and International Affairs* 13 (1999): 81-98.

11. Aboriginal and Torres Strait Islander Social Justice Commissioner, *Social Justice Report 2008* (Sydney: Australian Human Rights Commission, 2008), pp. 147-98, 152; cf. Gregory Philips, "Healing and Public Policy," in *Coercive Reconciliation: Stabilise, Normalise, Exit Aboriginal Australia*, ed. Jon Altman and Melinda Hinkson (Melbourne: Arena, 2007), pp. 141-50; David Cooper, *Closing the Gap in Cultural Understanding: Social Determinants of Health and Indigenous Policy in Australia* (Darwin: Aboriginal Medical Services Alliance NT, 2011).

12. Notably Christopher Marshall, *Beyond Retribution: A New Testament Vision for Justice, Crime and Punishment* (Grand Rapids: Eerdmans, 2001); Ched Myers and Elaine Enns, *Ambassadors of Reconciliation*, Vol. 1: *New Testament Reflections on Restorative Justice and Peacemaking* (Maryknoll, NY: Orbis, 2009).

BIBLICAL RESONANCES IN AUSTRALIAN PUBLIC DISCOURSES

A landmark event in Australia occurred in February 2008, when the Prime Minister Kevin Rudd delivered a formal Apology to the "stolen generations," that is, to Indigenous people who had been removed from their families by government agencies. This was a lyrical moment in the nation's life. The language of the speech embodied the narrative progression of sin and repentance, and Rudd wrote it himself after attending Sunday morning worship at St John's Anglican Church in Canberra. Much of the commentary at the time referred to removing a stain on the nation's soul, but also reflected on the difficulty of repenting of the "sins of the fathers" rather than one's own generation.

When not simply deflecting responsibility, such discussions have rightly drawn a distinction between guilt and shame: guilt arises from personal involvement, as opposed to shame that can properly be felt for the crimes of earlier generations, and for inheriting the unjustly gained wealth of previous generations through colonialism. Such acknowledgment of shame, however, arises precisely from a sense of participation within a larger narrative of identity, whether for example the history of a church, or a national narrative. It is also worth noting in passing that the imperative to "confess the iniquity of their ancestors" is particularly strong in some of the later traditions of the Hebrew Bible (as in Lev. 26:40). In spite of the rejection of intergenerational guilt in other biblical texts, this biblical example of confession may equally be seen as more a matter of shame, although it entails a clear commitment to a covenantal or constitutional framework that sets higher standards of future behavior.

At least two questions came to the fore in the months that followed Prime Minister Rudd's Apology: How would this lyrical moment of governmental repentance become embedded in the larger national narrative? In what ways would Aboriginal and Torres Strait Islander people be moved to forgiveness? Subsequent legislative attempts to provide reparations for the stolen generations have failed. The fate of two bills in 2008 was symptomatic of the government's inability to embody the Prime Minister's Apology in institutional change.[13] Under circumstances such as these, we may ask how a coherent narrative of reconciliation can be embodied in political life, even if one were to adopt Susan Dwyer's "realist" advice that removes the necessity for forgiveness on the part of Indigenous peoples.[14]

---

13. Calma, *Social Justice Report 2008*, pp. 147-50.

14. Dwyer, "Reconciliation for Realists," 22-23. Contrast Philpott's more thorough discussion of Jewish, Christian and Islamic approaches to forgiveness in *Just and Unjust Peace*, pp. 251-285.

The discourses of reconciliation and healing rose to prominence especially in the wake of the churches' advocacy around the time of Australia's Bicentenary celebrations in 1988, marking two hundred years since the arrival of the first British settlers. The heads of fourteen church bodies produced a document entitled "Towards Reconciliation in Australian Society," which was delivered to the Commonwealth Government by the Jesuit priest and lawyer, Frank Brennan. It was a deliberate attempt to secularize Christian conceptions of reconciliation, and in the course of time, defenders of the concept would emphasize its inter-religious and multicultural foundations.[15]

The Prime Minster at the time, Bob Hawke, affirmed the initiative from the churches as well as Indigenous aspirations for a treaty. In 1988 he responded warmly to the so-called Barunga Statement from the chairs of the Aboriginal Land Councils in the Northern Territory, and interestingly, this Statement built on an earlier tradition of activism in Aboriginal churches. For example, the Yirrkala Petition in 1963 grew out of paintings that were installed in a local church, protesting the Commonwealth Government's unilateral grant of mining rights over customary land. Many of the leaders from Yirrkala, then and since, have affirmed Yolgnu sovereignty — notably Reverend Djiniyini Gondarra, a custodian of local law and a Uniting Church minister. A fierce critic of federal policies in the Northern Territory, he has led workshops around Australia adapting a traditional Yolgnu ceremony to promote reconciliation and healing.[16] Like the majority of Aboriginal people who live in remote communities, the Yolgnu people overwhelmingly identify as Christian while maintaining traditional laws and customs. Reverend Gondarra's political practice of reconciliation raises a key question that is shared by Indigenous Christians the world over: how is it possible to balance the various claims of Indigenous, state, and divine sovereignty in the everyday business of life?

One of the applicants in the historic "native title" decision of the High Court in 1992 was Father David Passi, an Anglican priest. He often referred to a biblical sanction that established traditional tribal tenure, "Do not move an everlasting boundary stone, set up by your ancestors" (Prov. 22:28).[17] The use of this warrant from Scripture connects immediately with the wisdom

15. Notably, Evelyn Scott, Chairperson, Council for Aboriginal Reconciliation, "The Importance of Reconciliation for Multiculturalism," 7 October 2000. Available at http://www.austlii .edu.au/au/orgs/car/media/071000.htm.

16. Cf. Fiona Magowan, *Melodies of Mourning: Music and Emotion in Northern Australia* (Crawley: University of Western Australia Press, 2007), p. 191.

17. Graham Paulson and Mark Brett, "Five Smooth Stones: Reading the Bible through Aboriginal Eyes," *Colloquium* 45 (2013): 199-214, 203.

traditions, and we have already noted in Chapter Seven how the protection of boundary stones is part of Job's self defense in Job 24:1–8. These wisdom traditions stand apart from covenantal theology, but the protection of divinely established borders is endorsed also in the law and the prophets, for example where Isaiah depicts the delusions of an Assyrian king:

> By the strength of my hand I have done this,
>> and by my wisdom, because I have understanding.
> I removed the boundaries of the peoples;
>> I plundered their treasures. . . .
> As one reaches into a nest,
>> so my hand reached for the wealth of the nations.
> As men gather abandoned eggs,
>> so I gathered all the countries;
> not one flapped a wing,
>> or opened its mouth to chirp. (Isa. 10:13–14)

The fantasy that the empire experiences no resistance, figured here as the flapping and chirping of birds, fits remarkably well with the ideology of *terra nullius*. In Australian Aboriginal societies, birds often have a totemic status, and they have appeared in many testimonies to traditional law.

Hermeneutical imagination could easily draw the conclusion that the British assertion of sovereignty was much like Assyria's in its disregard for traditional borders, a point that was even made by nineteenth-century missionaries by reference to the King James Version of Acts 17:26 — "And [God] hath made of one blood all nations of men for to dwell on all the face of the earth, and hath determined the times before appointed, and the bounds of their habitation."[18] It would take two centuries of settlement in Australia before the High Court's determination of native title would render "the bounds of their habitation" a challenge to the British Crown.

Indigenous claims to sovereignty are not free from paradox, whether within the spheres of law, politics or theology. Internationally, Indigenous assertions of self-determination have not generally been framed as secession movements, proposing perhaps new machinery for taxation, trade, defense, and so on, in order to establish a new state. The aspiration for autonomy is more mod-

---

18. See, e.g., Richard Broome, *Aboriginal Australians: A History since 1788*, 4th ed. (Crows Nest: Allen & Unwin, 2010), p. 31; cf. Allen Dwight Callahan, *The Talking Book: African Americans and the Bible* (New Haven: Yale University Press, 2006), pp. 115-16.

erate and selective, presuming ongoing respectful relationships and cultural acceptance on the part of the majority population, often proposing alternative conceptions of Indigenous sovereignty.[19]

The notion of unique Indigenous rights presents particular difficulties for the liberal tradition within which citizenship rights are supposed to be distributed equally within a state, ideally on an individual rather than corporate basis. From this individualist tradition of politics, even the discovery of native title by the High Court of Australia was perceived as a threat to reconciliation. Hence, Senator Nick Minchin could claim that native title would become "a vehicle for creating a lot of damage to the reconciliation process itself" since "Aboriginal people have these special rights that other Australians don't have."[20] But the suggestion was spurious even given a presumption that all citizens should share the same rights: Indigenous peoples had been denied compensation for compulsory acquisition of their land, which was supposed to be available to all Australians under the Constitution since 1901. This is an inconvenient truth that has been rendered largely invisible by a veil of racism. Even in the High Court's *Mabo* judgment, compensation for the extinguishment of native title could — even in theory — only be made available from 1975, the date of the *Racial Discrimination Act*. Dispossession before that time could not be addressed in native title claims.[21] To date, however, there has been no successful litigation that required the payment of compensation for the Crown's extinguishment of native title. Reconciliation without reparations rings hollow.

Legally, there are particular ironies in the fact that the discovery of native title was enabled precisely by the British common law, rather than European civil law. For our present purposes, the key difference between the two systems turns on the question of who holds underlying title. In Renaissance times, continental Europe revived the Roman idea of land holding in an "allodial" title that granted full *dominium* to the landowner.[22] In effect, a private *dominium*

19. Notably, George E. Tinker, *American Indian Liberation: A Theology of Sovereignty* (Maryknoll, NY: Orbis, 2008), esp. pp. 78-83.

20. "Chorus of Criticism for Howard's Negotiator," *Sydney Morning Herald,* June 1, 1996, p. 4.

21. Lisa Strelein, *Compromised Jurisprudence: Native Title Cases since Mabo* (Canberra: Aboriginal Studies Press, 2006), pp. 20-23. See the discussion in Chapter Two above of *Mabo v. Queensland* [No. 2] (1992) 175 CLR 1, 111 and the similar implications drawn out by *Tee-Hit-Ton Indians v. United States*, 348 U.S. 272, 279 (1955).

22. See, e.g., Joshua Getzler, "Roman Ideas of Land Ownership," in *Land Law*, ed. S. Bright and J. Dewar (Oxford: Oxford University Press, 1988), pp. 81-106; Samantha Hepburn, "Feudal Tenure and Native Title: Revising an Enduring Fiction," *Sydney Law Review* 27 (2005): 49-86.

over property created a kind of "petty sovereignty," in deliberate opposition to feudal arrangements. Where a feudal lord could acquire labor by virtue of the peasants' residence on his land, allodial title yielded no such peasant obligations; labor had to be purchased within the emerging capitalist economy. This is the story of emancipation that capitalism can tell, and we will return to it below, since it is really only the first chapter of a much larger and complex narrative about the kinds of alienation that capitalism has wrought.

Colonial Australia continued with certain feudal assumptions, particularly in promoting leasehold tenure over land that was still owned by the Crown. At the same time, the common law preserved medieval ideas about peasant usufruct rights on common land, and it was these old ideas about land use that eventually informed the High Court's judgment in *Wik* (1996) that the grant of a lease by the Crown did not thereby extinguish native title; while very different from each other in the source of their authority, leasehold and native title rights could co-exist. In contrast to the simple *dominium* that characterizes the use of private land, the 40% of Australia's landmass under leasehold tenure was then framed as space for ongoing negotiation, and by implication, for the restoration and maintenance of relationships between Indigenous and non-Indigenous Australia.

If one considers the current complexities of leasehold tenure, within which different parties have to negotiate the usufruct of the land, some analogies with the Priestly imaginary might be ventured at this point. In principle at least, the rights of "native and immigrant" must both be respected, although in practice the power of each party will condition any negotiations. The modern state maintains its hold over the underlying tenure of the land, although this claim on the part of the state contradicts the Indigenous law and custom that recognize no such jurisdiction. The contradiction resides at a metaphysical level, as it were, and the residual political issues effectively turn on the question of how to be a good neighbor. The Priestly imaginary renders the political world in essentially the same terms.

The social challenges presented by "native title" in settler colonial states might seem very specific — arising from peculiar tenure arrangements that are merely local accidents of history — but the principles at stake here actually have broader application. Even if an expression of Indigenous sovereignty has secured exclusive rights within a particular territory or reservation, some similar challenges will remain. To what extent will the dominant culture make space for Indigenous norms and customs within the wider society, and to what extent will any inter-cultural communion transform the hegemony of market capitalism?

The Priestly imaginary offers a model for thinking about these questions which suggests that the current generation never has exclusive rights to their lands and resources, and that human identity politics are always embedded in the larger webs of the created order. The national imaginary, on the other hand, provokes the question whether the assertion of exclusive jurisdictions will almost inevitably give rise to reiterated patterns of violence. This is a key concern that sits behind a number of Christian critiques of the very idea of national identity.

CHRISTIAN CRITIQUES OF NATIONAL IDENTITY

Of particular concern here is the so-called "neo-orthodoxy" taught in divinity schools and universities since World War II, which has been rigorously critical of any attempt to preserve national or ethnic identity in ecclesial contexts. A significant impetus for neo-orthodoxy again came from the experience of Nazi Germany, where the Confessing Church's resistance to the German Christian movement was compelled to oppose any conflation of national and Christian identities.[23] This sharp critique of ethnicity is also understandable when considered in light of the colonial projects that too readily combined national hubris with Christian identity — not least when Protestant nationalisms of the nineteenth century laid self-conscious claims to being the New Israel.[24] Yet this strain of anti-nationalist theology has also given rise to a theological assimilationism within which all Christians are called to relativize, if not extinguish, their old ethnic identities in the unified body of Christ. From this perspective, and contrary to the historic uses of Acts 17:26 mentioned above, any affirmation of self-determination or sovereignty on the part of particular groups, even Indigenous groups, would appear problematic. In order to appreciate the complexity of the issues at stake here, I want to turn to the strongest possible version of this argument, which to my mind has been provided by the black theologian Willie James Jennings.

As discussed in our Introduction, Jennings has in his compelling work *The Christian Imagination* argued that racist and colonial assumptions will continue to infect the life of the Christian churches to the extent that they

23. Doris L. Bergen, *Twisted Cross: The German Christian Movement in the Third Reich* (Chapel Hill: University of North Carolina Press, 1996).

24. See especially Anthony D. Smith, *Chosen Peoples: Sacred Sources of National Identity* (Oxford: Oxford University Press, 2003); Mark G. Brett, *Decolonizing God: The Bible in the Tides of Empire* (Sheffield: Phoenix, 2008), pp. 8-15.

continue to appropriate the story of Israel. He proposes instead to read the scriptures from the perspective of the Gentiles (the common translation of Hebrew *goyim*). He is even critical of those who have promoted the use of Indigenous divine names in biblical translations. As we have seen, both Job and Priestly tradition adopted the Canaanite name "El" for the Creator, and this kind of appropriation anticipates many similar instances in the history of biblical translation, as is demonstrated by Lamin Sanneh in his classic study on theology and translation.[25] Sanneh, however, emphasizes that vernacular translations of the Bible yielded cultural receptions that the missionary translators could not control, and ironically, Indigenous resistance to imperial rule has often been shaped by biblical typologies.

In response to this irony, Jennings argues that "If the practice of translation disrupted colonist hegemony, it did so by making room for something else, cultural nationalism."[26] This would not be news to Sanneh, who himself acknowledges that there is a sense in which "mission begot cultural nationalism."[27] So even in the well-known cases of Indigenous Christian resistance to colonialism, Jennings objects to the theological logic of supersessionism in appropriating Israel's story, and argues that cultural nationalism carries "racial, social, political, and economic signatures that cannot be divorced from ecclesial embodiments or the violence of nation states."[28]

It seems to me, however, that Jennings does not adequately distinguish between the many different kinds of cultural self-assertion. Aboriginal communities in Australia, for example, are far from being nation states, and as mentioned above, their advocacy of self-determination is often linked to demands for cultural acknowledgment from the wider population. Shortly after native title was first discovered in the Torres Strait, the then Social Justice Commissioner, Michael Dodson, proposed a model of double citizenship (one belonging to the Commonwealth and one belonging to each Indigenous nation), but even in this case he explicitly excluded the secession of new nations.[29] Just as the constituent state governments maintain certain sovereign

25. Sanneh, *Translating the Message: The Missionary Impact on Culture* (Maryknoll: Orbis, 1989). To mention just one example, Zulu biblical translations came to adopt the traditional name for God, *uNkulunkulu* (pp. 171-72).

26. Jennings, *The Christian Imagination* (New Haven: Yale University Press, 2010), p. 157.

27. Sanneh, *Translating*, p. 106; cf. Brian Stanley, ed., *Missions, Nationalism and the End of Empire* (Grand Rapids: Eerdmans, 2003).

28. Jennings, *Imagination*, 161.

29. Michael Dodson, "Aboriginal and Torres Strait Islander People and Citizenship," Address delivered at the Complex Notions of Civic Identity Conference, University of New South

powers under federal arrangements, so also Dodson proposed a layered approach to sovereignty and jurisdiction, which would promote more respectful relationships within the public domain, and require the acknowledgment of corporate rather than merely individual rights.

Since this proposal for double citizenship was advanced in 1993, the native title system has in fact turned away from the idea of domestic nations (and, by implication, away from the kinds of sovereignty exercised by the First Nations in North America). Australian jurisprudence has arrived at the conclusion that native title is not actually a property right, a remarkable example of legal casuistry that seems to confirm the ongoing structural racism in the law.[30] But the process for resolving native title claims has at least generated the need for negotiated settlements — mainly outside the courts — with the participation of state and federal governments, corporations and other third parties who share the use of Crown lands. While this process must be considered unjust according to many measures, it has necessitated the building of relationships through shared management of lands and waters, against the tide of private ownership that admits only of exclusive property rights.[31] The outcomes are culturally hybrid, but they can claim some continuity with the logic of communal access to natural resources that is so fundamental to Indigenous societies.

As Patrick Dodson has pointed out, there should be a clear analogy between a community of Christian believers and a community of native title holders in so far as they both provide alternatives to merely private property. In practice, however, Christian social visions in the West are often hard to distinguish from liberal political theory and politics.[32] Even when politicians affirm the work of faith-based organizations, the policy framework has assumed a "welfare state" equivalent of older charitable practices. Efforts to address social disadvantage have customarily been underpinned by ideals of distributive justice, rather than promotion of diverse polities within civil society.[33]

Wales, 20 August 1993. Available at http://www.humanrights.gov.au/news/speeches/aboriginal-and-torres-strait-islander-people-and-citizenship-dodson-1993.

30. See Noel Pearson, "Land Is Capable of Ownership," in *Honour Among Nations? Treaties and Agreements with Indigenous People*, ed. Marcia Langton et al. (Melbourne: Melbourne University Press, 2004), pp. 83-100.

31. Cf. the ideas of multiple or complex spatiality in Michael Keith and Steve Pile, *Place and the Politics of Identity* (New York: Routledge, 1993), esp. p. 23; John Milbank, *The World Made Strange: Theology, Language, Culture* (Oxford: Basil Blackwell, 1977), pp. 268-92.

32. Patrick L. Dodson, Jacinta K. Elston and Brian F. McCoy, "Leaving Culture at the Door: Aboriginal Perspectives on Christian Belief and Practice," *Pacifica* 19 (2006): 249-62, 254.

33. Michael Ignatieff, *The Needs of Strangers* (London: Vintage, 1984); Iris M. Young, *Justice and the Politics of Difference* (Princeton: Princeton University Press, 1990).

Patrick Dodson's critique of the dominant economic assumptions points to the need for some historical understanding of how modern Western Christianity has arrived at this point, particularly since the legitimation of private property within capitalist arrangements was in many respects a late-comer to Christian ethics. Most notably perhaps, the biblical and classical aversion to the payment of interest was reversed only in Reformation times.[34] The church's accommodation of capitalism will be further discussed in the concluding chapter, but at this point at least one qualification is necessary.

Although capitalist cultures appear to be founded on individualism, they continue to make use of national measures of well-being like the Gross Domestic Product. In spite of the growing number of international trade agreements, economic solidarity remains salient at the level of the nation state, and this is also the level at which the exercise of political sovereignty continues to be effective, regardless of the enormous power wielded by transnational corporations. But this begs the question: given the ongoing life of smaller polities (not least the Indigenous polities within settler colonial societies) why is national identity still commonly regarded as the most effective form of political solidarity today?

Some commentators have entertained the hypothesis that the rise of nation states can be interpreted as a secularizing domestication of Christendom's claim to political sovereignty. Michael Oakeshott once observed that "when some kings in the sixteenth century claimed a *plenitude potestas* they were aping a claim made centuries before on behalf of the popes."[35] Protestantism fractured the unity of Catholic Christendom, and after protracted religious wars, the Treaty of Westphalia in 1648 gave birth to the idea of a world comprised of separate, national jurisdictions. This much is common knowledge, one might say, although in their wide-ranging comparative study of empires, Jane Burbank and Frederick Cooper conclude that "the idea of 'Westphalian sovereignty' — a world of bounded and unitary states interacting with other

34. See, e.g., the discussion in John W. Rogerson, *According to the Scriptures? The Challenge of Using the Bible in Social, Moral and Political Questions* (London: Equinox, 2006), pp. 95-98; Michael Wykes, "Devaluing the Scholastics: Calvin's Ethics of Usury," *Calvin Theological Journal* 38 (2003): 27-51.

35. Oakeshott, *Lectures in the History of Political Thought*, ed. T. Nardin and L. O'Sullivan (Exeter: Imprint Academic, 2006), p. 276. See further Carl Schmitt, *Political Theology: Four Chapters on the Concept of Sovereignty*, trans. George Schwab (Chicago: University of Chicago Press, 2005) and the alternative proposals in Roger Haydon Mitchell, *Church, Gospel, and Empire: How the Politics of Sovereignty Impregnated the West* (Eugene, Ore.: Wipf and Stock, 2011).

equivalent states — has more to do with 1948 than with 1648."[36] The global spread of the national ideal was in practice a product of the twentieth rather than the seventeenth century, and ironically, the foundation of the United Nations in 1948 came together with the overwhelming realization that a nation's citizens sometime need to be protected from their own government.

The *Universal Declaration of Human Rights* in 1948 did not contemplate, however, the kinds of the economic, social, and cultural rights that were articulated in the *Declaration on the Rights of Indigenous Peoples* (2007). Significantly, in 2007, a number of settler colonial states initially refused to be signatories — Canada, the USA, New Zealand, and Australia — a fact that of course did not go unnoticed by Indigenous leaders. The United Nations Permanent Forum on Indigenous Issues moved on to examine the religious roots of this resistance in the "doctrine of discovery," beginning particularly with the fifteenth-century papal decrees that enabled the division of Latin America between the Spanish and the Portuguese (discussed above in Chapter Two).

In Australia's case, however, the "doctrine of discovery" had long been secularized, and legal imagination had no need of a theology of election, let alone a medieval doctrine of papal jurisdiction. Yet there is still something residually religious in the making of Australian settler sovereignty. As James Perkinson suggests, national identity has been sacralized when it incorporates the possibility of dying in service to one's country. Dying for the state only becomes intelligible when it ultimately serves the redemption of the nation, or as he puts it: "A politics becomes soteriological at the point where the identification absolutizes itself in its willingness to face or somehow justify death in the name of securing the boundaries and fulfillment of that identity."[37]

The historian Graeme Davison translates this into plainer discourse when he suggests that the business of imagining the Australian nation has been facilitated by a basic stock of biblical and classical narratives which give shape to experience, and that in our case it is an *Odyssey* model of heroic and tragic journeys that underpins the "ANZAC" memory — a military defeat endured

---

36. Jane Burbank and Frederick Cooper, *Empires in World History: Power and the Politics of Difference* (Princeton: Princeton University Press, 2010), p. 183; cf. Jean L. Cohen, *Globalization and Sovereignty: Rethinking Legality, Legitimacy, and Constitutionalism* (Cambridge: Cambridge University Press, 2012), pp. 28-29.

37. James W. Perkinson, *White Theology: Outing Supremacy in Modernity* (New York: Palgrave Macmillan, 2004), p. 66; cf. William T. Cavanaugh, *Migrations of the Holy: God, State, and the Political Meaning of the Church* (Grand Rapids: Eerdmans, 2011), pp. 7-35, "Killing for the Telephone Company."

at Gallipoli in 1915, which has risen to iconic status in annual public rituals.[38] As we have seen above, Anne Curthoys interprets the ANZAC symbolism as part of a larger pattern of rendering the white settler identity *as victim*, a pattern that draws on the biblical typology of exodus and conquest. Just as the oppressed Israelites in Egypt find divinely ordained reasons to conquer Canaan, Curthoys suggests, a pioneer society becomes free to subdue a new land, and impose its constitutional imagination as one finds in Deuteronomy.

Whether borrowing plots from the *Odyssey*, Exodus, or Deuteronomy, it is evident that Australian national narratives cannot rely on the European Romantic assumptions of deep primordial ties to country. But the issue that concerns us particularly here is the theological evaluation of the exodus-conquest story, including the genocidal dimension of its national imagination, past and present.[39]

We have already discussed, in Chapter Four above, the national social imaginary within which the exodus-conquest narratives are situated, and within which they were debated already in ancient Israel. Whether one chooses to read only the surface of these narratives, or alternatively explore their social depths, they should be seen as narratives "from below." When the quest for national liberation expands into imperial fantasies, as perhaps in the portrait of King Solomon's career, it is significant that the northern tribes find it necessary to secede and to create their own kingdom. Where this secession is described in 1 Kings 12 we find a reuse of the exodus typology, but this time with Solomon in the role of Pharaoh.[40] The conquest literature in the book of Joshua was formed over a long period, as already noted, and it was decisively

38. Graeme Davison, "Narrating the Nation in Australia," Menzies Lecture 2009, Menzies Centre for Australian Studies, King's College, London. Cf. Bill Ashcroft, "The Sacred in Australian Culture," in *Sacred Australia: Post-Secular Considerations*, ed. Makarand Paranjape (Melbourne: Clouds of Magellan, 2009), pp. 21-43; Agnes Heller, "European Master Narratives about Freedom," in *Handbook of Contemporary European Social Theory*, ed. Gerard Delanty (London: Routledge, 2006), pp. 257-65.

39. Marilyn Lake and Henry Reynolds, *Drawing the Global Colour Line: White Men's Countries and the Question of Racial Equality* (Melbourne: Melbourne University Press, 2008). For examples of Christian resistance to white colonialism, see especially Henry Reynolds, *This Whispering in Our Hearts* (Sydney: Allen & Unwin, 1998); Bain Attwood, *Rights for Aborigines* (Sydney: Allen & Unwin, 2003); Robert Kenny, *The Lamb Enters the Dreaming: Nathanael Pepper and the Ruptured World* (Melbourne: Scribe, 2007).

40. Keith Bodner, *Jeroboam's Royal Drama* (Oxford: Oxford University Press, 2012). Cf. Yoram Hazony's defence of the "limited state," which finds its legitimacy in the middle position between anarchic disorder and imperial hubris. Hazony, *The Philosophy of Hebrew Scripture* (Cambridge: Cambridge University Press, 2012), pp. 153-54, 160.

shaped as Israel's response to the aggression of the Assyrian empire. Accordingly, I have argued that Deuteronomy and Joshua were historically not shaped out of settler colonial experience, and this might go part way to explaining why the exodus narrative has inspired not only colonial imagination, but also anti-colonial and liberation movements.[41]

Commenting on the critique of the exodus in postcolonial biblical interpretation, Peter Lewis comments simply that "Australian Indigenous theologians at this stage have demonstrated less concern [with this problem] and often use the Mosaic phrase 'Let my people go' as a call to liberation."[42] In short, the Mosaic literary motifs do not belong to biblical texts in some essentialist way, regardless of the social contexts within which they are reread and reinterpreted. The exodus yields different meanings, depending on the social location of reading, and part of the task of reconciliation within the churches is to understand why this is so. In the hands of powerful churches and nations, the exodus material is potentially damaging, whereas in the hands of weaker groups, it can inspire well-founded resistance.

I suggested in Chapter One that postcolonial repentance includes not only confessing to the collusion of Christianity and colonialism but, as a consequence, resolutely resisting new temptations to exercise mastery over others. In hermeneutical terms, we may perhaps conclude that the most relevant biblical traditions for white Christians would be those that have relinquished political sovereignty, such as we find in the Priestly imaginary. But it does not follow that such a self-emptying ethic can also be imposed on Indigenous Christians, as if their cultural identities no longer have relevance.[43]

---

41. See, e.g., Callahan, *The Talking Book*, pp. 88-137; Taylor Branch, *Parting the Waters: America in the King Years, 1954-63* (New York: Simon & Schuster, 1988). Cf. Mark G. Brett, "Sovereignty and Treaty in Religious Imagination," in Paranjape, ed., *Sacred Australia*, pp. 96-118.

42. Lewis, "Terra Nullius Amnesiacs: A Theological Analysis of the Persistence of Colonisation in the Australian Context and the Blocks to Real Reconciliation," in *Colonial Contexts and Postcolonial Theology: Storyweaving in the Asia-Pacific*, ed. Mark G. Brett and Jione Havea (New York: Palgrave Macmillan, 2014), p. 197 n.44; cf. Djiniyini Gondarra, "Overcoming the Captivities of the Western Church Context," in *The Cultured Pearl: Australian Readings in Cross-Cultural Theology and Mission*, ed. Jim Houston (Melbourne: Joint Board of Christian Education, 1988), p. 180.

43. See, e.g., George Rosendale, *Spirituality for Aboriginal Christians* (Darwin: Nungalinya College, 1993), p. 19; Rainbow Spirit Elders, *Rainbow Spirit Theology* (Melbourne: HarperCollins, 1997), p. 69; cf. Alain Epp Weaver, *States of Exile: Visions of Diaspora, Witness and Return* (Scottdale: Herald Press, 2008), 42; Mark G. Brett, "Interpreting Ethnicity: Method, Hermeneutics, Ethics," in *Ethnicity and the Bible*, ed. Brett (BIS 19; Leiden: E. J. Brill, 1996),

Accordingly, in her important attempt to rethink the theology and practice of Christian "self-emptying," the feminist theologian Sarah Coakley emphasizes that properly conceived *kenosis* or vulnerability does not in fact imply self-extinction, but rather, the opening up of space within the hospitality of God: "this special 'self-emptying' is not a negation of self, but the place of the self's transformation and expansion into God."[44] This clarification arises particularly from an awareness that people who have suffered trauma need to reaffirm their identity in order to begin the process of healing.[45] Coercive reconciliation (e.g., imposing the requirement of forgiveness on Indigenous people) is not reconciliation at all, but rather, simply another kind of abuse.[46] There is no substitute for patient negotiation and relationship building, acknowledging the particularity of each new context, especially where power and resources are held unequally. [47]

In relation to biblical hermeneutics, we may wish to conclude that a recovery of the self, perhaps even within a national imaginary, is justifiable when a communal identity has been pushed to the edge of its very life. This is where one could question Willie James Jennings' critique of national identity in Christian theology. To be clear however, the dignity of the First Nations is usually expressed through complex relationships within a larger nation state, and in this respect their claims to sovereignty do not match the Westphalian ideal.[48]

Translating these issues into ecclesial contexts, similar issues arise where Indigenous or immigrant groups establish separate churches or denominations in order to find a more secure sense of participation. The Aboriginal and Torres Strait Islander Congress within the Uniting Church in Australia has for example found it necessary to govern itself, rather than be assimilated within the larger church, although it remains within the larger denomination. As Miroslav Volf has argued in theological terms, the symbolism of "embrace"

---

pp. 16-21, in dialogue with Daniel Boyarin, *A Radical Jew: Paul and the Politics of Identity* (Berkeley: University of California Press, 1994), esp. pp. 252-59.

44. Sarah Coakley, *Powers and Submissions: Spirituality, Philosophy and Gender* (Oxford: Blackwell, 2002), pp. 36-37. See further, Aristotle Papanikolaou, "Person, Kenosis and Abuse: Hans Urs von Balthasar and Feminist Theologies on Conversation," *Modern Theology* 19 (2003): 41-65.

45. Judith Herman, *Trauma and Recovery: The Aftermath of Violence from Domestic Abuse to Political Terror*, 2nd ed. (New York: Basic Books, 1997); Ida Kaplan, *Rebuilding Shattered Lives* (Parkville: Victorian Foundation for Survivors of Torture Inc., 1998), esp. pp. 71-129.

46. Miroslav Volf, "The Social Meaning of Reconciliation," *Interpretation* 54 (2000): 158-72.

47. See, e.g., Marcia Langton, et al., eds, *Settling with Indigenous People: Modern Treaty and Agreement-making* (Sydney: The Federation Press, 2006).

48. Nor does the UN *Declaration on the Rights of Indigenous Peoples* create a new right of succession.

affirms the integrity of persons in relationship, and makes clear that reconciliation is not simply a ruse for assimilation.[49] What is at stake in reconciliation is the restoration of respectful relationships, not the dissolution of selves.

CONCLUSION

Regardless of what transpires at the level of national politics, the churches have a particular calling to embody a theology of embrace in their practices of reconciliation, and to demonstrate the alternatives to reiterated patterns of conflict. A holistic vision is needed, which includes financial compensation and the building of new ecclesial institutions, in addition to practices of apology, forgiveness, and hospitality to the other, all of which will enrich the churches' own corporate self-understandings. Having clarified what reconciliation might look like in practice, then the churches' public advocacy on Indigenous issues will become more intelligible to the wider society.

49. Miroslav Volf, *Exclusion and Embrace: A Theological Exploration of Identity, Otherness, and Reconciliation* (Nashville: Abingdon, 1996).

9. Undocumented Immigrants, Asylum Seekers, and Human Rights

We are living in an age of unprecedented forced displacement. The United Nations refugee agency (UNHCR) reported that by the end of 2014 there were around 59.5 million displaced people worldwide.[1] Of these, 19.5 million people were classified as refugees. The disparity between the two figures reveals the terminological and legal complexities that beset the human misery of displacement. During 2015, the number of Syrian refugees passed the 4 million mark, and with large groups streaming into Europe, the crisis received renewed attention in Western media. But the countries that host the largest refugee populations are Turkey, Pakistan, Lebanon (one in every five persons), Iran, Ethiopia, Jordan, and Kenya.[2] In 2014, 1.7 million people submitted applications for asylum — which is to say, they applied for official refugee status. 121,200 of these applications were received in the United States,[3] reflecting the tip of the iceberg of the population regarded as illegally resident or "undocumented" in that country.

The scale of the displacement seems overwhelming, although in countries like Australia, the political charge attached to these issues is out of all proportion to the international statistical comparisons. The raw numbers of people seeking asylum in Australia, especially when considered in re-

---

1. *Global Trends: Forced Displacement in 2014* (Geneva: UNHCR, 2015), available at http://unhcr.org/556725e69.html and accessed 7 March 2016.

2. In 2011, Syria hosted the third largest group of displaced people in the world, but by the end of 2012 it had dropped to fifth place as a host country, as 647,000 fled civil war in that year. See the *UNHCR Global Trends 2012*, available at http://www.unhcr.org/51bacb0f9.html and accessed 7 March 2016.

3. UNHCR, *Forced Displacement in 2014*, p. 28.

lation to national wealth, barely rate a mention in international analyses, yet national elections in Australia have been known to turn on "border protection" policies.

What, then, can biblical theology and ethics hope to contribute to these debates? The question is a pressing one for faith communities, and it is not without relevance for democratic contexts where a large proportion of citizens identify as Christian. In this chapter I will suggest that scriptural sanctions for the provision of asylum can be drawn from a wide range of traditions and genres, but on closer inspection of the complex issues at stake, the sanctions that have the most public relevance are arguably the ones found in Priestly literature and in the creation theology of Job. It is not that citations from these texts may therefore be effective in public debate, but rather, that these texts can provide a more compelling framework for faith communities to engage with the issues at stake, bearing in mind that other traditions of ethical reasoning will bring quite different perspectives to the issues.[4]

One might imagine that it would be enough to list the obligations to the stranger that appear throughout the scriptures, such as in Exodus 22:21; Leviticus 19:10, 34; Deuteronomy 14:29; 23:7; Isaiah 61:5; Jeremiah 7:6; and Luke 10:25-37.[5] M. Daniel Carroll's book *Christians at the Border* has been influential in surveying these texts, especially in the United States, although some scholars with a commitment to biblical norms have countered his arguments by discriminating between different classes of strangers in the Hebrew Bible. James Hoffmeier, for example, has argued that the biblical obligation is precisely to the "stranger" (the *ger* in Hebrew) who might be understood by analogy as a "properly processed alien," as opposed to an undocumented immigrant who can claim no protection from the state. This semantic correlation is then linked to a sanctification of state authorities, notably with reference to Romans 13, and an argument that Christians are therefore called to submit to the laws of the state, including immigration laws.[6] We will return to Hoffmeier's approach below, but here I will simply note in passing how anomalous the surface meaning of Romans 13 is when considered against the wider background of the Bible's

4. Cf. Erin K. Wilson, "Be Welcome: Religion, Hospitality and Statelessness in International Politics," in *Hospitality and World Politics*, ed. Gideon Baker (Basingstoke: Palgrave Macmillan, 2013), pp. 145-70.

5. See, e.g., M. Daniel Carroll, *Christians at the Border: Immigration, the Church, and the Bible* (Grand Rapids: Baker, 2008). A second edition was published in 2013.

6. James K. Hoffmeier, *The Immigration Crisis: Immigrants, Aliens and the Bible* (Wheaton: Crossway, 2009).

relentlessly reiterated critique of unjust monarchies and empires, including the Roman empire of Paul's own day.[7]

Directly opposed to the acknowledgment of state authority, Christian "cosmopolitan" arguments for hospitality to strangers fundamentally reject the relevance of nation state jurisdictions and take up more philosophical approaches to the issues.[8] Neither the philosophical nor the biblical approaches to hospitality seem to pay much attention to the complexity of biblical literature on the theme of borders and how this literature might contribute to a contemporary political theology. Even Esther Reed, who does provide some valuable theological reflection on borders, tends to agree that "a Christian theology of the political should be far more occupied with secular authority, government, power, office, and civil polity than with land, territory, borders, and sovereignty."[9] In the long run this may well be justifiable, but the making of state sovereignties in colonial history was deeply indebted to the assumptions of Christendom, and addressing the secularized legacies of colonial history is a matter that deserves detailed theological work. A relative indifference to land, borders, and Indigenous sovereignty is part of the historic problem, and in this respect a globalized cosmopolitanism resurrects a colonial logic even as it rails against the arbitrariness of national borders that seal off the majority of the world's fragile populations from life-giving resources.

Our discussion in Chapter Two above retraced the steps by which divine sovereignty was secularized first in the making of modern European states, and secondly in the fabrication of colonial sovereignties.[10] Such retrospective

---

7. See, among many studies, Tom Wright, "Paul and Caesar: A New Reading of Romans," in *A Royal Priesthood? A Dialogue with Oliver O'Donovan*, ed. Craig Bartholomew et al. (Grand Rapids: Zondervan, 2002), pp. 173-93; Richard Horsley, ed., *Paul and Empire: Religion and Power in Roman Imperial Society* (Harrisburg: Trinity Press International, 1997); Christopher D. Stanley (ed.), *The Colonized Apostle: Paul through Postcolonial Eyes* (Minneapolis: Fortress, 2011).

8. Notably Luke Bretherton, "The Duty of Care to Refugees, Christian Cosmopolitanism, and the Hallowing of Bare Life," *Studies in Christian Ethics* 19 (2006): 39-61. Cf. Giorgio Agamben, *Homo Sacer: Sovereign Power and Bare Life* (Stanford: Stanford University Press, 1998); also his *State of Exception* (Chicago: University of Chicago Press, 2005); cf. Jacques Derrida, *On Cosmopolitanism and Forgiveness* (New York: Routledge, 2001) and the lucid overview in Andy Lamey, *Frontier Justice: The Global Refugee Crisis and What to Do about It* (St Lucia: University of Queensland Press, 2011), pp. 177-218.

9. Esther D. Reed, "Refugee Rights and State Sovereignty: Theological Perspectives on the Ethics of Territorial Borders," *Journal of the Society of Christian Ethics* 30 (2010): 59-78, at 61. Portions of this article were revised within chapter 6 of Esther D. Reed, *Theology for International Law* (London: Bloomsbury, 2013).

10. See especially Lisa Ford, *Settler Sovereignty: Jurisdiction and Indigenous People in Amer-*

analysis helps to underline the constructed nature of modern nation states, but once established, they are far from being merely discursive products that can be undone by cleverly told histories or subtle philosophical paradoxes. Reed argues that in beginning to consider borders as at least relatively meaningful in theological terms, there is value in reconsidering the following list of biblical texts:[11]

You have set all the borders of the earth. (Ps. 74:17)

When the Most High apportioned the nations, when he divided humankind, he fixed the boundaries of the peoples according to the number of the gods; Yhwh's own portion was his people, Jacob his allotted share. (Deut. 32:8–9)[12]

These are the borders by which you shall divide the land as an inheritance among the twelve tribes of Israel. (Ezek. 47:13)

He has made from one blood every nation to dwell on all the face of the earth, and has determined their preappointed times and the boundaries of their dwellings. (Acts 17:26)

As noted in our previous chapter, Acts 17:26 has figured in many historic defenses of Indigenous rights.

Given the diversity of these texts, it would indeed be hazardous to suggest that we could find here biblical warrants for sanctifying the borders created in "postcolonial Africa, the disputed territories of the West Bank and Gaza Strip, Nagorno-Karabakh, the seabed of Antarctica, or the state of Jammu and Kashmir, and more."[13] Reed resiles from such a naïve hermeneutic, and from

---

ica and Australia, 1788-1836 (Cambridge, Mass.: Harvard University Press, 2010). Perhaps Australian legislators could be mindful that our nation's ancestors were "Irregular Maritime Arrivals," to use the current bureaucratic discourse. Cf. Allen Buchanan and Margaret Moore, States, Nations, and Borders: The Ethics of Making Boundaries (Cambridge: Cambridge University Press, 2003).

11. Reed, "Refugee Rights and State Sovereignty," p. 63; Reed, Theology for International Law, pp. 226-27.

12. On the complexity of this and other texts in the Hebrew Bible that refer to borders, see Mark G. Brett, Decolonizing God: The Bible in the Tides of Empire (Sheffield: Sheffield Phoenix, 2008), pp. 55-61, 102.

13. Reed, "Refugee Rights and State Sovereignty," p. 63.

the reification of borders in general, but she goes on to argue nevertheless that there is a properly ethical status for borders within a conception of state sovereignty explicated as responsibility before God:

> The ancient hope that God will judge the nations — retold in Matthew 25:31–35 as the Son of Man judging the nations based upon how they have responded to the requirements of the gospel for the treatment of the hungry, poorly clothed, imprisoned, and so on — invites an explication of the dynamic and norms of answerability.[14]

This appeal to the parable of the sheep and the goats in Matthew 25 interestingly reveals a weakness in James Hoffmeier's hermeneutical dependence on the Hebrew terminology of the *ger*, which he considers the appropriate biblical correlate for properly processed immigrants today. In Matthew 25:38, 44 the hungry, thirsty, naked, or imprisoned stranger is an undifferentiated *xenos* (rather than *paroikos*, as the customary Greek translation of *ger* might lead us to expect). The unsettling suggestion in the parable is that not even the "righteous" have discerned that the *xenos* is Christ, and this can hardly lead hermeneutically to an unreserved confidence in immigration authorities. On the contrary, the parable points precisely to the theological danger of categorizing strangers.[15]

While Reed's argument focuses on an ethic of answerability, rather than one of hospitality, there is an inevitable conceptual linkage between affirming borders and affirming the idea of a homeland.[16] Home and migration are reciprocally defining. Equally, a concept of home is logically implied by what is now called "forced migration" in recent research, and increasingly, biblical studies of exile are being reframed in dialogue with modern studies of forced

14. Reed, "Refugee Rights and State Sovereignty," pp. 63, 66, and 72.

15. See Brett, *Decolonizing God*, p. 186, invoking Emmanuel Levinas, *Otherwise than Being, or, Beyond Essence,* trans. Alphonso Lingis (Dordrecht: Kluwer, 1991). On the theme of categorization, Bretherton, "The Duty of Care to Refugees," takes up Agamben's concept of "bare life"; Reed provides an exemplary discussion of the British legal case *Regina v. Immigration Officer at Prague Airport* to illustrate the current complexity of understanding national and racial borders under European human rights legislation. Cf. Alison Kesby, "The Shifting and Multiple Border and International Law," *Oxford Journal of Legal Studies* 21 (2007): 101-19.

16. A related point emerges in Luke Bretherton's discussion of refugees in *Christianity and Contemporary Politics* (Oxford: Wiley-Blackwell, 2010), pp. 126-74. In this revision of his earlier essay on refugees, mentioned above (n. 8), Bretherton here places more emphasis on hospitality and the provision of sanctuary, notably pp. 140, 155-60, practices which require at least some affirmation of "the moral licitness of borders" (p. 158).

migration.[17] In exploring the contribution of the biblical literature to public debates about a state's obligations to provide asylum, we need to give consideration to the obligations of hospitality in the broader political sense.[18]

Reed rightly suggests that rights and responsibilities are reciprocally defining, but defining the scope of international responsibility raises complex issues. Most defenses of refugee rights today assume that seeking asylum is a legally enforceable right (e.g., under domestic legislation arising from the UN *Convention Relating to the Status of Refugees* 1951), but the presumption that all state parties have the same legal obligations, regardless of their capacity and resources, raises significant questions.[19] Thus, for example, Australian political discussion tends to be focused on the hundreds of asylum seekers arriving in small boats instead of the millions of displaced people living in countries that lack adequate resources to care for them. "Answerability," in this context, cannot simply be about the legal accountability of individual nations as they respond to the numbers of displaced people who arrive at their particular borders.

When considering the secular developments of international law after 1948, it is evident that signatories to United Nations' Declarations, Covenants and Conventions are primarily state parties who are formalizing their answerability before the international community. Following the horrors of World War II, the overwhelming consensus was that an international instrument was needed that could uphold the rights of individuals against the powers of a state, in particular a state like Nazi Germany. When considering the long prehistory of human rights, however, it is also clear that their foundations were laid in conceptions of answerability to a divine Creator, particularly in contexts where the wellbeing of fragile persons was at risk. The story of the Christian churches'

17. See especially John Ahn, *Exile as Forced Migration: A Sociological, Literary, and Theological Approach on the Displacement and Resettlement of the Southern Kingdom of Judah* (BZAW 417; Berlin: de Gruyter, 2011); Brad E. Kelle, Frank R. Ames, and Jacob L. Wright, eds., *Interpreting Exile: Displacement and Deportation in Biblical and Modern Contexts* (SBLAIL 10; Atlanta: SBL, 2011).

18. We are not primarily concerned here with domestic practices of hospitality in the sense of providing short-term accommodation for travelers. On this narrower topic, see T. Raymond Hobbs, "Hospitality in the First Testament and the 'Teleological Fallacy,'" *Journal for the Study of the Old Testament* 95 (2001): 3-30. Hobbs draws a sharp distinction between domestic and political hospitality and can find no analogy between the two. In his semantic analysis, a refugee or immigrant (*ger*) is never offered domestic hospitality, a finding that amounts to a tautology.

19. See Lamey, *Frontier Justice*, p. 348, on the necessity for what has come to be termed "burden sharing."

involvement in drafting the documents behind the 1948 Universal Declaration of Human Rights is perhaps less well known than it should be.[20]

Accordingly, I will at this point briefly review some of the history of human rights thinking, before turning to theological consideration of the specific obligations arising under the UN *Convention Relating to the Status of Refugees* (1951) and subsequent legal initiatives.

REWINDING THE HISTORY OF HUMAN RIGHTS

There is no organic development from ancient biblical texts to modern human rights, but a number of compelling arguments have shown that the Hebrew Bible does indeed contain the roots of a conception of divinely conferred rights (one of the senses of the term *mishpat*) that belong to marginalized persons.[21] I will investigate below some of the key texts that support this view, but it is worth noting at this point that examples can be found in all the major genres of ethics in the Hebrew Bible — law, prophecy, and wisdom. Rather than being isolated examples that are easily overwhelmed by the dominant paradigm of justice as a "right order" mediated by monarchs (another use of *mishpat*), this triangulation across genres provides a substantial foundation for modern understandings of rights.

Some theologians have argued that all modern talk of human rights is inherently individualistic and incompatible with the Bible's communitarian logic, but this rejection of the Bible's relevance does not do justice to the variety of ways in which the biblical traditions have influenced the recognition of human rights. These rights were not born into secular liberalism; they were adapted within that environment in the context of new conceptions of human flourishing. A simplistic historical account of seventeenth-century Europe might suggest that in this modern period the "divine right of kings" gave way to a new secular model of sovereignty within which the inherent rights of the

20. John Nurser, *For All Peoples and All Nations: Christian Churches and Human Rights* (Washington: Georgetown University Press, 2005).

21. This is acknowledged by Oliver O'Donovan, *The Desire of the Nations: Rediscovering the Roots of Political Theology* (Cambridge: Cambridge University Press, 1996), p. 248, even though he strenuously criticizes modern theories of rights. See the important works of James Barr, "Ancient Biblical Laws and Modern Human Rights," in *Justice and the Holy: Essays in Honor of Walter Harrelson*, ed. Douglas A. Knight and Peter J. Paris (Atlanta: Scholars, 1989), pp. 21-33; Eckart Otto, "Human Rights: The Influence of the Hebrew Bible," *Journal of Northwest Semitic Languages* 25 (1999): 1-14.

people finally prevailed over medieval theological hierarchies. But a closer examination of history clearly reveals that secularity was initially forged in *theological* debates,[22] and some philosophical and legal commentators even doubt whether the discourse of human rights can be successfully maintained without its religious moorings.[23]

Certainly, the modern discourse of human rights plays a key role in the philosophical construction of liberal democracies, which themselves depart substantially from the older conceptions of natural law.[24] In this liberal tradition, citizens are often seen as participants in a virtual social contract — rather than a divinely constituted covenant[25] — within which individuals are willing to relinquish some aspects of their autonomy to the state in exchange for security of life and property. Essentially the role of the state is to protect the "life, liberty and property" of its citizens, or perhaps even the "pursuit of happiness," as the American Declaration of Independence proclaimed in 1776. This political tradition is linked closely to the life of modern nation states, and accordingly it entails an inevitable tension between the flourishing of the individual state over against the common good of humanity as such.[26]

Conceptions of natural rights were discussed by Catholic lawyers already

22. See the magisterial overview provided by Charles Taylor, *A Secular Age* (Cambridge, Mass.: Belknap Press, 2007).

23. See, e.g., Michael J. Perry, "Is the Idea of Human Rights Ineliminably Religious?," in Perry, The *Idea of Human Rights: Four Inquiries* (Oxford: Oxford University Press, 1998), pp. 11-41; Nicholas Wolterstorff, *Justice: Rights and Wrongs* (Princeton: Princeton University Press, 2008); cf. Hans Küng and Jürgen Moltmann, eds., *The Ethics of World Religions and Human Rights* (London: SCM, 1990); Joseph Runzo, Nancy M. Martin, and Arvind Sharma, *Human Rights and Responsibilities in the World Religions* (Oxford: Oneworld, 2003).

24. David Harvey, *A Brief History of Neoliberalism* (Oxford: Oxford University Press, 2005), pp. 175-82; O'Donovan, *Desire of Nations*, pp. 240-41.

25. See, however, David Novak's argument that a social contract is actually strengthened by agreements between a number of covenantal communities, in "Oliver O'Donovan's Critique of Autonomy," *Political Theology* 9 (2008): 327-38, and Novak, *Covenantal Rights* (Princeton: Princeton University Press, 2000). Cf. Eric Nelson, *The Hebrew Republic: Jewish Sources and the Transformation of European Political Thought* (Cambridge, Mass.: Harvard University Press, 2010).

26. Notably, Hannah Arendt, *The Origins of Totalitarianism* (London: George Allen and Unwin, 1967), p. 293. Lamey's *Frontier Justice* represents an extended response to Arendt, arguing that her skepticism could be legally overcome if the rights of asylum seekers were entrenched in national constitutions, conceived as "portable," and supported by rights to legal representation and review. Should such provisions for procedural justice be adopted, as undoubtedly they should be, they would not in themselves provide positive and richly textured patterns of hospitality within a national culture.

in the twelfth century, and Brian Tierney has shown how these antecedents work their way through the centuries to the complex secular theology of Hugo Grotius.[27] In the thirteenth century, for example, St. Bonaventure argued in his *Defence of the Mendicants* that although love among Christians might give rise to the practice of sharing goods in common, there was a more basic community of goods from which people could draw in sustaining their natural existence, on the basis of "the right that naturally belongs to man as God's image and noblest creature." The right to these goods held in common could be exercised by virtue of "natural necessity" and could not be renounced.[28] It would take some centuries before the idea of "inalienable" rights would take revolutionary shape, but when Oliver Cromwell assaulted the monarchy in the seventeenth century, and asserted the rights of the people against the Crown, it was still on the basis of a biblical covenant theology within which "the people" relate directly to God, making kings and priests largely unnecessary.[29] Later forms of nationalism moved between ethnic and civic extremes, excising monarchs and religion to greater and lesser degrees depending on the local permutations.

Protestant revolutionaries in Europe did not invent their ideas out of nothing; they were re-reading the Bible with renewed political interest. What they found, especially in the prophetic books, was a relentless critique of kings and priests. We now know that this ancient tradition of prophetic critique was very unusual within the surrounding cultures of Mesopotamia, Egypt, and Assyria.[30] Kings were more likely to be considered divine or semi-divine, and given this exalted status, they were the ones who made the law. In Israel this was pointedly not so: kings were not originally part of the divine plan for government, and when they did arrive on the scene it was a matter of divine regret and accommodation to human desire, at least as 1 Samuel 8 suggests. Kings exercised *mishpat* in the sense of "judgment" (usually very badly, according to

27. Brian Tierney, *The Idea of Natural Rights* (Atlanta: Scholars Press, 1997); cf. Oliver O'Donovan, "The Justice of Assignment and Subjective Rights in Grotius," in Oliver O'Donovan and Joan Lockwood O'Donovan, *Bonds of Imperfection: Christian Politics Past and Present* (Grand Rapids: Eerdmans, 2004), pp. 167-203.

28. See the translation in Oliver O'Donovan and Joan Lockwood O'Donovan, *From Irenaeus to Grotius: A Sourcebook in Christian Political Thought 100-1625* (Grand Rapids: Eerdmans, 1999), p. 317.

29. Liah Greenfeld, *Nationalism: Five Roads to Modernity* (Cambridge, Mass.: Harvard University Press, 1992); Mark G. Brett, "Nationalism and the Hebrew Bible," in *The Bible in Ethics*, ed. John W. Rogerson, Margaret Davies, Mark Daniel Carroll R. (Sheffield: JSOT Press, 1995), pp. 136-63.

30. See especially Otto, "Human Rights."

the Deuteronomists), but they did not make the foundational statutes handed down in Mosaic tradition. In the course of time, the accommodation of monarchs in Israelite religion took on different forms, ranging from the strong affirmations in Zion-Jerusalem theology[31] to the constraint of kings under divine law in Deuteronomistic theology,[32] and to a qualified indifference to monarchs in Priestly tradition, as we have seen in Chapter Five.

According to the biblical story that describes the introduction of kingship into Israel's polity, Samuel warns the people that the king's "justice" (*mishpat*) would turn out to be an oppressive regime of accumulation. The Crown's view of social order would not just require taxation, but also the acquisition of sons, daughters, and land: "he will take the best of your fields, vineyards, and olive groves and give them to his underlings" (1 Sam. 8:11, 14). James Barr's otherwise admirable discussion of rights in the Hebrew Bible lacks some literary subtlety when it comes to this text, since he suggests that "the *mishpat* of the king" in 1 Samuel 8:9, 11 (usually watered down in translation as the "ways" or "practices" of the king) should be distinguished semantically from the *mishpat* of the "the poor, the orphan, the *ger* or dependent foreigner."[33] There are indeed two different notions of justice at issue here — the king's "right order" on the one hand, and the rights of the marginalized on the other — but the wordplay in Hebrew is crucial. In 1 Samuel 8, the force of Samuel's speech is clearly that of a warning; he presumes that the social order imposed by a king is a bad thing and to be avoided, and therefore the use of *mishpat* in 8:9, 11 is better seen as ironic — if this is justice, who would want it?

Ironically, as in social contract theory, Israel seems willing in the Samuel narrative to engage in a trade-off, accepting the social benefits along with the impositions that the new polity entails.[34] Set against this trade-off, Samuel's warning against kingship in 1 Samuel 8 fits with the later prophetic denunciations of the wealthy, including kings, where the prophets assert that they did not become rich because God had blessed them in accord with their righteousness, but rather, they

---

31. This is the tradition that seems to have captivated Oliver O'Donovan in his use of the Hebrew Bible in *The Desire of the Nations*. See the detailed response to O'Donovan's proposals in J. Gordon McConville, *God and Earthly Power: An Old Testament Political Theology* (London: T & T Clark, 2006).

32. Bernard Levinson, "The First Constitution: Rethinking the Origins of Rule of Law and Separation of Powers in Light of Deuteronomy," *Cardozo Law Review* 27 (2006): 1853-88.

33. Barr, "Ancient Biblical Laws," p. 26.

34. Mark G. Brett, "Narrative Deliberation in Biblical Politics," in *The Oxford Handbook of Biblical Narrative*, ed. Danna Nolen Fewell (New York: Oxford University Press, 2016), pp. 540-49.

are wealthy as a result of their exploitative behaviour.[35] In this respect at least, the prophets join with Job in rejecting an ideology of right order. In the case of Samuel, he eventually finds a middle position in 1 Samuel 10:25 by imposing legal constraints on the Crown: "Samuel told the people the rights and duties (*mishpat*) of the kingship, and he wrote them in a book and laid it up before Yhwh."

While we do not find the specifically modern vocabulary of "inherent" or "human" rights in biblical law, analogous concepts can be found there nonetheless. The *mishpat* may in some contexts be relatively limited, as illustrated by the "right (*mishpat*) of the firstborn" (Deut. 21:17) or the "right of redemption" (Jer. 32:7–8). Unlike such instances of "special rights" arising from family position or institutional function, the rights of the widow, orphan, and alien belong naturally to persons as such. Barr suggests: "any child could become an orphan, any woman a widow," and the inclusion of the *ger* only strengthens the case, since if they were foreigners, then their right was not generated by specifically Israelite citizenship.[36] Even Deuteronomy's national perspective on answerability to God seems to provide for these non-Israelite rights:

> You shall not oppress a hired person who is poor and needy, whether your brother Israelite or your stranger (*ger*) residing in your land or in your gates. You must pay him his wages on the same day, before the sun sets, for he is needy and depends on them to sustain his life. Otherwise, he may appeal above you to Yhwh, and you will be guilty of sin. . . . You shall not subvert the right (*mishpat*) of a resident alien or an orphan. (Deut. 24:14–15, 17)

If one considers the probability, however, that the Deuteronomic *gerim* laws arose in the seventh century BCE particularly in response to forced migration from the northern kingdom of Israel to the southern kingdom of Judah, then Barr's argument is potentially weakened. A *ger* need not be a non-Israelite but simply an Israelite from another tribe, as can be illustrated from a number of narratives in the Deuteronomistic History. In order to found his argument for a conception of "natural right," Barr would have been better served perhaps by attending to the example of Job, who founds his protection of the marginalized widow, orphan, and alien explicitly on the basis of a universal creation theology rather than with reference to Deuteronomic or even Levitical divine commands:

---

35. See the overview in Walter Houston, *Contending for Justice: Ideologies and Theologies of Social Justice in the Old Testament*, 2nd ed. (London: T&T Clark, 2008).

36. Barr, "Ancient Biblical Laws," p. 26.

> Did not He who made me in the belly make them,
> and form me in the one womb? (Job 31:15)

Barr does however identify a key issue here, which is that the underlying logic of covenantal commands made to Israel assumes that they are only binding on Israel.

In some respects, this is also the case in the Holiness Code in Leviticus, where the holiness of Israel turns on their laws being different from the laws of other nations. While there are some differences of interpretation even within the Priestly tradition itself, there is a consensus that holiness is constituted by difference; as in many cultures, the sacred is set off from the profane. The Holiness School established a graded hospitality that provides the possibility for some cultic inclusion (with circumcision marking the boundary). Yet as we saw in Chapter Five above, the Holiness School opened Israel's social borders and even asserted a kind of equality under the law for "natives and immigrants" who live beside each other in the land. In short, Barr's argument for the natural or universal rights of *gerim* can be established on broader canonical foundations, which in the case of the Priestly tradition situate the particularity of Israelite law within a universal horizon of answerability to God.[37]

This canonical breadth was forged over time through inner-biblical conversations, and it is worth noting here that the eighth-century prophets expressed their concern for the marginalized by focusing on widows, orphans, and the poor, without mentioning *gerim* — the key term which can be variously translated as stranger, alien, sojourner, refugee or immigrant. Before the seventh century BCE, these rights of the vulnerable are not extended to the *gerim* with any consistency.

While the first chapter of the book of Isaiah may well have been subject to editing in later centuries, the narrower scope of marginalized persons is preserved in Isaiah 1:17, where the prophet exhorts his audience to defend the widow and orphan:[38]

37. Mark G. Brett, "Natives and Immigrants in the Social Imagination of the Holiness School," in *Imagining the Other and Constructing Israelite Identity in the Early Second Temple Period*, ed. Ehud Ben Zvi and Diana Edelman (LHBOTS 456; London: T & T Clark, 2014), pp. 89-104; cf. James Barr, *Biblical Faith and Natural Theology* (Oxford: Clarendon, 1993); Jon D. Levenson, "The Universal Horizon of Biblical Particularism," in *Ethnicity and the Bible*, ed. Mark G. Brett (BIS 19; Leiden: Brill, 1996), pp. 143-69.

38. This detail is overlooked by Nicholas Wolterstorff in his discussion of the "archaeology of rights," where he includes Isaiah 1:17 in his discussion of the "quartet of the vulnerable"

> Seek justice (*mishpat*),
>   rescue the oppressed,
> defend the orphan,
>   plead for the widow.

The Hebrew verbs in this verse all have a legal connotation, e.g., "plead" for the widow can be accurately translated as "plead the case of the widow." While the prophet may well have had in mind here the customary law practiced in the city gate, rather than any written statutes associated with the authority of Moses, it is the inherent rights of the vulnerable that are at issue. Similarly, in Isaiah 10:1-2, matters of legal process are again placed in the foreground and contrasted with a true justice that may or may not be delivered legally:

> Woe to those who make iniquitous decrees,
>   who write oppressive statutes,
> to turn aside the needy from fair judgment
>   and to rob the poor of my people of their justice (*misphat*),
> that widows may be your spoil,
>   and that you may make the orphans your prey! (Isa. 10:1-2)

The *mishpat* of the poor is here an inherent right that "belongs" to the vulnerable,[39] yet it has to be defended by strenuous human effort — even when legal systems and the Crown do not actually deliver justice.

By the time we reach Deuteronomy and the later prophets, Jeremiah and Ezekiel, a concern for *gerim* has become a standard test of moral concern, along with the rights of the widow, orphan and the poor (e.g., Jer. 7:6; Ezek. 14:7). While there are a number of competing explanations for this, it seems to me that the best way to understand the standardized inclusion of *gerim* is to see it reflecting a new level of awareness that arose in the seventh century. After the fall of the northern kingdom, there was a flood of refugees who headed south into Judah, leaving evidence in the archaeological record of dramatic rises in population.[40]

— widows, orphans, the poor and resident aliens. Wolterstorff, *Justice: Rights and Wrongs* (Princeton: Princeton University Press, 2008), pp. 75-76.

39. Barr ("Ancient Biblical Laws," p. 25) following Gerhard Liedke's wording "das, was den Armen usw. 'gehört'" in *ThWAT*, 2:1005. See the translation in Liedke, "שפט to judge," in *Theological Lexicon of the Old Testament*, Vol. 3, ed. Ernst Jenni and Claus Westermann, trans. Mark E. Biddle (Peabody, Mass.: Hendrickson, 1997), p. 1395.

40. Frank Crüsemann, *The Torah: Theology and Social History of Old Testament Law* (Ed-

Theologically, an analogy was discovered between the experience of Assyrian imperial aggression and the older experience of living under the imperial power of Egypt. What appears to be an older law in Exodus 22:21, "you shall not *wrong* or *oppress* the refugee," is reinterpreted in a way that mimics the Assyrian treaty discourse of love: "*Love* the refugee (*ger*), because you were refugees in Egypt" (Deut. 10:19). The irony in this shift of terminology towards an Assyrian model is that it may well have been focusing attention on the victims of Assyrian aggression.[41] This is however the sort of ironic mimicry that has been illuminated in postcolonial studies.

The prophetic traditions also contain several significant visions of an international law (*torah* or *mishpat*) that offers peace and justice beyond Israel. The late wisdom traditions find no tension between the universal torah of creation and the particular Torah of Israel, but the book of Isaiah is arguably still in the process of brokering this settlement. Jerusalem is seen as the centre of redemption, even if the offer of salvation goes to the ends of the earth. Isaiah 42:1 envisages a justice "for the nations," as does Isaiah 2:3–4, where the nations converge in pilgrimage on Jerusalem. This is a torah given at Zion, not at Sinai, and the change of geographical symbolism may well indicate a shift from the particularities of a national theology to an imperial imagination.[42]

---

inburgh: T. & T. Clark, 1996), pp. 182-85; cf. Israel Finkelstein, "The Settlement History of Jerusalem in the Eighth and Seventh Centuries BC," *Revue Biblique* 115 (2008): 499-515; Aaron A. Burke, "An Anthropological Model for the Investigation of the Archaeology of Refugees in Iron Age Judah and Its Environs," in Kelle, Ames, and Wright, eds., *Interpreting Exile*, pp. 41-56.

41. See, e.g., Simo Parpola, "Assyria's Expansion in the 8th and 7th Centuries and Its Long-term Repercussions in the West," in *Symbiosis, Symbolism and the Power of the Past*, ed. William G. Dever and Seymour Gitin (Winona Lake, Ind.: Eisenbrauns, 2003), pp. 99-111; Brett, *Decolonizing God*, pp. 79-93; William Morrow, "'To Set the Name' in the Deuteronomic Centralization Formula: A Case of Cultural Hybridity," *Journal of Semitic Studies* 55 (2010): 365-83.

42. J. J. M. Roberts, "The End of War in the Zion Tradition: The Imperialistic Background of an Old Testament Vision of Worldwide Peace," in *Character Ethics and the Old Testament*, ed. M. Daniel Carroll R. and Jacqueline E. Lapsley (London: Westminster John Knox, 2007), pp. 119-28; cf. Baruch J. Schwartz, "Torah from Zion: Isaiah's Temple Vision (Isaiah 2.1-4)," in *Sanctity of Time and Space in Tradition and Modernity*, ed. Alberdina Houtman, Marcel Poorthuis and Joshua J. Schwartz (Leiden: Brill, 1998), pp. 12-26; Irmtraud Fischer, "World Peace and Holy War — Two Sides of the Same Theological Concept: YHWH as Sole Divine Power (A Canonical-Intertextual Reading of Isaiah 2:1-5, Joel 4:9-21 and Micah 4:1-5," in *Isaiah's Vision of Peace in Biblical and Modern International Relations*, ed. Raymond Cohen and Raymond Westbrook (New York: Palgrave Macmillan, 2008), pp. 151-65; Mark G. Brett, "Unequal Terms: A Postcolonial Approach to Isaiah 61," in *Biblical Interpretation and Method: Essays in Honour of Professor John Barton*, ed. Katharine J. Dell and Paul M. Joyce (Oxford: Oxford University Press, 2013), pp. 243-56.

But however these changes are construed, we encounter in Isaiah 2:3–4 the symbolism of an international law that brings peace between nations:

> They shall beat their swords into ploughshares,
>   and their spears into pruning-hooks;
> nation shall not lift up sword against nation,
>   neither shall they learn war any more.

In much later centuries, Judaism and Christianity have each conceived their own versions of internationalism, and both have developed universal conceptions of natural rights that necessarily extend beyond any narrow definition of covenant community.[43]

There have also been a number of attempts to ground human rights christologically, which are more problematic unless perhaps they are understood in terms of a cosmic Christology that establishes the kinship of all of God's creatures. The biblical starting point that is best suited to this kind of project ironically arises from a dialogue with ancient Hellenistic cosmology.[44] A Christian embrace of the entire created order opens up an environmental hospitality that builds on the covenant with all creatures in Genesis 9, or more generally, on the Priestly theology in the Hebrew Bible.[45] Turning from anthropocentrism to an ecotheology in which human rights take their place *within* "the gift of continuing creation," we also take up responsibilities for the rights of other creatures.[46] These responsibilities have already been linked to our main topic in this chapter in so far as the number of ecological refugees is likely to increase dramatically with the rise of sea levels, notably in the Pacific region.

---

43. See the notable discussions in Jonathan Sacks, *The Dignity of Difference: How to Avoid the Clash of Civilizations*, 2nd ed. (London: Continuum, 2003); Albino Barrera, *Economic Compulsion and Christian Ethics* (Cambridge, UK: Cambridge University Press, 2005).

44. See especially Vicky S. Balabanski, "Hellenistic Cosmology and the Letter to the Colossians: Towards an Ecological Hermeneutic," in *Ecological Hermeneutics: Biblical, Historical and Theological Perspectives*, ed. David G. Horrell et al. (London: T & T Clark, 2010), pp. 94-107.

45. The classic argument for deriving human rights from the "image of God" in Genesis 1 is dependent on the inclusive monotheism of the Priestly tradition. See Schmid, "Political Theology of the Priestly Document"; Jeremy Waldron, "The Image of God: Rights, Reason and Order," in *Christianity and Human Rights: An Introduction*, ed. John Witte Jr. and Frank S. Alexander (Cambridge, UK: Cambridge University Press, 2010), pp. 216-35; cf. J. Richard Middleton, *Liberating Image: The Imago Dei in Genesis 1* (Grand Rapids: Brazos Press, 2005).

46. Cf. Whitney Bauman, *Theology, Creation, and Environmental Ethics: From* creatio ex nihilo *to* terra nullius (New York: Routledge, 2009), p. 166.

CONCLUSION

For the atheist defenders of human rights, the historical complexity of the Hebrew Bible's legacy is sufficient to demonstrate that such ancient scriptures are irrelevant to modern ethical and legal debates. But for those of us whose identities are still marked by this tradition, another conclusion is possible: the significance of a living tradition is always constituted by internal debates about the meaning and values that constitute that tradition. As it has done for centuries, the Bible still inspires religious motivations to support the common good, including the protection of inherent rights that are secured by a universal theology of creation. This is not the only approach to human rights, and we need to seek clarity in public discourse as to alternative approaches, but in recent years, the Christian commitment to human rights has often been much thinner than it ought to have been.

While the inflation in the sheer number of rights may be problematic, not to mention the associated complexities of legislation, jurisprudence, and parliamentary freedoms, there can be no doubt that Christian practice should err on the side of hospitality to asylum seekers, whatever the status of their documentation. To be sure, the lessons drawn from colonial history should cause us to draw back from the cosmopolitan utopia that acknowledges no homelands to which particular groups are attached, since it is precisely a homeland's jurisdiction that gives rise to special accountabilities. We can expect some tensions and incommensurability in the way that rights and responsibilities are exercised, and beyond the narrowly legal imperative not to oppress a stranger, ecclesial communities have a positive charge to love the stranger as themselves, in practices of hospitality exercised beyond the constraints of national interest.

10. Justice for the Earth

While there have been significant fluctuations in the earth's climate in the past, the clear majority of climate scientists now agree that the overall rise in global temperatures over recent decades can be linked to the human production of greenhouse gases.[1] The global community is facing the first fruits of anthropogenic climate change: extreme weather events, the accelerated extinction of species and loss of biodiversity, and the advent of climate refugees. Yet during 2011–2012, the United States Congress contemplated no less than seven bills that were designed to reduce the Environmental Protection Agency's powers to regulate greenhouse gas emissions. There are a range of factors that might influence this apparent disconnection between science and politics in America, and the issues are of course configured differently in other areas of the world, but recent research has shown that one of the drivers in attitudes to climate change is religion. Notably, evangelical Christians in America are among the groups most sceptical of climate science, and this may be attributed at least in part to their characteristic emphasis on personal salvation, but also to an ambivalence about science and its relationship to creation theology.[2]

The theological conversation about these issues is well established, and in

1. "IPCC, 2013: Summary for Policymakers," in *Climate Change 2013: The Physical Science Basis. Contribution of Working Group I to the Fifth Assessment Report of the Intergovernmental Panel on Climate Change*, ed. T. F. Stocker et al. (Cambridge: Cambridge University Press, 2013).

2. Wylie Carr, Michael Patterson, Laurie Yung, and Daniel Spencer, "The Faithful Skeptics: Evangelical Religious Beliefs and Perceptions of Climate Change," *Journal for the Study of Religion, Nature and Culture* 6.3 (2012): 276-99; cf. Michael Northcott, *An Angel Directs the Storm: Apocalyptic Religion and American Empire* (London: IB Taurus, 2004).

spite of ongoing disagreements, evangelical biblical scholars and theologians have also joined the environmental cause.[3] Many conservative churches, however, appear untouched by the scholarly outpouring, and specialists therefore need to confront the question of how to shape resources that can transform attitudes within particular streams of religious tradition, and at the local level.[4] In providing an overview of the key issues in the current discussions, this chapter seeks to evaluate the ways in which biblical traditions might inform Christian attitudes to environmental policy.

This chapter may be read as a response to the recent challenge laid down by an economics commissioner from the British government's Sustainable Development Commission, Timothy Jackson. Instead of reframing the issues in conventional economic terms (e.g., by suggesting that the human enterprise is a "wholly owned subsidiary" of natural ecosystems[5]) Jackson argues in *Prosperity without Growth* that the now dominant conceptions of prosperity also have to be dismantled and replaced with alternative understandings of human flourishing.[6] One might be tempted to think that the Bible could assist with this task, so we also need to reflect on how it has popularly come to be understood as part of the problem. Cautioned by Jeremiah's complaint that even prophets and priests may preach "wellbeing" where there is no real wellbeing, we turn now to a review of how biblical traditions relate to the earth.[7]

---

3. See the overview provided by Katherine K. Wilkinson, *Between God and Green: How Evangelicals Are Cultivating a Middle Ground on Climate Change* (Oxford: Oxford University Press, 2012); Daniel I. Block and Noah J. Toly, eds., *Keeping God's Earth: The Global Environment in Biblical Perspective* (Downers Grove: InterVarsity, 2010).

4. In addition to his numerous academic projects in this area, Norman Habel has for example established a website that provides resources inserted into the ecumenical liturgical calendar as a "Season of Creation," http://seasonofcreation.com. See further the multi-faith resources at the "Australian Religious Response to Climate Change" website at http://www.arrcc.org.au/.

5. Harold A. Mooney and Paul R. Ehrlich, "Valuing Ecosystem Services: Philosophical Bases and Empirical Methods," in *Nature's Services: Societal Dependence on Natural Ecosystems*, ed. Gretchen C. Daily (Washington, DC: Island Press, 1997), p. 17.

6. Timothy Jackson, *Prosperity without Growth: Economics for a Finite Planet* (London: Routledge, 2011), esp. pp. 30, 86, 91. Among other similar contributions, see the Social Progress Index 2013, http://www.socialprogressimperative.org/data/spi.

7. In Jeremiah 6:13-14, the key term for wellbeing is normally translated as "peace," but the Hebrew *shalom* can encompass personal health, communal prosperity and justice, and ecological flourishing.

RECONCILING WITH THE EARTH

Climate change has reached traumatic proportions in particular episodes around the globe, and rising sea levels imply that it is probably already too late to save the Pacific nations of Tuvalu, Kiribati, and the Marshall Islands. Theological responses in Oceania will necessarily include the embrace of diaspora migrations,[8] and the vocation of the churches to expand their practices of hospitality to climate refugees has been mentioned in the previous chapter of this volume. But we might also reconsider in this context some of the elements of reconciliation as discussed by Daniel Philpott: (1) acknowledgment of wrongdoing; (2) reparations, in this case, compensatory measures vis-à-vis the earth; (3) punishment of environmental offenders; (4) apologies, for example to the poorest populations whose ecological footprint is small but who will suffer the consequences of climate change disproportionately; (5) the establishment of just institutions that enable the healing of the global earth community.

Following Philpott's analysis, a sixth theme might be forgiveness on the part of the wronged, the non-human species. Perhaps this is an overly anthropocentric way of framing the problem, but it is precisely the restoration of relationships that is at issue.[9] As Michael Northcott suggests, "At the heart of the ecological crisis is the refusal of modern humans to see themselves as creatures, contingently embedded in networks of relationships with other creatures."[10] Given our earlier discussion, it is worth acknowledging here that this kind of refusal is not characteristic of Indigenous cultures, and some understanding of the inability of colonial ideology to grasp this point is also relevant to the matters at stake in this chapter.

Lynn White's essay from 1967, "The Historical Roots of Our Ecological Crisis," has become something of a classic in laying sweeping blame at the feet of Christianity, but a more detailed analysis would focus attention on the intersections of modernity, colonialism, and Christianity.[11] Instead of reading

8. Jione Havea, "Opening Borders, for Diaspora Is Home," in *Climate Change, Culture Change: Religious Responses and Responsibilities*, ed. Anne Elvey and David Gormley-O'Brien (Melbourne: Mosaic, 2013), pp. 65-77.

9. See the proposals in Anne Elvey, "Can There Be a Forgiveness That Makes a Difference Ecologically? An Eco-Materialist Account of Forgiveness as Freedom (*aphesis*) in the Gospel of Luke," *Pacifica* 22 (2009): 148-70.

10. Michael Northcott, *A Moral Climate: The Ethics of Global Warming* (London: Darton, Longman and Todd, 2007), 16; Michael Northcott, *A Political Theology of Climate Change* (Grand Rapids: Eerdmans, 2013).

11. Peter Harrison, "'Fill the Earth and Subdue It': Biblical Warrants for Colonization in

the creation theology of Genesis 1 in the context of its own ancient imaginary, colonial Christianity and economics isolated the injunction to "subdue the earth" (Gen. 1:28) and absorbed it into the popular philosophical discourses of the day. In the history of colonialism, John Locke was perhaps the most significant figure in providing a modern philosophical bridge. And it was the modern division between mind and matter that shaped a new kind of instrumental attitude to the natural world, very different from the older strains of Christianity.[12] Modern philosophy endowed the mind with this autonomous status precisely by disengaging rationality from its religious traditions.

In the introduction to a collection of essays entitled *Decolonizing Knowledge*, Frédérique Apffel-Marglin argues that Christian theology conditioned the Western habit of sharply distinguishing between humans and other living beings, and that this is not the case in non-Western religions. She refers particularly to the influential biologist J. B. S. Haldane, who moved in the 1960s from Britain to India because he sensed that the cultural climate there would be more favorable to the development of his biological research. She mentions that Haldane found no such sharp distinction between humans and other species in Hindu, Buddhist, and Jain cosmology. When the reader turns to a later essay in this same volume, we find a citation of Haldane that is not so sweepingly dismissive of Christian theology: "this may well be a perversion of Christianity," Haldane asserts. "St Francis seems to have thought so."[13]

At the risk of stating the obvious, a public engagement between religious traditions would be well served by clarifying points of connection, as well as divergence, and this passing allusion to St. Francis on Haldane's part points to the possibility of a much more constructive inter-religious dialogue on ecological matters.[14] If we are genuinely seeking a global solidarity, then Senator

---

Seventeenth Century England," *Journal of Religious History* 29/1 (2005): 3-24; Whitney Bauman, *Theology, Creation, and Environmental Ethics: From* creatio ex nihilo *to* terra nullius (New York: Routledge, 2009), pp. 67-87; cf. Barbara Aneil, *John Locke and America: The Defence of English Colonialism* (Oxford: Clarendon, 1996).

12. Charles Taylor, *Sources of the Self: The Making of Modern Identity* (Cambridge, Mass.: Harvard University Press, 1989), p. 149; Frédérique Apffel-Marglin, "Introduction: Rationality and the World," in *Decolonizing Knowledge: From Development to Dialogue*, ed. Frédérique Apffel-Marglin and Stephen Marglin (Oxford: Clarendon, 1996), pp. 1-40, 4.

13. Apffel-Marglin, "Rationality and the World," 28; Francis Zimmerman, "Why Haldane Went to India," in Apffel-Marglin and Marglin, eds., *Decolonizing Knowledge*, p. 287, quoting from Haldane's essay "The Unity and Diversity of Life" published in 1959.

14. See further, Leonardo Boff, *Cry of the Earth, Cry of the Poor* (Maryknoll: Orbis, 1997); Ibrahim Abdul-Matin, *Green Deen: What Islam Teaches about Protecting the Earth* (San Fran-

John Kerry's recent appeal for faith-based initiatives around climate change[15] may be more fruitful than the disregard commonly shown to Christianity in postcolonial theory.[16] Re-examination of Genesis 1–3 will also be necessary in clarifying some points of connection.

EARTHING THE HUMAN IN GENESIS 1–3

These chapters include a mix of traditions that bring together stories of creation, crime, consequences, and re-adjustments — all set within the primordial time before ordinary human life begins. Primordial time (as in the Dreaming of Aboriginal Australians[17]) is not just ordinary, historical time, since it bears directly on the shape of current experience. The narratives of Genesis 1–3 do not simply string together episodes that may be of antiquarian interest; they configure the human and non-human condition.

Even John Locke's philosophical writings are not entirely without value for understanding this biblical material, we may note in passing. For example, in opposing a monarchist reading of Scripture in his day, Locke observed that what we find in Genesis 1:28 is a divine command for all humankind (including women) to rule over creation, not a divine command "for certain particular men to rule over the rest."[18] Therefore, he argued, Genesis 1 did not well serve the monarchist's cause. In this respect, Locke anticipated the later work of biblical scholars who discovered that the "image of God" discourse was indeed found elsewhere in ancient Western Asia, but only as a character-

cisco: Berrett-Koehler, 2010); Celia Deane-Drummond and Heinrich Bedford-Strohm, eds., *Religion and Ecology in the Public Sphere* (London: T&T Clark International, 2011).

15. Kerry announced in August 2013 that a project on climate change would be taken up by the State Department's Office of Faith-Based Community Initiatives: http://www.cnsnews .com/news/article/kerry-climate-change-challenges-us-safe-guarders-gods-creation.

16. Regarding postcolonial theory, see Catherine Keller's critique of Gayatri Spivak in Keller, *God and Power: Counter-Apocalyptic Journeys* (Minneapolis: Fortress, 2005), pp. 126-32, and the more promising engagements in Stephen D. Moore and Mayra Rivera, eds., *Planetary Loves: Spivak, Postcoloniality and Theology* (New York: Fordham University Press, 2011).

17. See Deborah Bird Rose, "Consciousness and Responsibility in an Australian Aboriginal Religion," in *Traditional Aboriginal Society*, ed. William H. Edwards (Melbourne: Macmillan, 2nd ed. 1998), pp. 239-51.

18. Jeremy Waldron, *God, Locke and Equality: Christian Foundations of John Locke's Political Thought* (Cambridge: Cambridge University Press, 2002), p. 22, referring particularly to Locke, *Treatise*, I §630. Cf. Phyllis Bird, *Missing Persons and Mistaken Identities: Women and Gender in Ancient Israel* (Minneapolis: Fortress, 1997), pp. 134-38.

istic of kings. As suggested in Chapter Five above, Genesis 1:28 represents a democratization of human dignity that is part of a Priestly movement away from monarchic sovereignty as it had been expressed in Israel. What was originally conceived as an implied critique of monarchy by the authors of Genesis 1 (the point that Locke had already sensed), has more recently been reduced to a mere anthropocentrism.

Moreover, the idea that humanity is called on in Genesis 1 to "rule" implies not just a critique of monarchy but also a willingness on the part of God — here named Elohim — to share the management of the created order. Rather than seeing the rule of creation as an exclusively divine prerogative exercised at a transcendent distance, humans also have responsibilities.[19] Indeed, the earth itself is twice called on to co-create with God (Gen. 1:11, 24), as is the sea (1:20), so non-human participation is essential as well. In this respect, the recent proposals for seeing creation as a kind of divine self-emptying, or *kenosis*, are not entirely dissimilar to what we find in Genesis 1.[20]

There is no sharp distinction between creatures in so far as they all share *nephesh*, a term that has been translated either as breath, soul or life itself. Genesis 1 refers to the non-human *nephesh* creatures (1:20–21, 24, 30), and Genesis 2:7 makes clear that the first human made from the earth is also a *nephesh* creature. When the first covenant is established with Noah, according to Priestly tradition, the original vegetarian order of Genesis 1:29–30 is overturned on one condition: "only you shall not eat flesh with its *nephesh*-blood in it" (9:4). Carnivorous behavior must maintain a sense of the sacred. Having stipulated that the shedding of human *nephesh*-blood will be held to account (9:5–6), Noah's covenant then extends over every "*nephesh*-creature," human and non-human together, and this covenant is explicitly said to be eternal (9:12, 15–16). When the Priestly narrative of creation concludes with the summary "these are the generations (*toledot*) of the heavens and the earth" in Genesis 2:4, it is evident that the humans belong to the vast lineage

---

19. Terence E. Fretheim, *Creation Untamed: The Bible, God, and Natural Disasters* (Grand Rapids: Baker, 2010), p. 41.

20. See especially John Polkinghorne, ed., *The Work of Love: Creation as Kenosis* (Grand Rapids: Eerdmans, 2001). New Testament notions of incarnation arguably reiterate *kenosis* in ways that envisage an enduring divine connection with all creation. See especially Kathleen P. Rushton, "The Cosmology of John 1:1-14 and Its Implications for Ethical Action in This Ecological Age," *Colloquium* 45 (2013): 137-53; Vicky S. Balabanski, "Hellenistic Cosmology and the Letter to the Colossians: Towards an Ecological Hermeneutic," in *Ecological Hermeneutics: Biblical, Historical and Theological Perspectives*, ed. David G. Horrell et al. (London: T & T Clark, 2010), pp. 94-107.

systems of creation, and human wellbeing is inextricably tied to the wellbeing of non-human creatures.

The formula "these are the *toledot* of . . . " is repeated several times in Genesis, and it appears to be a structuring principle used by the Priestly writers in order to introduce each new episode in their complex narratives about the ancestral families. But in the case of Genesis 2:4, the formula rounds off the Priestly creation story of the cosmos, and introduces another creation story in which the human (*'adam*) is made from the land (*'adamah*), as indeed are the animals (2:7, 19). This is no doubt a deliberate wordplay which emphasizes a humble kinship with the earth, rather than a glorious image of divinity as found in Genesis 1:27. A similar kind of inversion is found in the human vocation in the second story, which is "to serve and protect" the Garden of Eden (2:15) rather than "rule and subdue" the earth (1:28).

Indeed, the Garden of Eden story begins with the question of who would serve the land: "when no plant of the field was yet in the earth and no grasses of the field had yet sprung up — for Yhwh Elohim had not caused it to rain upon the earth, and there was no *'adam* to serve the land" (2:5).[21] The subsequent alienation that arises between the human and God includes alienation from the land (3:17), and the hope of reconciliation with the land then becomes a leitmotif of Israel's story, and at the same time a hope that illuminates in symbolic terms the struggles of all humanity: Israel's experience reflects the human condition.[22] Even the peculiar combination of divine names in Genesis 2–3, "Yhwh Elohim," seems to highlight this thematic doubling: Israel's Yhwh is at the same time the Elohim of the nations, and Yhwh's unfolding relationship with Israel and her land provides a kind of model for other peoples in relation to *their* lands, suspended as they are in similar tensions between alienation and redemption.

THE NATURAL WORLD IN THE PROPHETS

Notwithstanding the reservations commonly expressed about anthropocentrism in prophetic texts, none of the visions of the Prophets sever the human

21. The Hebrew word *'abad*, often translated here as "till," is otherwise most commonly translated as "serve," in the sense of "work for." See especially Ellen Davis, *Scripture, Culture, and Agriculture: An Agrarian Reading of the Bible* (Cambridge: Cambridge University Press, 2009), pp. 28-33.

22. André LaCocque, *The Trial of Innocence: Adam, Eve, and the Yahwist* (Eugene, Ore.: Cascade, 2006).

interconnections with non-human creatures.[23] For example, while the national traditions reflected in Hosea and Jeremiah imagine the undoing of creation and the mourning of the earth on account of Israel's own failures (especially Hos. 4:1–3 and Jer. 4:23–28), redemption is seen as a renewing of relationships within the whole created order, and Hosea uses covenantal discourse in order to make that very point: "I will make for them a covenant on that day with the beasts of the field, the birds of the heavens, and the creatures that move on the land" (Hos. 2:18).

The later traditions of Isaiah reconfigure the human connections with nature within an imperial imaginary, as we have seen. Israel's future salvation is accordingly linked not only to an inclusion of the other nations, but to the redemption and re-creation of the whole earth. Isaiah 65 adopts poetic license in speaking of "new heavens and a new earth" (v. 17), including a paradoxical reconciliation within nature that has wolves lying down with lambs (v. 25), but this does not literally imply the utter extinction of the old earth, any more than it implies the complete extinction of the old Israel or the old heavens.[24]

The prophetic visions for the redemption of society and nature tend to be focused on a very specific place: the city of Jerusalem with its symbolic centre Mount Zion.[25] In fact, both the national and imperial imaginaries agree on this geographical locus. The utopian restorations envisaged in Isaiah 40–66, for example, have their centre there, as do the visions of a resettled Judah in Ezekiel 40–48. The all too familiar patterns of harm and destruction between nations and between species all come to an end in the peace "on all my holy mountain," according to Isaiah 65:25. In Isaiah 62:1–4, redemption is figured as a new marriage between Jerusalem and the land. These traditions reflect an ineluctable particularity in conceiving of this locus of redemption for the created order — as do the concluding chapters of the New Testament where the restored Zion is figured as a marriage of heaven and earth.[26]

23. Hilary Marlow, *Biblical Prophets and Contemporary Environmental Ethics: Re-Reading Amos, Hosea, and First Isaiah* (Oxford: Oxford University Press, 2009).

24. See further Dermot Nestor, "If Not Now, When? The Ecological Potential of Isaiah's New Things," in *Creation Is Groaning: Biblical and Theological Perspectives*, ed. Mary Coloe (Collegeville, Minn.: Liturgical Press, 2013), pp. 33-56.

25. Donald Gowan, *Eschatology in the Old Testament* (Edinburgh: T&T Clark, 1986), pp. 97-120.

26. N. T. Wright, *The Resurrection of the Son of God* (Minneapolis: Fortress Press, 2003), p. 470, suggests that Revelation 21 provides "an integrated vision of a new creation in which 'heaven' and 'earth,' the twin halves of created reality, are at last united."

EXPOSING ANTHROPOCENTRISM

The Holiness Code's picture of the earth "vomiting" out its recalcitrant inhabitants presents a stronger challenge to anthropocentrism than what we find
in the prophetic traditions. Leviticus 18:24–28 claims that "the land will vomit
you out for defiling it," and in this context the land does not discriminate between Israelites and non-Israelites; all are equally accountable for maintaining
the purity of the environment. The conceptual framework for understanding
defilement in the holiness legislation cannot, of course, be mapped directly
on to modern environmental concerns, but informed uses of Scripture in recent theological reflection do not contemplate such literalism. With a proper
awareness of the historical and cultural distance between ancient authors of
Scripture and current faith communities, it is nevertheless possible to discern
analogies with our current dilemmas.[27] The land itself has agency, and according to the Holiness Code, it even has a right to rest from human exploitation. If
people persist in disrespectful behavior, the land will enjoy the Sabbath years
owing to it while Israel languishes in exile: "then shall the land rest and make
up for her Sabbaths" (Lev. 26:34).

So far we have touched on biblical texts that are situated within national
and imperial imaginaries, each of which have their own perspective on human
responsibility within the natural order, but the book of Job presents a much
more radical position on these matters. As we have seen in Chapter Seven, the
Joban poet comes closer to the deep ecologists and to their critique of human
stewardship. In Job 38–41, we encounter the idea that the creatures of the earth
have their own ways, are subject to their own divine laws, and they can even
offer their own instruction apart from Israel's Torah. In this context, not only
is human flourishing displaced from the centre of things, but the very idea
of human rule over creation is satirized. The fearsome Leviathan is adduced
in chapter 41 as the parade example of creatures that cannot be subdued or
exploited (41:6–9). At the end of Job 41, instead of humankind, the mysterious
ocean beast has his own measure of sovereignty: "He looks down on all that
are haughty; he is king over all the children of pride" (41:34).

The Joban attack on anthropocentrism is so thorough that one might begin
to doubt the validity of even modest attempts to exercise human stewardship
of creation — such as found in the divinely given vocation "to serve and protect" the Garden of Eden in Genesis 2:15. The skeptical wing of the wisdom

---

27. See for example, Brent A. Strawn, "On Vomiting: Leviticus, Jonah, Ea(a)rth," *Catholic
Biblical Quarterly* 74 (2012): 445-64.

tradition punctures delusions of human grandeur, but overall, it also serves to reinforce the connections between the human and non-human creatures. The diverse perspectives of the biblical canon converge in agreement on the unity of life given by the divine Creator. Psalm 104:29-30, for example, articulates this unified vision where it speaks of "spirit" or "breath" as a life force given by Yhwh to all creatures in a continuous process of creation:

> When you hide your face,
> they are troubled;
> when you take away their breath (*ruach*),
> they die and return to their dust.
> When you send out your spirit (*ruach*),
> they are created; and you renew the face of the land.

From this perspective, there is no sharp distinction between the species. Even the biblical apocalypses point to a vision of all creatures participating in worship[28] — a unity of praise rising from "every creature in heaven and on earth and under the earth and in the sea," as the book of Revelation puts it (Rev. 5:13). The apocalyptic imagination does not extinguish the old earth, but rather, envisages earth's renewal when the hubris of human empires finally gives way to the rule of God.

While postcolonial critics are wont to criticize the idea of a unified divine rule as the sublimation of Empire, it is necessary to bear in mind that environmental sensibilities demand in fact a sense of planetary solidarity. Instead of creation arising out of capricious divine violence (the common understanding in ancient Mesopotamia and the Levant), the revolutionary claim in Genesis was that God creates a stable order, while Job asserts that the cosmos has been given its own divine laws to obey. The presumption of a unified stable order is exactly the kind of faith that must underlie much later scientific attempts to discover natural laws. When the venerable tradition of natural theology eventually mutated into modern science, the foundations of this modern inquiry had already long been laid in biblical convictions about the law-like behavior of the natural world.[29]

28. Richard Bauckham, *Living with Other Creatures: Green Exegesis and Theology* (Waco, Tex.: Baylor University Press, 2011), pp. 163-84; cf. Howard N. Wallace, "*Jubilate Deo omnis terra*: God and Earth in Psalm 65," in *The Earth Story in the Psalms and the Prophets,* ed. Norman C. Habel (The Earth Bible 4; Sheffield: Sheffield Academic Press, 2001), pp. 51-64.

29. Peter Harrison, "The Development of the Concept of Law of Nature," in *Creation: Law and Probability*, ed. Fraser Watts (Minneapolis: Fortress, 2008), pp. 13-35; Harrison, *The Fall of*

BIBLICAL RESOURCES FOR ENVIRONMENTAL ETHICS

In light of this overview of biblical testimony, we are now in a position to re-frame the questions with which we began: how might these scriptures inform Christian practices in relation to nature, and more specifically, how might these practices inform a public policy of "prosperity without growth"? An obvious beginning point would be the new discussion of asceticism in an environmental key.[30] Whereas ascetic practices in earlier ages might have re-lied on a sharp distinction between souls and bodies, this distinction is now considered seriously problematic, not least for reasons that can be derived from closer examination of both the Hebrew and Christian scriptures.[31] The idea of overcoming the desires of the body for the sake of the soul belongs indeed to a dominant philosophy in early Christianity, from which theology is now repenting. Today, one might rather say that overcoming the desires of consumption for the sake of God's creation lies at the heart of Christian environmental ethics.

Practices of self-restraint in consuming the earth's resources arguably have the same kind of self-emptying (or kenotic) norms, which have been described in the preceding chapters in relation to practices of reconciliation and of hospi-tality to refugees. Translating such norms into an environmental context would imply suspending the borders of the anthropocentric self, and reconnecting with species on the brink of extinction — thereby entering more fully into the self-emptying love of God. Rather than focusing on an inner life of spirituality, *kenosis* calls human life outwards into networks of new relationships animated by love.[32] One might regard this as a new meeting of St. Francis's rule of life and *ahimsa* (as discussed in Chapter One).

This way of articulating Christian ethics clearly intersects with a number of

---

Man and the Foundations of Science (Cambridge University Press, 2007); Harrison, *The Bible, Protestantism, and the Rise of Natural Science* (New York: Cambridge University Press, 1998); James Barr, *Biblical Faith and Natural Theology* (Oxford: Clarendon Press, 1993); William P. Brown, *The Seven Pillars of Creation: The Bible, Science, and the Ecology of Wonder* (Oxford: Oxford University Press, 2010).

30. See, e.g., Sallie McFague, *Blessed Are the Consumers: Climate Change and the Practice of Restraint* (Minneapolis: Fortress, 2013); Larry L. Rasmussen, *Earth-Honoring Faith: Reli-gious Ethics in a New Key* (Oxford: Oxford University Press, 2013), pp. 239-54, "Asceticism and Consumerism."

31. Joel B. Green, *Body, Soul, and Human Life: The Nature of Humanity in the Bible* (Grand Rapids: Baker, 2008), which includes a fruitful dialogue with natural sciences.

32. Cf. Charles Taylor's notion of "networks of agape" in *A Secular Age* (Cambridge, Mass.: Belknap, 2007), pp. 277, 158, 282.

other religious traditions, and this intersection is of no small significance in the formation of public policies. A key difficulty for Christian theology, however, arises ironically in the question of how to connect this kenotic approach to ethics with an understanding of God's own character. Most notably for the present discussion, some strands of popular theology seem to assume that *kenosis* can be understood as a temporary anomaly in the life of God, expressed in the incarnation of Jesus. On this understanding, a distant and omnipotent God, who creates and redeems humanity essentially by demonstrations of sovereign power, might accommodate an incarnational, self-emptying moment in the life of God without it becoming a defining indicator of divine character. As suggested above, ecological theology in recent decades is almost unanimous in its criticism of this view, although it seems that many churches have barely started to absorb this broad consensus.

No doubt the complexities of almost any academic argument are not likely to achieve a popular acclaim, especially when the implications cut so deeply into entrenched economic interests. And of course, it is not just the wealthy classes in Western nations who rely on fossil fuels for their livelihood; the economic transformations required by ecological traumas in the future will be very widely felt. Once again, as in our discussion of reconciliation and national sovereignties, it is necessary to pay attention to the question of how any call to restraint and *kenosis* is heard in a world marked by dramatic economic differences.

For example, in addressing a North American middle class, Sallie McFague can legitimately frame her account of restraint as a saintly dispersal of the self, but her message seems discordant if it is read in contexts of economic deprivation:

> The defining characteristic of the universal self, the inclusion of all others in one's understanding of who one is, points to the stretching of one's own body (and bodily needs) beyond the limits of one's own skin: the world becomes my body, and I must therefore consider all the world's physical needs and not just my own.[33]

There is a wealth of philosophical and mystical notions that might inform the idea of a universal self, but in relation to public ethics, it is doubtful whether this kind of universality can be given practical effect. A notable exception, one might think, was provided by Mahatma Gandhi's Hindu cosmology and his

33. McFague, *Blessed Are the Consumers*, p. 202.

reinterpretation of *ahimsa*, but it must be borne in mind that his practice of non-violence was shaped within an affirmation of the national political self.[34] In my view, Gandhi's model of mysticism illustrates the political implications that may arise in the quest for healthy postcolonial relationships. An interpretation of *kenosis* that calls only for self-sacrifice or restraint has not grasped the centrality of the practical task of renewing relationships through affirming the weaker parties.[35]

Human societies — like the ecosystems within which they are embedded — are in the first instance interlinked by networks of actual relationships; they have an embodied particularity that cannot be reduced to universal principles or abstract generalities. In Australia, for example, it is apparent that our interest in Aboriginal spirituality has grown in inverse proportion to the erosion of Western cultural resources, but popular interest is focused not so much on the irreducibly particular tribal traditions and their local care of country, but rather in the general idea of connectedness to the earth. A general embrace of animism, however, is not respectful of the actual Aboriginal people who claim no jurisdiction beyond the boundaries of their own traditional lands and waters.

Local patterns of life are permeated in complex ways by relationships with bodies half the globe away, but it is not humanly possible to care for all persons and animals with equal levels of attention all at once. The extensive feminist literature on the tensions between "care" and "justice" points to these realities of human finitude. While religious traditions persistently pull at the limits of what might be thinkable in practices of care and justice, each of these spheres of ethics have their own characteristic sets of norms, even when they are overlapping and mutually defining.[36] The old adage "think globally and act locally" still has some value in this context, although acting locally will also require new patterns of thinking locally as we come to terms with the substantial contribution of the Indigenous knowledges to environmental practices.[37]

34. Cf. Rasmussen's brief comments on Gandhi in *Earth-Honoring Faith*, pp. 322-23.

35. Mark G. Brett, "Diaspora and Kenosis as Postcolonial Themes," in *Decolonizing the Body of Christ: An Interdisciplinary Conversation,* ed. David Joy and Joseph Duggan (London: Palgrave, 2012), pp. 127-40; cf. John Milbank, "The Midwinter Sacrifice," in *The Blackwell Companion to Postmodern Theology,* ed. Graham Ward (Oxford: Blackwell, 2001), pp. 107-30.

36. One of the most impressive philosophical attempts to identify the overlaps can be found in Nicholas Wolterstorff, *Justice in Love* (Grand Rapids: Eerdmans, 2011).

37. See for example Fikret Berkes, *Sacred Ecology: Traditional Ecological Knowledge and Resource Management,* 2nd ed. (New York: Routledge, 2008); Serena Heckler, ed., *Landscape, Process and Power: Re-evaluating Traditional Environmental Knowledge* (New York: Berghan

It is perhaps the very dilemma in relating local and global ethics that should shape our appreciation of the tension between national and non-national imaginaries in the biblical literature. The finite scope of actual relationships inevitably implies that the primary sphere of human and ecological responsibility will be local, even when that local context is continually being influenced by global or planetary factors, or indeed, by networks of actual relationships that have a global reach. Instead of imagining the construction of global, cosmopolitan citizenship, we will need to bring the inevitably local features of our identities, however hybridized, to the task of thinking about the health of our shared planet. Instead of speaking broadly about the interconnectedness of all things, we will need to engage in the harder work of learning the intricate idioms of our own ecosystems.

On the other hand, a communitarian retreat into merely local practice (or into what postcolonial theorists tend to call the "interstices" of Empire) will not be enough. Collaborations at every level will be necessary — local, national, international — if we are to begin the political, economic, and cultural transformations that will make a difference to the wellbeing of future generations. Gayatri Chakravorti Spivak puts the breadth of intersecting challenges well when she says "The necessary collective efforts are to change laws, relations of production, systems of education, and health care. But without the mind-changing one-on-one responsible contact, nothing will stick."[38] And this comment links us back to the irreducibly relational dimension of postcolonial redemption that Willie James Jennings has described as "the space of communion":

> The space of communion is always ready to appear where the people of God reach down to join the land and reach out to join those around them, their near and distant neighbors. This joining involves first a radical remembering of the place, a discerning of the histories and stories of those from whom that land was the facilitator of their identity... so that land is never simply released to capitalism and its autonomous, self-perpetuating turnings of space inside commodity form.[39]

Books, 2009); Steve Heinrichs, ed., *Buffalo Shout, Salmon Cry: Conversations on Creation, Land Justice and Life Together* (Waterloo: Herald Press, 2013).

38. Gayatri Chakravorti Spivak, *A Critique of Postcolonial Reason: Toward a History of the Vanishing Present* (Cambridge: Harvard University Press, 1999), p. 383.

39. Willie James Jennings, *The Christian Imagination: Theology and the Origins of Race* (New Haven: Yale University Press, 2010), pp. 286-87.

CONCLUSION

The Joban critique of anthropocentrism might lead us to be sceptical of the idea that a global cooperation (should it ever be achieved) will be able to control the climate of the planet. But neither that kind of scepticism, nor quibbling about the politics of climate science, can provide a warrant for human irresponsibility. There is no escaping the fact that the human species is turning parasitic on the earth's resources, and communities of faith need to find a new sense of responsibility for planetary inequities, now and into the future. In the unfolding of the biblical narratives, the earth plays a constitutive role in redemptive imagination.[40]

Working with any party who has seriously grasped these challenges, we need new institutions that can evaluate the effectiveness of ecological initiatives, and promote transformed understandings of human wellbeing. Perhaps taking a cue from the Priestly theologians in Genesis 1 who named the Creator "Elohim" rather than Yhwh, we may also conclude that doing justice for the earth will require broadly based inter-faith collaborations.

The majority of Christians today live in non-Western countries, and the international churches enjoy significant opportunities for interlinking resources and practices in most parts of the world. Rather than assuming that all nations need the same kinds of targets for reducing consumption, the poorer nations will need the right kind of resources in promoting their own development. Our future is interconnected with the future of creation, and the challenges ahead will inevitably include a revision of economic arrangements, which is the subject of the final chapter in this volume.

40. See, for example, Brendan Byrne, "Creation Groaning: An Earth Bible Reading of Romans 8.18-22," in *Readings from the Perspective of Earth*, ed. Norman C. Habel (The Earth Bible 1; Sheffield: Sheffield Academic Press, 2000), pp. 193-203, and the popular discussion in N. T. Wright, *Surprised by Hope: Rethinking Heaven, the Resurrection, and the Mission of the Church* (New York: HarperCollins, 2008).

11. Economics and Redemption

The stability of current economic arrangements is, on closer inspection, best understood as an illusion. Climate change has provoked widespread doubts about unfettered industrial expansion, and the financial crisis in 2008–2009 that emerged from the American secondary mortgage market illustrated the fragility of global financial systems. When large corporations suddenly rediscovered a Keynesian interest in Government assistance, the hypocrisy of neo-liberal ideology was exposed for all to see. Subsequently, the accumulation of sovereign debt in Western nations has seen a number of countries lurch from crisis to crisis, as parliaments debate the implications of lifting the ceiling of national debt.[1] In the developing world, the traumas of "structural adjustment" have been well known for decades as external financial agencies intervened in cases of sovereign debt with a battery of demands for economic change. The presumption, however, that Western nations will lead the world in economic enlightenment has also been unmasked as mere prejudice as China begins to assert itself.[2] Given the enormous complexity of these issues, in what possible ways might biblical ethics contribute to the formation of public policy?

1. Robert W. Kolb, *Sovereign Debt: From Safety to Default* (Hoboken, NJ: John Wiley & Sons, 2011).
2. See John Farndon, *China Rises: How China's Astonishing Growth Will Change the World* (London: Virgin Books, 2007).

HOW THE BIBLE LOST ITS ECONOMIC RELEVANCE

A growing number of critics have begun to agitate for alternatives to the still dominant "neo-classical" approaches to modern economics, and some have wondered whether a better grasp on economic history can help.[3] The central difficulty here is that the changes wrought by industrialization and capitalism render such ancient analogies tenuous at best. One of the most influential, if overly generalizing, analyses of these changes is to be found in Karl Polanyi's classic work from 1944, *The Great Transformation*. Polanyi described the ways in which ancient economies were organized around culturally embedded principles of reciprocity and redistribution, rather than facilitated by markets relatively autonomous of their cultural context. While Polanyi's work has been repeatedly criticized for its lack of attention to the evidence for trade in the ancient world, and in particular for his misinterpretation of the Roman economy, one must also acknowledge that such trade was largely the business of elites, rather than the vast majority of populations engaged in subsistence agriculture. The "disembedding" of an economic sphere was indeed a central achievement of modernity.[4]

Ancient imperial economies seem to have extracted resources more by force and tribute than by trade. The comparatively larger settlements in ancient Israel that archaeologists have described as "market towns" provided social networks of exchange largely without the aid of coinage.[5] Money arrived in later periods, in league with imperial taxation. Social stratification is certainly evident in ancient Israelite and Judean society, but the major factors in economic life were kinship relations, local patterns of exchange, and religious expectations — along with the periodic arrivals of imperial armies, taking

3. Notably Michael Hudson and Baruch Levine, eds., *Privatization in the Ancient Near East and Classical World* (Cambridge, Mass.: Peabody Museum of Archaeology and Ethnology, 1996); Michael Hudson and Baruch Levine, *Urbanization and Land Ownership in the Ancient Near East* (Cambridge, Mass.: Peabody Museum of Archaeology and Ethnology, 2000); Michael Hudson, "Debt Forgiveness and Redemption: Where Do the Churches Now Stand?" *Geophilos* 2 (2002): 8-33.

4. Karl Polanyi, *The Great Transformation: The Political and Economic Origins of Our Time*, 2nd ed. (Boston: Beacon, 2001). See especially Gareth Dale, *Karl Polanyi: The Limits of the Market* (Cambridge: Polity, 2010); Charles Taylor, *A Secular Age* (Cambridge, Mass: Belknap, 2007), pp. 159-85.

5. See the useful synthesis of archaeological evidence in William Dever, *The Lives of Ordinary People in Ancient Israel: Where Archaeology and the Bible Intersect* (Grand Rapids: Eerdmans, 2012); cf. Roger S. Nam, *Portrayals of Economic Exchange in the Books of Kings* (BIS 112; Leiden: Brill, 2012).

plunder and demanding tribute. Perhaps not surprisingly, the economic ideals expressed in biblical literature move between a domestic agrarian utopia in which each family has their own "vine and fig tree" and the counter-imperial vision in Isaiah 60 that has the wealth of nations arriving in Jerusalem rather than in the capital of the Persian Empire.[6] Somewhere in the middle of this spectrum lies the pragmatic suggestion within a national imaginary, famously expressed in 1 Samuel 8, that landowners might consent to providing a native king with provisions and resources in exchange for protection and social order.[7]

It does not appear possible to explain ancient Mesopotamian economies in neoclassical terms.[8] The principles for explaining modern market mechanisms are largely irrelevant to understanding ancient Western Asia. For example, it seems that a season of bumper crops in ancient Mesopotamia would not lead to a dramatic decline of "commodity prices," and during lean years debts would accrue at a stable rate.[9] If debt balances could not be cleared at harvest time, then the whole system would eventually become unworkable unless a monarch's declaration of debt release could be enacted from time to time. This is the wider economic context that sits behind much of the biblical discourse of social justice.[10] In ancient Israel, agrarian loans provided an essential element of social glue, but charging interest on such loans was consistently regarded as iniquitous by all the legal and prophetic biblical traditions that touch on

6. Brent Strawn, "'A World under Control': Isaiah 60 and the Apadana Reliefs from Persepolis," in *Approaching Yehud*, ed. Jon L. Berquist (Atlanta, Ga.: Society of Biblical Literature, 2006), pp. 85-116.

7. See especially Jonathan Kaplan, "1 Samuel 8:11-18 as 'A Mirror for Princes,'" *Journal of Biblical Literature* 131 (2012): 625-42. Cf. Yoram Hazony's comments on the "limited state," in *The Philosophy of Hebrew Scripture* (Cambridge: Cambridge University Press, 2012), esp. pp. 153-54, 160.

8. See especially Johannes Renger, "On Economic Structures in Ancient Mesopotamia," *Orientalia* 18 (1994): 157-208, critically reviewing the attempts of Morris Silver, *Prophets and Markets: The Political Economy of Ancient Israel* (Boston: Kluwer Nijhof, 1983); Silver, *Economic Structures of the Ancient Near East* (London: Croom Helm, 1985).

9. See, e.g., Michael Hudson, "How Interest Rates Were Set, 2500 BC–1000 AD," *Journal of the Economic and Social History of the Orient* 43 (2000): 132-61; Hudson, "The Archaeology of Money: Debt Versus Barter Theories of Money's Origins," in *Credit and State Theories of Money: The Contributions of A. Mitchell Innes*, ed. L. Randall Wray (Cheltenham: Edward Elgar, 2004), pp. 99-127, 116; Philippe Guillaume, *Land, Credit and Crisis: Agrarian Finance in the Hebrew Bible* (Sheffield: Equinox, 2012).

10. Moshe Weinfeld, *Social Justice in Ancient Israel and in the Ancient Near East* (Jerusalem: Magnes, 1995); Walter Houston, *Contending for Justice: Ideologies and Theologies of Social Justice in the Old Testament*, 2nd ed. (London: T&T Clark, 2008).

economic topics. Extinguishing this biblical norm has been one of the most significant and systematic achievements of modernity.[11]

The biblical aversion to interest persisted for more than a millennium of Christian history until John Calvin turned the hermeneutical tide in Reformation times (although Calvin was in many respects responding theologically to the institutional changes that were already well established in proto-capitalist Europe).[12] In the second half of the eighteenth century, Adam Smith attempted a balance of "moral sentiments" and political economy, and by the end of that century most expert writers on the subject apparently stopped regarding the Bible as importantly relevant to economics. The science of political economy took leave of biblical warrants at this time, not least because it was commonly framed by "natural" theology.[13]

Adapting Smith's ideas in the 1820s and 1830s, leading American economists were convinced that their own discipline was "*the* redeeming science of modern times" and that given appropriate implementation it would lead to "liberty, peace and abundance."[14] Francis Wayland's best selling textbook on political economy in antebellum America asserted that "the Creator has subjected the accumulation of the blessings of this life to some determinate laws," laws which provided for free trade and a worldwide division of labor. John McVickar went so far as to suggest that forbidding trade among nations would be "contrary to the will of God," while the promotion of international trade "inclines nations to drop the sword from their hands" and engage in

11. Timothy Gorringe proposes the abolition of interest in a single, sweeping paragraph in Gorringe, *Capital and the Kingdom: Theological Ethics and Economic Order* (Maryknoll, NY: Orbis, 1994), p. 167. This can hardly be taken as a serious invitation to conversation with economists, and one might have expected at least some engagement with Islamic finance. Constrast Ian Harper and Lachlan Smirl, "Usury," in *The Oxford Handbook of Christianity and Economics*, ed. Paul Oslington (Oxford: Oxford University Press, 2014), pp. 564-80.

12. Michael Wykes, "Devaluing the Scholastics: Calvin's Ethics of Usury," *Calvin Theological Journal* 38 (2003): 27-51; Bruce R. Scott, *Capitalism: Its Origins and Evolution as a System of Governance* (New York: Springer, 2011), ch.5 "Creating Capitalism in Europe, 1400-1820," pp. 141-84.

13. Stewart Davenport, *Friends of the Unrighteous Mammon: Northern Christians and Market Capitalism, 1815-1860* (Chicago: University of Chicago Press, 2008); Paul Oslington, "Natural Theology as an Integrative Framework for Economics and Theology," *St Mark's Review* 199 (2005): 56-65; Paul Oslington, ed., *Adam Smith as Theologian* (London: Routledge, 2011); Peter Harrison, "Adam Smith and the History of the Invisible Hand," *Journal of the History of Ideas* 72 (2011): 29-49.

14. John McVickar, *Outlines of Political Economy* (New York: Wilder and Campbell, 1825), p. 188, cited in Davenport, *Unrighteous Mammon*, p. 83.

more civilized forms of behavior.[15] Indeed, the civilizing influence of trade can be seen as a key doctrine of modernity.[16]

It must be said, however, that this civilizing doctrine yielded peculiar anomalies in reflection on colonial contexts where certain economic laws were held to be inapplicable. Nineteenth-century economists claimed, for example, that the inverse relationship between profits and wages did not apply in the colonies, and Indigenous peoples were manifestly excluded from the emerging markets at the time. John R. McCulloch noted ominously that "on the first settling of any country abounding in large tracts of unappropriated land, no rent is ever paid," thereby incorporating into economic theory (or more specifically, into the theory of "rent" in its more technical economic sense) a dubious set of assumptions about the productive use of Indigenous lands.[17]

A PERSONAL ASIDE

The discourse of economic civilization has played a significant role in Australia's history of racism, both in relation to Asian immigration policies and Indigenous issues. My own interest in economics increased dramatically in 2005 when I began working for an Aboriginal representative body, and in effect, took on the political task of advocating for the reconstruction of traditional economies, using native title legislation as a legal foothold. This advocacy was an exercise in reconciliation, or at least bridge-building, attempting to link native title rights and interests to broader strategies of economic development. Negotiations with the Victorian state government took place at a policy level since native title jurisprudence has demonstrated a notoriously deficient economic hermeneutic. Instead of accepting that the use of Indigenous lands and waters would reflect contemporary circumstances, the Australian Federal and High Court ruled that native title rights and interests must be seen as essentially the same rights and interests as were exercised two centuries ago when the British first asserted sovereignty, e.g., hunting, fishing, and gathering

15. Francis Weyland, *The Elements of Political Economy*, 4th ed. (New York: Leavitt, Lord, 1854), 15; John McVickar, "Introductory Lecture to a Course on Political Economy," *Banner of the Constitution* 1/35 (1830): 273, cited in Davenport, *Unrighteous Mammon*, pp. 61 and 80-81.

16. Albert O. Hirshman, *The Passions and the Interests: Political Arguments for Capitalism before Its Triumph* (Princeton: Princeton University Press, 1977); Taylor, *A Secular Age*, pp. 159-85.

17. See Davenport, *Unrighteous Mammon*, p. 99. On Mill's contributions in the same period, see Duncan Bell, "John Stuart Mill on Colonies," *Political Theory* 38 (2010): 34-64.

resources on traditional country. Native title rights have therefore generally been defined in law as non-commercial. It is more than ironic, then, when social commentators still criticize Indigenous peoples for not taking commercial advantage of their traditional lands and waters, a critique that was of course foundational to the colonial enterprise.[18]

Interestingly, Australian Indigenous people commonly express their desire to find links between traditional uses of natural resources and the business of contemporary economic life.[19] In other words, they are looking for a kind of "fusion of horizons" between traditional culture and contemporary economic participation. Such participation could be described as "critical traditionalism," to use Ashis Nandy's terminology — a hermeneutic that seeks to revitalize the best features of traditional cultures, notably their ecological, spiritual, and communal values.[20] Instead of allowing movements of capital to roll over an undeveloped *terra nullius*, critical traditionalism looks for a cultural match between trade arrangements and local participation, or as Jon Altman puts it, an economic hybridity.[21]

My experience with the formation of native title policy has caused me to rethink some of the analogous questions for faith communities about how the Bible might contribute traditional norms to modern economic life — not because Scripture needs to be deployed directly in democratic debates, but because a significant number of faith communities still have an in-principle interest in how biblical traditions might continue to shape their own public participation. At the very least, the question of how to manage the considerable resources of the churches should be a high priority for discussion. But beyond that narrowly ecclesial focus, there are a number of other questions

18. Mark G. Brett, *Decolonizing God: The Bible in the Tides of Empire* (Sheffield: Sheffield Phoenix Press, 2008), pp. 7-31.

19. See, for example, Aboriginal and Torres Strait Islander Social Justice Commissioner, *Native Title Report 2004,* Australian Human Rights Commission, 2005, 72-79 available at http://www.hreoc.gov.au/social_justice/ntreport04/.

20. See, e.g., Ashis Nandy, "Cultural Frames for Social Transformation: A Credo," *Alternatives* 12 (1987): 125-52, reprinted in Nandy, *Bonfire of Creeds: The Essential Ashis Nandy* (New Delhi: Oxford University, 2004), pp. 17-29. Cf. Vandana Shiva, *Staying Alive: Women, Ecology, and Development* (London: Zed, 1989); Shiva, *Earth Democracy* (Cambridge, Mass.: South End, 2005).

21. See especially Jon Altman, "What Future for Remote Indigenous Australia? Economic Hybridity and Neo-liberal Turn," in *Culture Crisis: Anthropology and Politics in Aboriginal Australia,* ed. Jon Altman and Melinda Hinkson (Sydney: University of New South Wales Press, 2010), pp. 259-80.

about how the churches and faith-based agencies might contest the dominant assumptions of economic growth and human wellbeing in the public domain.

DISTINGUISHING POLICY VALUES FROM ECONOMIC THEORIES

The Bible consistently expresses concern for the poor, in all its major traditions and genres, yet the ways in which this imperative might bear on public policy today is still a controversial matter. Even the Christian members of the Labor Party in Britain or Australia would probably be bemused by the defense of Christian socialism provided by Metropolitan Geevarghese Mar Osthathios of the Syrian Orthodox Church in India. In his book *The Sin of Being Rich in a Poor World* he argues that human participation in Trinitarian *perichoresis* should bring about a classless society.[22] This is no doubt the kind of argument that Rawls and Habermas would prefer to see translated into a more widely accessible discourse, but even given a sufficiently perspicuous translation, there would still be room to debate the best kinds of policies that might lead to this classless goal.

Within Catholic social thought we can find claims, for example, that "the free market is the most efficient instrument for utilizing resources," while at the same time noting that efficiency should not be equated with justice. Rather, "an appropriate judicial framework" is required, it is suggested, in order to ensure the dignity of labor.[23] A string of papal encyclicals over the past few decades have maintained a principled distance from neo-liberal economic theory, especially in so far as such theory undermines the Catholic tradition of virtue ethics, e.g., *Laborem Exercens* (1981), *Sollicitudo Rei Socialis* (1987), *Centesimus Annus* (1991), *Caritas in Veritate* (2009), and *Evangelii Gaudium* (2013). The contribution from Pope Francis, contains some blunt criticism at points:

> In this context, some people continue to defend trickle-down theories which assume that economic growth, encouraged by a free market, will

22. *The Sin of Being Rich in a Poor World: Holy Trinity and Social Justice* (Tiruvala: Christava Sahitya Samithi, 2004).

23. Pontifical Council for Justice and Peace, *Compendium of the Social Doctrine of the Church* (London: Burns & Oates, 2005), pp. 169-70; cf. Daniel K. Finn, ed., *The True Wealth of Nations: Catholic Social Thought and Economic Life* (Oxford: Oxford University Press, 2010); Daniel K. Finn, ed., *The Moral Dynamics of Moral Life: An Extension and Critique of* Caritas in Veritate (Oxford: Oxford University Press, 2012).

inevitably succeed in bringing about greater justice and inclusiveness in the world. This opinion, which has never been confirmed by the facts, expresses a crude and naïve trust in the goodness of those wielding economic power and in the sacralized workings of the prevailing economic system. Meanwhile, the excluded are still waiting. (*Evangelii Gaudium,* 2013, §54)

There is no doubting the evidence that market liberalization in India and China has yielded dramatic effects in producing new middle classes, but the focus of this papal critique seems to be on the continuing and expanding disparities that are masked by utilitarian measures such as a Gross Domestic Product (GDP).[24]

Ironically, the Catholic ethicist Albino Barrera has pointed out that the global agricultural market is not actually free, and that it is the market protectionism of most OECD countries that blocks the progress of less developed nations. The effects fall disproportionately on the poor, he suggests: "The cost of such policies is shifted to the nations that are the most dependent on agriculture and the ones with the least resources to deal with disruptions in food markets, the LDCs [Less Developed Countries]."[25] He therefore argues that the checks on the global market should be provided more by international human rights considerations than by trade protectionism, and he draws particularly on the biblical traditions and Catholic tradition in reinforcing his human rights arguments.[26]

Barrera is concerned to discover the line below which economic conditions become unacceptably coercive — as, for example, when parents in Thailand might find it unavoidable that a daughter should enter the sex industry in order to support her family. Barrera identifies such cases as unacceptable "economic compulsion," and he wants to use human rights arguments to establish appropriate benchmarks in legislation, regulation, and in institutional practice that can constrain the amoral functioning of markets. He has no doubt as to

24. While GDP is only one of the many instruments utilized by economists, it is a prominent element in political rhetoric fixated on "growth."

25. Albino Barrera, *Economic Compulsion and Christian Ethics* (Cambridge: Cambridge University Press, 2005), pp. 199-200.

26. Barrera has more recently provided a comprehensive overview of biblical economic norms in his *Biblical Economic Ethics: Sacred Scripture's Teachings on Economic Life* (Lanham, MD: Lexington Books, 2013); cf. the less detailed discussion in Richard A. Horsley, *Covenant Economics: A Biblical Vision of Justice for All* (Louisville: Westminster John Knox, 2009), who also concludes with a call for comprehensive systems of worker protection, rather than providing a root and branch critique of capitalism.

the efficiency of markets; the key problems turn on the social effects of such remarkable efficiency.

In his subsequent book *Market Complicity and Christian Ethics*, Barrera provides a more complex analysis that includes the social and environmental implications of globalized trade arrangements — the negative "externalities" to market operations that impact on innocent third parties. One of his examples illustrates a difficulty, however, with the suggestion that the poor would benefit from liberalizing the OECD agricultural market. Environmentally motivated investments in ethanol, he notes, have yielded immediate problems for food prices in less developed nations, as more land is devoted to ethanol production.[27] This is one of many examples that demonstrate the complexity of market operations, and the need for constant monitoring of unintended effects yielded by policy changes. Even if a consensus could be secured around the kinds of economic rights that should underpin international trade arrangements, there would still be room to debate the legal and regulatory structures that would best secure these rights year by year.

The difficulties are multiplied by the various kinds of complicity in market structures that elude legal constraints — such as when consumers buy cheaper goods and services without regard for, or knowledge of, the damage they may be causing to workers and environments hidden from immediate view. But the protection of workers' rights and wages in one country will often prompt transnational corporations to shift their operations to another country where labor can be legally exploited, thereby impacting on the working classes even in the wealthier nations — as car makers in the USA and Australia have found to their cost. Barrera pithily observes, "the prices consumers pay for their cheaper imports do not reflect the total societal costs incurred."[28]

These wider costs are immediately felt in local communities affected by dramatic job losses, but attempts to factor such costs into government policy and legislation can often be dismissed by neo-liberal governments as socialist ideology. At best, a neo-liberal approach might concede that socially responsible investment strategies could be regarded as a worthy initiative if they were freely adopted by particular companies who are competing in a small, sensitized market. One might imagine that support for this sensitized market from faith-based organizations would be uncontroversial, but in fact we find religious objections from both right and left branches of political theology.

27. Albino Barrera, *Market Complicity and Christian Ethics* (Cambridge: Cambridge University Press, 2011), pp. 148-50.
28. Barrera, *Market Complicity,* p. 187.

When it comes to political debates about economic policies, it would seem more important to focus attention on policy values and norms, rather than on the detail of economic theories as such. Communities of faith can agree that the Bible consistently urges action on behalf of the poor, for example, but it does not underwrite a particular economic theory — Marxist, Keynesian, or any other. A public debate might converge on the ethical principles for evaluating economic policies, without thereby directly shaping the bureaucratic or legal machinery of such policies. Commenting on the relationship between faith and public commitments, Gustavo Gutiérrez makes a significant point that is also relevant to the task of economic hermeneutics:

> To assert that there is a direct, immediate relationship between faith and political action encourages one to seek from faith norms and criteria for particular political options. . . . Confusions are created which can result in a dangerous politico-religious messianism which does not sufficiently respect either the autonomy of the political arena or that which belongs to an authentic faith, liberated from religious baggage.[29]

Rather than attempting to assimilate theology to economics, or perhaps even attempting to resurrect the laws of an ancient agrarian economy, communities of faith need to inhabit exactly this kind of tension between the spheres of faith and public practice.

That is not to say that we lack substantive proposals for how theology might be assimilated to particular economic theories. For example, in his book *Divine Economy: Theology and the Market*, D. Stephen Long provides a detailed analysis of five essentially "pro-capitalist" theologians whose work can be situated on a spectrum from neo-classical positions (e.g., Michael Novak) to Keynesian ones (e.g., Ron Preston). Long demonstrates how a single theological doctrine can yield contrasting consequences for economic theory. Thus, for example, the doctrine of original sin is shaped by Novak into an argument for an unfettered market, whereas for Preston it "reveals the need for the presence of a strong state."[30] It is not important for our present purposes to resolve this difference. At this point I simply wish to agree with Long that the relationship between biblical norms and particular public policies will be one that is

29. Gustavo Gutiérrez, *A Theology of Liberation*, trans. Caridad Inda and John Eagleson (Maryknoll: Orbis, 1973), p. 236.

30. D. Stephen Long, *Divine Economy: Theology and the Market* (London: Routledge, 2000), 58, discussing Ron Preston, *Religion and the Ambiguities of Capitalism* (Cleveland: Pilgrim Press, 1991).

always subject to ongoing debates, and especially to debates about the effects of policies as their impact unfolds in particular contexts.

I would want to make the same point in relation to Christian theology that has been associated with economic theory on the Marxist end of the spectrum. Long suggests, for example, that liberation theology tends towards a secularizing project that leaves the wider framework of biblical narrative and norms behind.[31] His critique suggests that salvation has been displaced by liberation, and the idea of freedom has taken on an almost idolatrous independence from other elements of Christian faith. To my mind, a great irony in this critique is that it seems more directly applicable to free market Christianity.[32] Contrary to this oft-repeated critique of liberation theology, Gutiérrez distinguishes between different kinds of liberation: political liberation, the liberation of the human being in history, and the liberation from sin that leads into communion with God. He insists that "These three levels mutually affect each other but they are not the same."[33] Sin is the most fundamental obstacle to communion with God, for example, but it is also the root of social injustices, exploitation, slavery, racism, and so on. The effects of overcoming sin will impact on all these issues, since communion with God is a fundamentally social reality. But it does not follow that Gutiérrez' liberation theology is logically wedded to Marxist economic analysis. If we take more seriously his cautious comments on the relative independence of the public sphere, then his position comes closer to my own suggestion that public theology necessarily sits at the intersection of sacred and secular discourse without collapsing into either.

As argued in Chapter One, faith commitments might provide the underlying motivations for political or economic engagement, but when it comes to public participation, there are both limits and possibilities that need to be worked through in actual dialogue concerning particular issues. Among the priority issues that will demand public cooperation in the future, we can expect to see a dramatic rise in policies designed to address climate change, and consequently, an expansion in the repertoire of sustainable economic practices. And as suggested in the previous chapter, this process must be connected to some fundamental debates about the nature of communal wellbeing, human flourishing, or in biblical language, redemption. Accordingly, in the next sec-

31. Long, *Divine Economy*, pp. 88-117; cf. John Milbank, *Theology and Social Theory: Beyond Secular Reason* (Oxford: Blackwell, 1990), p. 229.

32. See, e.g., Paul Heyne, "The Concept of Economic Justice in Religious Discussion," in *Morality of the Market: Religious and Economic Perspectives*, ed. Walter Block, Geoffrey Brennan, and Kenneth Elzinga (Vancouver: The Fraser Institute, 1985), pp. 463-82.

33. Gutiérrez, *Theology of Liberation*, pp. 175-76.

tion we will briefly review a few of the attempts to address these issues in biblical studies that are attuned to economic analysis.

LOCAL MODELS OF REDEMPTION

Instead of translating biblical principles into a public discourse of economic rights, the "Jubilee 2000" movement retained some of the particularity of biblical language, and enjoyed some success in advocating for the release of sovereign debts in particular Third World contexts. For many of the participants in this movement, there was a clear analogy between the ancient declarations of debt release and the agreement of international agencies to debt restructuring.[34] This was, of course, precisely an analogy rather than a straightforward biblical warrant, since the biblical law in Leviticus 25 assumes an agrarian society and explicitly excludes foreigners from its provisions.[35] As indicated above, the Jubilee had its roots in a much wider set of ancient cultural traditions, rather than being a uniquely biblical practice. So ironically, in this first example of economic engagement, the policy norms at issue did not in fact arise from specifically biblical visions but from an intercultural pattern of economic practice in ancient Western Asia. Moreover, some of the associated conditions of debt release included traumatic structural adjustments.

Ellen Davis developed a more rigorous agrarian hermeneutic in *Scripture, Culture and Agriculture*, which integrates biblical exegesis with a critique of modern agribusiness in order to produce a vision for ecologically sensitive economics. Especially in her chapter "Covenantal Economics: The Biblical Case for a Local Economy," she finds good reasons to be inspired by the agrarian model of family land, which in both its Deuteronomic and Priestly manifestations established enduring spiritual bonds between people and place. Her overall argument proposes that our modern culture has been led into grave danger by diverging from "the biblical ideal of healthy local communities with local food economies."[36] In practical terms, she proposes for example the embrace of local farmers' markets and an ethical aversion to imports.

34. On the ancient practice of debt tablet breaking, see for example John Bergsma, *The Jubilee from Leviticus to Qumran: A History of Interpretation* (VTSup 115; Leiden: Brill, 2007), pp. 20-26.

35. See further Mignon Jacobs, "Parameters of Justice: Ideological Challenges regarding Persons and Practices in Leviticus 25:25-55," *Ex Auditu* 22 (2006): 133-58.

36. Ellen Davis, *Scripture, Culture, and Agriculture: An Agrarian Reading of the Bible* (Cambridge: Cambridge University Press, 2009), pp. 101-119, 106; cf. Rajula Annie Watson, *A Christian Understanding of Land Ethics* (Delhi: ISPCK, 2004).

Davis's work is clearly stamped with biblical motifs of local "redemption" (conceived in ancient Israelite discourse as the restoration of families and their traditional lands) rather than an international language of economic rights. Some other attempts to promote the idea of "covenant economics" have been more accepting of the transition from rural to urban environments. Richard Horsley, for example, seems to assume that the basis of a livelihood in industrialized societies is not the possession of ancestral land but simply "having a job." But this individual reality requires an infrastructure of health, education and safety to underpin that employment.[37] Similarly, the Relationships Foundation in the UK highlights the ways in which an individual's employment within a modern corporation should be framed by principles of "covenantal" relationship that both constrain and enable the ethics of an organization. Unlike Davis's proposals, the explicit advocacy of biblical principles in this latter movement has no necessary consequences for a return to agrarian models of redemption.[38]

One of the leading Marxist interpreters of the Hebrew Bible, Roland Boer, is more directly disposed to an agrarian solution, not because he has any interest in rehabilitating biblical norms, but apparently because an embrace of subsistence economies is fast becoming the last solution left standing. After providing a taxonomy of ancient economies, he suggests that imperial exploitation and tribute relations are inherently unstable, in part because they are predicated on class divisions. Subsistence regimes, on the other hand, operate according to an "optimal rather than maximal engagement with nature."[39] Subsistence is the most resilient form of life, with the least impact on the environment.

The small commune is for Boer apparently the only sustainable alternative, but although there are numerous examples of local communes, it is very unclear how the transitions towards more comprehensive economic habits of this kind would be effected. In practice, a revolutionary transition from current arrangements to stable subsistence economies would be likely to en-

37. Richard A. Horsley, *Covenant Economics: A Biblical Vision of Justice for All* (Louisville: Westminster John Knox, 2009), p. 166.

38. See especially Michael Schluter and David Lee, *The R Factor* (London: Hodder and Stoughton, 1993); Michael Schluter and John Ashcroft, eds., *Jubilee Manifesto: A Framework, Agenda and Strategy for Christian Social Reform* (Leicester: InterVarsity Press, 2005); cf. Clive Beed and Clara Beed, "Biblical Ethical Principles and Its Critics," in *Public Theology in Law and Life*, ed. Brian Edgar, Paul Babie, and David Wilson (Adelaide: ATF Press, 2012), pp. 125-42.

39. Roland Boer, *The Sacred Economy* (Louisville: Westminster John Knox, 2015).

tail untold human misery. Ironically, this Marxist vision would probably be just as deadly in its consequences as the climate change denial of neo-liberal governments. A more promising alternative can be found in the so-called "transition town" movement that began in the UK and is now spreading internationally.[40]

There is a lot to be said for the strategic affirmation of local agrarian economies, but it needs to be acknowledged that there are certain achievements of the modern world that would never have arisen from within subsistence societies: our current health sciences and information technology, to mention just two of the most important examples. Unless societies are willing to live without these benefits, some kind of economic hybridity will be necessary into the future. And this inevitably means that we need to confront complex questions about equitable access to resources. Responding to Timothy Jackson's challenge in *Prosperity without Growth* discussed in our previous chapter, it will be essential for our discussion to include a more fundamental reconsideration of the notions of prosperity and wellbeing.

BIBLICAL *SHALOM* AND ECONOMIC APPROACHES TO WELLBEING

Perhaps the most fruitful philosophy of wellbeing in recent years has arisen from the so-called "capabilities approach" to development economics, which although allied with human rights frameworks has focused more specifically on human capabilities and agency. Amartya Sen established this approach with his influential account of poverty as more a matter of capabilities, rather than a deficit of income, utilities or other kinds of basic goods. Rejecting both utilitarian abstractions like a GDP and vague aspirations for "equality," this school proposes that wellbeing is best thought of as a basic set of capabilities that may take shape differently depending on the particularities of a culture. There is accordingly no definitive list of capabilities, but they most commonly relate to life expectancy, health and safety, education and employment opportunity, freedom of expression and religion, social affiliations, and connections with nature. Sen has argued that a closer description of their content cannot be clarified without the aid of deliberative political processes in particular cultural contexts.

In describing the sources of this philosophy from the point of view of

---

40. See especially, Rob Hopkins, *Localisation and Resilience at the Local Level: The Case of Transition Town Totnes,* PhD Thesis (Devon: University of Plymouth, 2010).

Indian tradition, Sen draws on Rabindranath Tagore and Mahatma Gandhi, along with earlier Indian thinkers. Martha Nussbaum, on the other hand, begins particularly with Aristotle in unpacking the significance of Sen's propositions.[41] Her use of Aristotle illustrates how generalized talk about equality and economic development is likely to be ineffective unless it emerges from concrete historical communities and their own conceptions of wellbeing and agency. Her critique of Aristotle, however, also illuminates his moral blind spots in presuming that the moral agents who engage in political deliberation were free, non-immigrant males. This deficiency in Aristotle's politics was remedied in the first instance, according to Nussbaum, by the Stoic teaching that all human beings have an inherent dignity — men and women, slave and free, native, and foreign. She acknowledges in her recent work *Creating Capabilities*, almost in passing, that "Later on, Christian ideas of human equality, themselves strongly influenced by Stoicism, joined with the Stoic ideas to strengthen notions of equal human entitlement."[42]

If, however, our attention is focused on contemporary challenges in international development, then understanding the precise extent of Stoic influence on early Christianity is not especially pertinent. Engaging with the existing international networks of Christian churches and their agencies would be more relevant in contemporary practice — at least for policy makers and community development agencies, if not for historians of ideas. Nussbaum's approach needs to demonstrate how people are motivated today to interpret their own moral traditions in the way she suggests. If one begins with communities of faith, for example, it may be significant to show how the Priestly tradition established not only the unity of all human beings in Genesis 1 but also a unity with non-human creatures in Genesis 9. With this background in mind, biblical resources might be drawn on in support of Nussbaum's particular formulation of the capabilities approach, which extends beyond the human rights tradition to include the rights of non-human animals.[43]

As made clear in Chapter Three, I am not claiming that complex herme-

41. E.g., Nussbaum, "Non-Relative Virtues: An Aristotelian Approach," in *Quality of Life*, ed. Martha Nussbaum and Amartya Sen (Oxford: Oxford University Press, 1993), pp. 242-69.

42. Martha C. Nussbaum, *Creating Capabilities: The Human Development Approach* (Cambridge, Mass.: Belknap, 2011), pp. 129-30. Connecting these Aristotelian roots with Aquinas and Christian tradition, see especially Sabina Alkire, *Valuing Freedoms: Sen's Capability Approach and Poverty Reduction* (Oxford: Oxford University Press, 2002).

43. See the extended argument in Martha C. Nussbaum, *Frontiers of Justice: Disability, Nationality, Species Membership* (Cambridge, Mass.: Belknap, 2006).

neutical issues can be resolved by listing particular biblical texts. A dialogue with Nussbaum would, for example, need to be shaped by a less mechanical reflection on the ongoing tension in the Hebrew Bible between the national and non-national imaginaries. In contrast with cosmopolitanism, she provides a strong defense of national sovereignties, which she takes to be an essential expression of a particular society's capacity to make laws of their own choosing: "The nation, then, has a moral role that is securely grounded in the Capabilities Approach, because the approach gives central importance to people's freedom and self-definition."[44] Yet, at the same time, Nussbaum proposes international standards of political legitimacy, so she also feels compelled to defend the internationalism of her approach from charges of cultural imperialism.[45] Resolving this tension can only come by way of the patient work of demonstrating how each tradition may arrive at the intersecting ideals that would secure the central capabilities. This tension between national and international aspects of Nussbaum's proposals might be seen as analogous with the tension between the national and imperial imaginaries in biblical literature.

Beyond such broad analogies, there is also a point of connection in the biblical notion of *shalom*. This term is used in the Hebrew Bible with reference to personal health, social justice, and ecological flourishing, all matters of concern to the capabilities approach.[46] In some contexts *shalom* is also translated as "peace" as opposed to "war," but the best overall translation is "wellbeing." The diverse usage of the term does not map on to a single concept, but rather to a network of concepts at times subject to dispute. We see this, for example, in Jeremiah 6–7, where the prophet claims that even religious leaders have failed to grasp the need to include social justice within their understanding of wellbeing. His outcry on behalf of "widows, orphans and strangers," and those who suffer unjust violence, may be taken as a principled commitment to all those who are vulnerable within society. Adding to this classical list of the vulnerable, today we would naturally include those who suffer various kinds of disability.[47]

44. Nussbaum, *Creating Capabilities*, p. 114, cf. pp. 92, 111.

45. See further the review of key issues in Sabina Alkire, "Human Development: Definitions, Critiques and Related Concepts," *Human Development Research Paper 2010/1* (New York: United Nations Development Program, 2010).

46. See, e.g., Perry B. Yoder and Willard M. Swartly, eds., *The Meaning of Peace: Biblical Studies*, 2nd ed. (Elkhart, Ind.: Institute of Mennonite Studies, 2001); Randy S. Woodley, *Shalom and the Community of Creation: An Indigenous Vision* (Grand Rapids: Eerdmans, 2012).

47. See further Hector Avalos, Sarah J. Melcher, Jeremy Schipper, eds, *This Abled Body: Rethinking Disabilities in Biblical Studies* (Atlanta: Society of Biblical Literature, 2007); Candida R.

Such hermeneutical extrapolations would, of course, mainly be of interest to faith communities who already hold the Hebrew Bible in high regard. Nevertheless, to borrow Ashis Nandy's terminology, it is precisely this kind of "critical traditionalism" that can underpin the motivation of faith-based agencies in many contexts internationally, where people can come to an agreement on the contours of the central capabilities. At the very least, Jewish and Christian scriptures should provoke faith communities to attend especially to the effects of any economic policy on the life of the poor and vulnerable.[48] We can reasonably expect that with increasing competition for natural resources beyond "peak oil," the transitions to more sustainable economies may well be traumatic for many, and caring for the vulnerable within those transitions will be of special concern.

WELLBEING BETWEEN NATIONS

I am suggesting that there are good reasons for faith communities to recover the older biblical notion of "redemption" — the restoration of family and land in local economies. And given convictions about the fundamental dignity of all human beings, there is also an imperative for the churches to provide resources to less developed countries, even if there is room to debate the particular contributions of NGOs and local institutions in the effective delivery of resources. As a general rule, local agency will be essential to enduring achievements, and it will always be necessary to examine the actual effects of policies in particular contexts, rather than assume that effective processes adopted in one cultural context will be immediately transferrable to others.[49] While faith-based agencies may focus their activities at the level of civil society within less developed nations, some engagement with governments would seem inevitable.

Most international development work requires specialized training and experience, and not everyone can express their ethical commitments in this

---

Moss and Jeremy Schipper, eds., *Disability Studies and Biblical Literature* (New York: Palgrave Macmillan, 2011).

48. From a Jewish point of view, see especially Joshua Berman, *Created Equal: How the Bible Broke with Ancient Political Thought* (Oxford: Oxford University Press, 2008), pp. 80-108, "Egalitarianism and Assets"; Jonathan Sacks, *The Dignity of Difference: How to Avoid the Clash of Civilizations*, 2nd ed. (London: Continuum, 2003), pp. 105-24; cf. George Gotsis and Sarah Drakopoulou-Dodd, "Economic Ideas in the Pauline Epistles of the New Testament," *History of Economics Review* 35 (2002): 13-34.

49. See the brief overview of these issues in Nussbaum, *Creating Capabilities*, pp. 113-22.

kind of work. But one pressing set of questions impinges on the life of faith communities everywhere: how to make worthwhile contributions to community development in poorer nations by participating in fair trade. For our present purposes we may set to one side an evaluation of Fair Trade branding as it is currently practiced, and consider the basic principles of exchange between nations.

Ethical or "political consumption" chooses goods or services on the basis of value considerations other than price, with a view to promoting the well-being of others. In local contexts, this kind of consumption would include support for farmers' markets, or the purchase of alternative energies, but it also includes within its scope international fair trade arrangements. Political consumption is deliberately opposed to the kind of consumerism that is reducible to personal benefit with little regard for relationships.[50] Theological attacks on consumerism are of course plentiful, but to the extent that such attacks do not actually impact on the institutional policies and purchasing behavior of faith communities, they have minimal practical effect. Political consumption helpfully moves beyond rhetoric to shape actual practice, while promoting critical reflection on the wider effects of our economic life.

In his defense of political consumption, Luke Bretherton argues that it is quite possible to promote economic networks of solidarity and friendship regardless of the character of governance in any particular context — whether it is capitalist, communist, or whatever it might be. Such networks of solidarity may not be very "efficient," he confesses, but they at least have the effect of de-familiarizing economic relations, particularly where they have been obscured by unthinking habits, or overwhelmed by self-interest. "What is important to consider is the ways in which the capillaries of friendship and forms of faithful witness can be forged and sustained within any hegemonic system."[51]

Bretherton draws attention to the prophet Jeremiah's recommendation to "seek the shalom of the city" even while the exiles were living in Babylon (Jeremiah 29). Jeremiah's advice seems to propel Israel's life beyond the kind of survival strategies of diaspora communities who adapt elements from a dominant culture only for purpose of resisting assimilation (strategies that postcolonial critics render in the jargon of *bricolage* or cultural hybridity). Beyond this ironic form of resistance to assimilation, Bretherton argues that

50. At this juncture it is worth remembering Albino Barrera's observation that neoclassical economic theory "does not differentiate needs from mere wants," whereas Christian ethics must make this distinction. Barrera, *Market Complicity*, p. 160.

51. Luke Bretherton, *Christianity and Contemporary Politics: The Conditions and Possibilities of Faithful Witness* (Oxford: Wiley-Blackwell, 2010), pp. 184 and 187.

sub-cultural communitarian withdrawal may in effect be overly subservient to the dominant culture by not expecting its transformation: "To frame Christian political witness in terms of tactical subcultural resistance forecloses the possibility of the irruption of God's sovereign acts of grace in the midst of the earthly city."[52] This is dense theological discourse, but at the very least it amounts to a call to keep the Christian vision of *shalom* wider than the local faith community, or even wider than the international networks of ecclesial friendship. Faith-based communities will have their own motivations for political consumption or community organizing, but seeking the *shalom* of others will necessarily include collaboration with a range of agencies who share overlapping ideals of wellbeing.[53]

This last point might also be translated into the kind of biblical theology discussed in Part Two of this volume where I have stressed the compatibility of the "non-Israelite" ethic in the book of Job and the idea of divine sovereignty in Priestly theology. I suggested that in relinquishing the national vision of political sovereignty, the Priestly vision reconfigures divine rule without the need for Judean kings, establishing much broader conceptions of the common good founded on a universal creation ethic and multinational relationships. These broader conceptions of the common good can be contrasted with the retreat into an exclusivist, communitarian model provided by Ezra-Nehemiah.

I would argue that a purely communitarian Christianity today is analogous in some respects with the social vision of Ezra-Nehemiah, and that both models of communal faithfulness threaten to extinguish the Priestly vision of divine sovereignty. The Priestly vision suggests that even under circumstances of foreign imperial rule, it is always possible for faith communities to live as if "natives and strangers" enjoy essentially the same standing before God. Precisely the particularist faith of the Priestly tradition enjoins everyday acts of love and justice towards others. Concern for the stranger was configured as a matter of economic redemption, restoring networks of family and land, yet this theological discourse did not draw a sharp distinction between the sacred and secular spheres in the domain of the economy. In this respect, I would support Bretherton's critique of sub-cultural communitarian withdrawal, as if it were the only way to embody a covenantal faithfulness today.

Israel's prophets made precisely this holistic point, calling their communities to hold justice and holiness together in practice. The historical unfold-

---

52. Bretherton, *Christianity and Contemporary Politics*, pp. 190-91.
53. Bretherton, *Christianity and Contemporary Politics*, pp. 71-125; cf. Ernesto Cortés, "Re-weaving the Social Fabric," *Boston Review* (June-September 1994): 12-14.

ing of the prophets' testimony began with the local ideal of subsistence, each family with their own "vine and fig tree," but eventually it was recognized that the local ideal was not sustainable unless the rapacious appetites of successive empires could learn to accept a global practice of justice. This ancient vision can have an enduring value, in spite of the dramatic changes wrought by modernity. Perhaps one justification for the national imaginary can still be found in the practicalities of local commitments: human finitude prohibits an equal care for the entire planet all at once. Nevertheless, grounded in their convictions concerning divine sovereignty, faith communities can continue to bear witness in their economic life to the necessary tension between local and global redemption, regardless of the political leverage that might be achieved in any particular context.

Bibliography

Abdul-Matin, Ibrahim. *Green Deen: What Islam Teaches about Protecting the Earth.* San Francisco: Berrett-Koehler, 2010.

Abernethy, Andrew T. "Eating, Assyrian Imperialism and God's Kingdom in Isaiah." In *Isaiah and Imperial Context: The Book of Isaiah in the Times of Empire*, edited by Andrew T. Abernethy, Mark G. Brett, Tim Bulkeley, Tim Meadowcroft, pp. 38-53. Eugene, Or.: Pickwick, 2013.

Aboriginal and Torres Strait Islander Social Justice Commissioner, *Social Justice Report 2008.* Sydney: Australian Human Rights Commission, 2008.

Abraham, Susan. *Identity, Ethics and Nonviolence in Postcolonial Theory: A Rahnerian Theological Assessment.* New York: Palgrave Macmillan, 2007.

Achenbach, Reinhard. "Der Pentateuch, seine Theokratischen Bearbeitungen und Josua – 2 Könige." In *Les Dernières Rédactions du Pentateuque, de L'Hexateuque et de L'Ennéateuque*, edited by Thomas Römer and Konrad Schmid, pp. 225-53. Bibliotheca ephemeridum theologicarum lovaniensium 203. Leuven: Leuven University Press, 2007.

Adam, Andrew K. M. *Faithful Interpretation.* Minneapolis: Fortress, 2006.

Adams, Nicholas. "A Response to Heuser: Two Problems in Habermas' Recent Comments on Religion." *Political Theology* 9 (2008): 552-56.

Agamben, Giorgio. *Homo Sacer: Sovereign Power and Bare Life.* Stanford: Stanford University Press, 1998.

————. *State of Exception.* Chicago: University of Chicago Press, 2005.

Ahn, Gregor. *Religiöse Herrscherlegitimation im Achämenidschen Iran: Die Voraussetzungen und die Strukturen ihrer Argumentation.* Acta Iranica 31. Leiden: Brill, 1992.

Ahn, John. *Exile as Forced Migration: A Sociological, Literary, and Theological Approach on the Displacement and Resettlement of the Southern Kingdom of Judah.* Beihefte zur Zeitschrift für die alttestamentliche Wissenschaft 417. Berlin: de Gruyter, 2011.

Albertz, Rainer. "The Canonical Alignment of the Book of Joshua." In *Judah and the Judeans in the Fourth Century*, edited by Oded Lipschits, Gary N. Knoppers, and Rainer Albertz, pp. 287-303. Winona Lake, Ind.: Eisenbrauns, 2007.

———. "Purity Strategies and Political Interests in the Policy of Nehemiah." In *Confronting the Past: Archaeological and Historical Essays on Ancient Israel in Honor of William G. Dever*, edited by Seymour Gitin, J. Edward Wright, and J. P. Dessel, pp. 199-206. Winona Lake, Ind.: Eisenbrauns, 2006.

Alkire, Sabina. "Human Development: Definitions, Critiques and Related Concepts." *Human Development Research Paper* 2010/1. New York: United Nations Development Program, 2010.

———. *Valuing Freedoms: Sen's Capability Approach and Poverty Reduction*. Oxford: Oxford University Press, 2002.

Altman, Jon. "What Future for Remote Indigenous Australia? Economic Hybridity and Neo-liberal Turn." In *Culture Crisis: Anthropology and Politics in Aboriginal Australia*, edited by Jon Altman and Melinda Hinkson, pp. 259-80. Sydney: University of New South Wales Press, 2010.

Andersen, Francis. *Job: An Introduction and Commentary*. Tyndale Old Testament Commentaries. Downers Grove: Intervarsity, 1976.

Aneil, Barbara. *John Locke and America: The Defence of English Colonialism*. Oxford: Clarendon, 1996.

Apffel-Marglin, Frédérique. "Introduction: Rationality and the World." In *Decolonizing Knowledge: From Development to Dialogue*, edited by Frédérique Apffel-Marglin and Stephen Marglin, pp. 1-40. Oxford: Clarendon, 1996.

Arendt, Hannah. *The Origins of Totalitarianism*. London: George Allen and Unwin, 1967.

Ashcroft, Bill. *Post-Colonial Transformation*. London: Routledge, 2001.

———. "The Sacred in Australian Culture." In *Sacred Australia: Post-Secular Considerations*, edited by Makarand Paranjape, pp. 21-43. Melbourne: Clouds of Magellan, 2009.

Ata, Samuel T. "Towards Peace and Reconciliation: Some Churches' Response with Specific Reference to the Post-Civil War in Solomon Islands." PhD Thesis Melbourne: Melbourne College of Divinity, 2013.

Attwood, Bain. *Possession: Batman's Treaty and the Matter of History*. Melbourne: Miegunyah Press, 2009.

———. *Rights for Aborigines*. Sydney: Allen & Unwin, 2003.

———. *Telling the Truth about Aboriginal History*. Crow's Nest: Allen and Unwin, 2005.

Audi, Robert, and Nicholas Wolterstorff. *Religion in the Public Sphere: The Place of Religious Convictions in Political Debate*. New York: Rowman and Littlefield, 1997.

Avalos, Hector, Sarah J. Melcher, Jeremy Schipper, eds. *This Abled Body: Rethinking Disabilities in Biblical Studies*. Atlanta: Society of Biblical Literature, 2007.

Badiou, Alain. *Saint Paul: The Foundation of Universalism*. Translated by Ray Brassier. Stanford: Stanford University Press, 2003. Translation of *Saint Paul: La Fondation de l'universalisme*. Paris: Presses Universitaires France, 1997.

Bakhtin, Mikhail. *Problems of Dostoevsky's Poetics*. Translated by Caryl Emerson. Minneapolis: University of Minnesota Press, 1984.

Balabanski, Vicky S. "Hellenistic Cosmology and the Letter to the Colossians: Towards an Ecological Hermeneutic." In *Ecological Hermeneutics: Biblical, Historical and Theo-*

logical Perspectives, edited by David G. Horrell, Cherryl Hunt, Christopher Southgate, Francesca Stavrakopoulou, pp. 94-107. London: T & T Clark, 2010.

Barr, James. "Ancient Biblical Laws and Modern Human Rights." In *Justice and the Holy: Essays in Honor of Walter Harrelson*, edited by Douglas A. Knight and Peter J. Paris, pp. 21-33. Atlanta: Scholars, 1989.

————. *Biblical Faith and Natural Theology*. Oxford: Clarendon, 1993.

Barrera, Albino. *Biblical Economic Ethics: Sacred Scripture's Teachings on Economic Life*. Lanham, Md.: Lexington Books, 2013.

————. *Economic Compulsion and Christian Ethics*. Cambridge: Cambridge University Press, 2005.

————. *Market Complicity and Christian Ethics*. Cambridge: Cambridge University Press, 2011.

Bauckham, Richard. *Living with Other Creatures: Green Exegesis and Theology*. Waco, Tex.: Baylor University Press, 2011.

Bauks, Michaela. "Die Begriffe מורשה und אחזה in Pg. Überlegungen zur landkonzeption der Priestergrundschrift." *Zeitschrift für die alttestamentliche Wissenschaft* 116 (2004): 171-88.

————. "Les notions de 'peuple' et de 'terre' dans l'oeuvre sacerdotale (Pg)," *Transeuphratène* 30 (2005): 19-36.

Bauman, Whitney. *Theology, Creation, and Environmental Ethics: From* Creatio ex Nihilo *to* Terra Nullius. London: Routledge, 2009.

Beed, Clive, and Clara Beed. "Biblical Ethical Principles and Its Critics." In *Public Theology in Law and Life*, edited by Brian Edgar, Paul Babie, and David Wilson, pp. 125-42. Adelaide: ATF Press, 2012.

Belich, James. *Replenishing the Earth: The Settler Revolution and the Rise of the Anglo-World, 1783-1939*. Oxford: Oxford University Press, 2009.

Bell, Duncan. "John Stuart Mill on Colonies." *Political Theory* 38 (2010): 34-64.

Bergen, Doris L. *Twisted Cross: The German Christian Movement in the Third Reich*. Chapel Hill: University of North Carolina Press, 1996.

Bergsma, John. "The Jubilee: A Post-exilic Priestly Attempt to Reclaim Lands?" *Biblica* 84 (2003): 225-46.

————. *The Jubilee from Leviticus to Qumran: A History of Interpretation*. Vetus Testamentum Supplements 115. Leiden: Brill, 2007.

Berkes, Fikret. *Sacred Ecology: Traditional Ecological Knowledge and Resource Management*. 2nd ed. New York: Routledge, 2008.

Berman, Joshua. *Created Equal: How the Bible Broke with Ancient Political Thought*. Oxford: Oxford University Press, 2008.

Bhabha, Homi. *The Location of Culture*. London: Routledge, 1994.

Binney, Judith. *Redemption Songs: A Life of the Nineteenth-Century Maori Leader Te Kooti Arikirangi Te Turuki*. Melbourne: Melbourne University Press, 1997.

Bird, Phyllis. *Missing Persons and Mistaken Identities: Women and Gender in Ancient Israel*. Minneapolis: Fortress, 1997.

Blenkinsopp, Joseph. "Abraham as Paradigm in the Priestly History in Genesis." *Journal of Biblical Literature* 128 (2009): 225-41.

Block, Daniel I., and Noah J. Toly, eds. *Keeping God's Earth: The Global Environment in Biblical Perspective.* Downers Grove: InterVarsity, 2010.

Blum, Erhard. *Die Komposition der Vätergeschichte.* Wissenschaftliche Monographien zum Alten und Neuen Testament 57. Neukirchen-Vluyn: Neukirchener Verlag, 1984.

Bodner, Keith. *Jeroboam's Royal Drama.* Oxford: Oxford University Press, 2012.

Boer, Roland. *The Sacred Economy.* Louisville: Westminster John Knox, 2015.

Boff, Leonardo. *Cry of the Earth, Cry of the Poor.* Maryknoll: Orbis, 1997.

Boyarin, Daniel. *A Radical Jew: Paul and the Politics of Identity.* Berkeley: University of California Press, 1994.

Boyarin, Daniel, and Jonathan Boyarin. "Diaspora: Generation and the Ground of Jewish Identity." In *Identities,* edited by K. Anthony Appiah and Henry Louis Gates, pp. 305-37. Chicago: University of Chicago Press, 1995.

Boyce, James. *1835: The Founding of Melbourne and the Conquest of Australia.* Melbourne: Black Inc., 2011.

Branch, Taylor. *Parting the Waters: America in the King Years, 1954-63.* New York: Simon & Schuster, 1988.

Brennan, Sean. "The Disregard for Legal Protections of Aboriginal Land Rights in Early South Australia." In *Coming to Terms: Aboriginal Title in South Australia,* edited by Shaun Berg, pp. 90-121. Kent Town, SA: Wakefield Press, 2010.

Bretherton, Luke. *Christianity and Contemporary Politics.* Oxford: Wiley-Blackwell, 2010.

———. "The Duty of Care to Refugees, Christian Cosmopolitanism, and the Hallowing of Bare Life." *Studies in Christian Ethics* 19 (2006): 39-61.

Brett, Mark G. "Abraham's 'Heretical' Imperative: A Response to Jacques Derrida." In *The Meanings We Choose: Hermeneutical Ethics, Indeterminacy and the Conflict of Interpretations,* edited by Charles Cosgrove, pp. 167-78. London: T&T Clark International, 2004.

———. *Biblical Criticism in Crisis?* Cambridge: Cambridge University Press, 1991.

———. *Decolonizing God: The Bible in the Tides of Empire.* Sheffield: Phoenix, 2008.

———. "Diaspora and Kenosis as Postcolonial Themes." In *Decolonizing the Body of Christ: An Interdisciplinary Conversation,* edited by David Joy and Joseph Duggan, pp. 127-40. London: Palgrave, 2012.

———. "Feeling for Country: Reading the Old Testament in the Australian Context." *Pacifica* (2010): 137-56.

———. "Four or Five Things to Do with Texts: A Taxonomy of Interpretative Interests." In *The Bible in Three Dimensions,* edited by David J. A. Clines, Stephen E. Fowl, and Stanley E. Porter, pp. 357-77. Sheffield: JSOT Press, 1990.

———. "The Future of Old Testament Theology." In *IOSOT Congress Volume: Oslo,* edited by André Lemaire and Magne Sæbø, pp. 465-88. Vetus Testamentum Supplements 80. Leiden: E. J. Brill, 2000. Reprinted in *Old Testament Theology: Flowering and Future,* edited by Ben C. Ollenburger, pp. 481-94. Winona Lake: Eisenbrauns, 2004.

———. "Genocide in Deuteronomy: Postcolonial Variations on Mimetic Desire." In *Seeing Signals, Reading Signs,* edited by Mark O'Brien and Howard N. Wallace, pp. 76-90. London: Continuum, 2004.

————. "Interpreting Ethnicity: Method, Hermeneutics, Ethics." In *Ethnicity and the Bible*, edited by Mark G. Brett, pp. 16-21. Leiden: E. J. Brill, 1996.

————. "Israel's Indigenous Origins: Cultural Hybridity and the Formation of Israelite Ethnicity." *Biblical Interpretation* 11 (2003): 400-412.

————. "Motives and Intentions in Genesis 1." *Journal of Theological Studies* 42 (1991): 1-16.

————. "Narrative Deliberation in Biblical Politics." In *The Oxford Handbook of Biblical Narrative*, edited by Danna Nolen Fewell, pp. 540-49. New York: Oxford University Press, 2016.

————. "National Identity as Commentary and as Metacommentary." In *Historiography and Identity (Re)formulation in Second Temple Historiographical Literature*, edited Louis Jonker, pp. 29-40. Library of the Hebrew Bible / Old Testament Series 534. London: Continuum, 2010.

————. "Nationalism and the Hebrew Bible." In *The Bible in Ethics*, edited by John W. Rogerson, Margaret Davies, and Mark Daniel Carroll R., pp. 136-63. *JSOT* Supplement Series 207. Sheffield: JSOT Press, 1995.

————. "Natives and Immigrants in the Social Imagination of the Holiness School." In *Imagining the Other and Constructing Israelite Identity in the Early Second Temple Period*, edited by Ehud Ben Zvi and Diana Edelman, pp. 89-104. Library of Hebrew Bible/ Old Testament Studies 456. London: T & T Clark, 2014.

————. "Permutations of Sovereignty in the Priestly Tradition." *Vetus Testamentum* 63 (2013): 383-92.

————. "Sovereignty and Treaty in Religious Imagination." In *Sacred Australia: Post-Secular Considerations*, edited by Makarand Paranjape, pp. 96-118. Melbourne: Clouds of Magellan, 2009.

————. "Unequal Terms: A Postcolonial Approach to Isaiah 61." In *Biblical Interpretation and Method: Essays in Honour of Professor John Barton*, edited by Katharine J. Dell and Paul M. Joyce, pp. 243-56. Oxford: Oxford University Press, 2013.

Brett, Mark G., and Jione Havea, eds. *Colonial Contexts and Postcolonial Theology: Story-weaving in the Asia-Pacific.* New York: Palgrave Macmillan, 2014.

Briant, Pierre. *From Cyrus to Alexander: A History of the Persian Empire.* Winona Lake, Ind.: Eisenbrauns, 2002.

Briggs, Richard. *Words in Action: Speech Act Theory and Biblical Interpretation.* Edinburgh: T & T Clark, 2001.

Broome, Richard. *Aboriginal Australians: A History since 1788.* 4th ed. Crows Nest: Allen & Unwin, 2010.

Brown, William P. *The Seven Pillars of Creation: The Bible, Science, and the Ecology of Wonder.* Oxford: Oxford University Press, 2010.

Brueggemann, Walter. *David's Truth in Israel's Imagination and Memory.* 2nd ed. Minneapolis: Fortress, 2002.

————. *Divine Presence and Violence: Contextualizing the Book of Joshua.* Eugene: Cascade, 2009.

————. *Theology of the Old Testament: Testimony, Dispute, Advocacy.* Minneapolis: Fortress, 1997.

―――. "Unity and Dynamic in the Isaiah Tradition." *Journal for the Study of the Old Testament* 29 (1984): 89-107.

Buber, Martin. *The Prophetic Faith.* Translated by Carlyle Witton-Davies. New York: Macmillan, 1949.

Buchanan, Allen, and Margaret Moore. *States, Nations, and Borders: The Ethics of Making Boundaries.* Cambridge: Cambridge University Press, 2003.

Bultmann, Christoph. *Der Fremde im antiken Juda: Eine Untersuchung zum sozialen Typenbegriff 'ger' und seinem Bedeutungswandel in der alttestamentlichen Gesetzgebung.* Forschungen zur Religion und Literatur des Alten und Neuen Testaments 153. Göttingen: Vandenhoeck & Ruprecht, 1992.

Bunimovitz, Shlomo, and Zvi Lederman. "A Border Case: Beth-Shemesh and the Rise of Ancient Israel." In *Israel in Transition: From Late Bronze II to Iron IIa (c. 1250-850)*, Vol. I, *The Archaeology*, edited by Lester L. Grabbe, pp. 21-31. Library of Hebrew Bible / Old Testament Studies 491. London: T&T Clark, 2008.

Burbank, Jane, and Frederick Cooper. *Empires in World History: Power and the Politics of Difference.* Princeton: Princeton University Press, 2010.

Burke, Aaron A. "An Anthropological Model for the Investigation of the Archaeology of Refugees in Iron Age Judah and Its Environs." In *Interpreting Exile: Displacement and Deportation in Biblical and Modern Contexts*, edited by Brad E. Kelle, Frank R. Ames, and Jacob L. Wright, pp. 41-56. Society of Biblical Literature Ancient Israel and Its Literature 10. Atlanta: SBL, 2011.

Butler, Judith, Jürgen Habermas, Charles Taylor, and Cornel West. *The Power of Religion in the Public Sphere.* New York: Columbia University Press, 2011.

Byrne, Brendan. "Creation Groaning: An Earth Bible Reading of Romans 8.18-22." In *Readings from the Perspective of Earth*, edited by Norman C. Habel, pp. 193-203. The Earth Bible 1. Sheffield: Sheffield Academic Press, 2000.

Cadwallader, Alan. *Beyond the Word of a Woman: Recovering the Bodies of the Syrophoenician Women.* Adelaide: ATF Press, 2008.

Calhoun, Craig, Eduardo Mendieta, and Jonathan VanAntwerpen, eds. *Habermas and Religion.* Cambridge, UK: Polity Press, 2013.

Callahan, Allen Dwight. *The Talking Book: African Americans and the Bible.* New Haven: Yale University Press, 2006.

Carr, Wylie, Michael Patterson, Laurie Yung, and Daniel Spencer. "The Faithful Skeptics: Evangelical Religious Beliefs and Perceptions of Climate Change." *Journal for the Study of Religion, Nature and Culture* 6.3 (2012): 276-99.

Carroll, M. Daniel. *Christians at the Border: Immigration, the Church, and the Bible*, 2nd ed. Grand Rapids: Brazos, 2013.

Cartwright, Michael G., and Peter Ochs, eds. *The Jewish-Christian Schism Revisited: John Howard Yoder.* Grand Rapids: Eerdmans, 2003.

Casanova, José. "Exploring the Postsecular: Three Meanings of 'the Secular' and Their Possible Transcendence." In *Habermas and Religion*, edited by Craig Calhoun, Eduardo Mendieta, and Jonathan VanAntwerpen, pp. 27-48. Cambridge, UK: Polity, 2013.

Casas, Bartolomé de las. *The Only Way to Draw All People to a Living Faith*, edited by Helen Rand. New York: Paulist, 1992.

Cavanaugh, William T. *Migrations of the Holy: God, State, and the Political Meaning of the Church*. Grand Rapids: Eerdmans, 2011.

Chalmers, Thomas. *On Political Economy: In Connection with the Moral State and Moral Prospects of Society*. Glasgow: Collins, 1832.

———. *On the Power, Wisdom and Goodness of God Manifested in the Adaption of External Nature to the Moral and Intellectual Constitution of Man*. Philadelphia: Carey, Lea and Blanchard, 1833.

Chamerovzow, Louis A. *The New Zealand Question and the Rights of Aborigines*. London: T. C. Newby, 1848.

Chapman, Siobhan. *Pragmatics*. Basingstoke: Palgrave Macmillan, 2011.

Chartrand, Paul L. A. H. "Reconciling Indigenous Peoples' Sovereignty and State Sovereignty." *Australian Institute of Aboriginal and Torres Strait Islander Studies Research Discussion Paper 26*, September 2009, available at http://www.aiatsis.gov.au/research/discussion.html.

Chatterjee, Partha. *The Nation and Its Fragments: Colonial and Postcolonial Histories*. Princeton: Princeton University Press, 1993.

Chesterman, John, and Brian Galligan, eds. *Citizens without Rights: Aborigines and Australian Citizenship*. Melbourne: Cambridge University Press, 1997.

Clarkson, Thomas. *A Portraiture of Quakerism*. London: Longman, Hurst, Rees and Orme, 1806.

Clayton, Lawrence A. *Bartolomé de Las Casas and the Conquest of the Americas*. Oxford: Wiley-Blackwell, 2011.

Clines, David J. A. *Job 1-20*. Word Biblical Commentary 17. Dallas: Word, 1989.

Coakley, Sarah. "Kenosis and Subversion: On the Repression of 'Vulnerability' in Christian Feminist Writing." In *Swallowing a Fishbone?*, edited by Daphne Hampson, pp. 82-111. London: SPCK, 1996.

———. *Powers and Submissions: Spirituality, Philosophy and Gender*. Oxford: Blackwell, 2002.

Cody, Aelred. "When Is the Chosen People called a Goy?" *Vetus Testamentum* 14 (1964): 1-6.

Cohen, Jean L. *Globalization and Sovereignty: Rethinking Legality, Legitimacy, and Constitutionalism*. Cambridge: Cambridge University Press, 2012.

Conversi, Daniele. "Conceptualizing Nationalism: An Introduction to Walker Connor's Work." In *Ethnonationalism in the Contemporary World: Walker Connor and the Study of Nationalism*, edited by Conversi, pp. 1-23. London: Routledge, 2002.

Cooper, David. *Closing the Gap in Cultural Understanding: Social Determinants of Health and Indigenous Policy in Australia*. Darwin: Aboriginal Medical Services Alliance NT, 2011.

Cortés, Ernesto. "Reweaving the Social Fabric." *Boston Review* (June-September 1994): 12-14.

Cosgrove, Charles. "Towards a Postmodern Hermeneutical Sacra." In *The Meanings We Choose: Hermeneutical Ethics, Indeterminacy and the Conflict of Interpretations*, edited by Charles H. Cosgrove, pp. 39-61. London: T & T Clark, 2004.

Cruse, Alan. *Meaning in Language: An Introduction to Semantics and Pragmatics.* Oxford: Oxford University Press, 2011.

Crüsemann, Frank. *The Torah: Theology and Social History of Old Testament Law.* Edinburgh: T. & T. Clark, 1996.

Curthoys, Ann. "Expulsion, Exodus and Exile in White Australian Mythology." *Journal of Australian Studies* (1999): 1-18.

Dale, Gareth. *Karl Polanyi: The Limits of the Market.* Cambridge: Polity, 2010.

Davenport, Stewart. *Friends of the Unrighteous Mammon: Northern Christians and Market Capitalism, 1815-1860.* Chicago: University of Chicago Press, 2008.

Davis, Ellen. *Scripture, Culture, and Agriculture: An Agrarian Reading of the Bible.* Cambridge: Cambridge University Press, 2009.

Davison, Graeme. "Narrating the Nation in Australia." Menzies Lecture, Menzies Centre for Australian Studies, King's College, London, 2009.

Deane-Drummond, Celia, and Heinrich Bedford-Strohm, eds. *Religion and Ecology in the Public Sphere.* London: T&T Clark International, 2011.

De Guglielmo, Antonine. "Job 12:7-9 and the Knowability of God." *Catholic Biblical Quarterly* 6 (1944): 478-79.

Dell, Katherine. "Plumbing the Depths of Earth: Job 28 and Deep Ecology." In *The Earth Story in Wisdom Traditions*, edited by Norman C. Habel and Shirley Wurst, pp. 116-25. Earth Bible 3. Sheffield: Sheffield Academic Press, 2001.

Derrida, Jacques. *On Cosmopolitanism and Forgiveness.* Translated by Mark Dooley and Michael Hughes. New York: Routledge, 2001.

Dever, William. *The Lives of Ordinary People in Ancient Israel: Where Archaeology and the Bible Intersect.* Grand Rapids: Eerdmans, 2012.

―――. *Who Were the Early Israelites, and Where Did They Come From?* Grand Rapids: Eerdmans, 2003.

Dodson, Michael. "Aboriginal and Torres Strait Islander People and Citizenship." Address delivered at the Complex Notions of Civic Identity Conference, University of New South Wales, 20 August 1993. Available at http://www.humanrights.gov.au/news/speeches/aboriginal-and-torres-strait-islander-people-and-citizenship-dodson-1993.

Dodson, Patrick. "Can Australia Afford Not to Be Reconciled?" Keynote address, National Indigenous Policy and Dialogue Conference, November 19, 2010. Available at http://www.recognise.org.au/wp-content/uploads/shared/downloads/270300fa878ecc9be603.pdf.

Dodson, Patrick L., Jacinta K. Elston, and Brian F. McCoy, "Leaving Culture at the Door: Aboriginal Perspectives on Christian Belief and Practice." *Pacifica* 19 (2006): 249-62.

Dozeman,Thomas B., Konrad Schmid, and Baruch J. Schwartz, eds. *The Pentateuch: International Perspectives on Current Research.* Forschungen zum Alten Testament 78. Tübingen: Mohr Siebeck, 2011.

Dwyer, Susan. "Reconciliation for Realists." *Ethics and International Affairs* 13 (1999): 81-98.

Dymond, Jonathan. *Essays on the Principles of Morality and on the Private and Political Rights and Obligations of Mankind.* 2 vols. London: Hamilton, Adams and Co., 1829.

Ebach, Jürgen. *Streiten mit Gott. Hiob*, Part 1: *Hiob 1-20*. Neukirchen-Vluyn: Neukirchener Verlag, 1996.

Echo-Hawk, Walter R. "Colonialism and Law in the Postcolonial Era." In *Coming to Terms: Aboriginal Title in South Australia*, edited by Shaun Berg, pp. 148-205. Kent Town: Wakefield Press, 2010.

Eco, Umberto. "Overinterpreting Texts." In *Interpretation and Overinterpretation*, edited by S. Collini, pp. 45-66. Cambridge: Cambridge University Press, 1992.

Elvey, Anne. "Can There Be a Forgiveness That Makes a Difference Ecologically? An Eco-Materialist Account of Forgiveness as Freedom ('aphesis) in the Gospel of Luke." *Pacifica* 22 (2009): 148-70.

Emerson, Michael O., and Christian Smith. *Divided by Faith: Evangelical Religion and the Problem of Race in America*. New York: Oxford University Press, 2000.

Eriksen, Thomas H. *Ethnicity and Nationalism: Anthropological Perspectives*. 3rd ed. London: Pluto, 2010.

Farndon, John. *China Rises: How China's Astonishing Growth Will Change the World*. London: Virgin Books, 2007.

Faust, Avraham. *Israel's Ethnogenesis: Settlement, Interaction, Expansion and Resistance*. London: Equinox, 2006.

Finkelstein, Israel. "The Settlement History of Jerusalem in the Eighth and Seventh Centuries BC." *Revue Biblique* 115 (2008): 499-515.

Finn, Daniel K., ed. *The Moral Dynamics of Moral Life: An Extension and Critique of Caritas in Veritate*. Oxford: Oxford University Press, 2012.

———, ed. *The True Wealth of Nations: Catholic Social Thought and Economic Life*. Oxford: Oxford University Press, 2010.

Fischer, Irmtraud. "World Peace and Holy War — Two Sides of the Same Theological Concept: YHWH as Sole Divine Power. A Canonical-Intertextual Reading of Isaiah 2:1-5, Joel 4:9-21 and Micah 4:1-5." In *Isaiah's Vision of Peace in Biblical and Modern International Relations*, edited by Raymond Cohen and Raymond Westbrook, pp. 151-65. New York: Palgrave Macmillan, 2008.

Fitzmaurice, Andrew. "Anticolonialism in Western Political Thought: The Colonial Origins of the Concept of Genocide." In *Empire, Colony, Genocide: Conquest, Occupation and Subaltern Resistance in World History*, edited by A. Dirk Moses, pp. 55-80. New York: Bergham, 2008.

Fleischacker, Samuel. *A Short History of Distributive Justice*. Cambridge: Harvard University Press, 2004.

Fleming, Daniel E. *The Legacy of Israel in Judah's Bible: History, Politics and the Reinscribing of Tradition*. Cambridge, Mass.: Cambridge University Press, 2012.

Ford, Lisa. *Settler Sovereignty: Jurisdiction and Indigenous People in America and Australia, 1788–1836*. Cambridge, Mass.: Harvard University Press, 2010.

Fowl, Stephen E. *Engaging Scripture*. Oxford: Blackwell, 1998.

Fretheim, Terence E. *Creation Untamed: The Bible, God, and Natural Disasters*. Grand Rapids: Baker, 2010.

Geertz, Clifford. *The Interpretation of Cultures*. New York: Basic Books, 1973.

Getzler, Joshua. "Roman Ideas of Land Ownership." In *Land Law*, edited by. S. Bright and J. Dewar, pp. 81-106. Oxford: Oxford University Press, 1988.

Gibbs, Robert. *Correlations in Rosenzweig and Levinas*. Princeton: Princeton University Press, 1992.

Goldenberg, David M. *The Curse of Ham: Race and Slavery in Early Judaism, Christianity, and Islam*. Princeton: Princeton University Press, 2003.

Gondarra, Djiniyini. "Overcoming the Captivities of the Western Church Context." In *The Cultured Pearl: Australian Readings in Cross-Cultural Theology and Mission*, edited by Jim Houston. Melbourne: Joint Board of Christian Education, 1988.

Gordis, Robert. *The Book of Job*. New York: Jewish Theological Seminary of America, 1978.

Gorman, Michael. *Inhabiting the Cruciform God: Kenosis, Justification, and Theosis in Paul's Soteriology*. Grand Rapids: Eerdmans, 2009.

Gorringe, Timothy. *Capital and the Kingdom: Theological Ethics and Economic Order*. Maryknoll, NY: Orbis, 1994.

Goswami, Manu. *Producing India: From Colonial Economy to National Space*. Chicago: University of Chicago Press, 2004.

Gotsis, George, and Sarah Drakopoulou-Dodd. "Economic Ideas in the Pauline Epistles of the New Testament." *History of Economics Review* 3 (2002): 13-34.

Gowan, Donald. *Eschatology in the Old Testament*. Edinburgh: T&T Clark, 1986.

Grattan, Michelle, ed. *Essays on Australian Reconciliation*. Melbourne: Bookman, 2000.

Green, Joel B. *Body, Soul, and Human Life: The Nature of Humanity in the Bible*. Grand Rapids: Baker, 2008.

Greenfeld, Liah. *Nationalism: Five Roads to Modernity*. Cambridge, Mass.: Harvard University Press, 1992.

Grotius, Hugo. *The Rights of War and Peace, Including the Law of Nature and of Nations*. Translated by A. C. Campbell. Pontefract: B. Boothroyd, 1814.

Guillaume, Philippe. *Land and Calendar: The Priestly Document from Genesis 1 to Joshua 18*. Library of Hebrew Bible / Old Testament Studies 391; New York: T&T Clark, 2009.

———. *Land, Credit and Crisis: Agrarian Finance in the Hebrew Bible*. Sheffield: Equinox, 2012.

Gutiérrez, Gustavo. *A Theology of Liberation*. Translated by Caridad Inda and John Eagleson. Maryknoll: Orbis, 1973.

Habel, Norman. "The Implications of God Discovering Wisdom in Earth." In *Job 28: Cognition in Context*, edited by Ellen van Wolde, pp. 281-98. Biblical Interpretation Series 64. Leiden: Brill, 2003.

Habermas, Jürgen. *Between Naturalism and Religion*. Translated by Ciaran Cronin. Cambridge: Polity, 2008.

———. "Interview with J. M. Ferry." *Philosophy and Social Criticism* 14 (1988): 436.

———. "On the Relation between the Secular Liberal State and Religion." In *The Frankfurt School on Religion*, edited by Eduardo Mendieta, pp. 337-46. New York: Routledge, 2004.

———. "Religion in the Public Sphere." *European Journal of Philosophy* 14 (2006): 1-25.

————. *The Theory of Communicative Action*. Volume 2: *Lifeworld and System*. Boston: Beacon, 1984.

Habermas, Jürgen, et al. *An Awareness of What Is Missing: Faith and Reason in a Post-secular Age*. Translated by Ciaran Cronin. Cambridge: Polity, 2010.

Habermas, Jürgen, and Joseph Ratzinger. *The Dialectics of Secularization: On Reason and Religion*. Translated by B. McNeil. San Francisco: Ignatius Press, 2006.

Hagedorn, Anselm C. "Local Law in an Imperial Context: The Role of Torah in the (Imagined) Persian Period." In *The Pentateuch as Torah: New Models for Understanding Its Promulgation and Acceptance*, edited by Gary N. Knoppers and Bernard M. Levinson, pp. 57-76. Winona Lake, Ind.: Eisenbrauns, 2007.

Halpern, Baruch H. *From Gods to God: The Dynamics of Iron Age Cosmologies*. Forschungen zum Alten Testament 63. Tübingen: Mohr Siebeck, 2009.

Hardt, Michael, and Antonio Negri. *Empire*. Cambridge: Harvard University Press, 2000.

Harper, Ian, and Lachlan Smirl. "Usury." In *The Oxford Handbook of Christianity and Economics*, edited by Paul Oslington, pp. 564-80. Oxford: Oxford University Press, 2014.

Harrison, Peter. "Adam Smith and the History of the Invisible Hand." *Journal of the History of Ideas* 72 (2011): 29-49.

————. *The Bible, Protestantism, and the Rise of Natural Science*. New York: Cambridge University Press, 1998.

————. "The Development of the Concept of Law of Nature." In *Creation: Law and Probability*, edited by Fraser Watts, pp. 13-35. Minneapolis: Fortress, 2008.

————. *The Fall of Man and the Foundations of Science*. Cambridge University Press, 2007.

————. "'Fill the Earth and Subdue It': Biblical Warrants for Colonization in Seventeenth Century England." *Journal of Religious History* 29/1 (2005): 3-24.

Harvey, David. *A Brief History of Neoliberalism*. Oxford: Oxford University Press, 2005.

Hauerwas, Stanley. *After Christendom? How the Church Is to Behave If Freedom, Justice, and a Christian Nation Are Bad Ideas*. Nashville: Abingdon, 1991.

Hauerwas, Stanley, and D. Stephen Long. "Interpreting the Bible as a Political Act." *Religion and Intellectual Life* 9 (1989): 134-42.

Havea, Jione. "Opening Borders, for Diaspora Is Home." In *Climate Change, Culture Change: Religious Responses and Responsibilities*, edited by Anne Elvey and David Gormley-O'Brien, pp. 65-77. Melbourne: Mosaic, 2013.

Hawk, L. Daniel. "Conquest Reconfigured: Recasting Warfare in the Redaction of Joshua." In *Writing and Reading War: Rhetoric, Gender, and Ethics in Biblical and Modern Contexts*, edited by Brad E. Kelle and Frank R. Ames, pp. 145-60. Society of Biblical Literature Symposium Studies 42. Atlanta: SBL, 2008.

————. *Every Promise Fulfilled: Contesting Plots in Joshua*. Louisville: Westminster/John Knox, 1991.

Hazlehurst, Kayleen M., ed. *Legal Pluralism and the Colonial Legacy*. Aldershot: Avebury, 1995.

Hazony, Yoram. *The Philosophy of Hebrew Scripture*. Cambridge: Cambridge University Press, 2012.

Heckler, Serena, ed. *Landscape, Process and Power: Re-evaluating Traditional Environmental Knowledge*. New York: Berghan Books, 2009.

Heimert, Alan, and Andrew Delbanco. *The Puritans in America: A Narrative Anthology*. Cambridge, Mass.: Harvard University Press, 2005.

Heinrichs, Steve, ed. *Buffalo Shout, Salmon Cry: Conversations on Creation, Land Justice and Life Together*. Waterloo: Herald Press, 2013.

Held, David. "Principles of Cosmopolitan Order." In *The Political Philosophy of Cosmopolitanism*, edited by Gillian Brock and Harry Brighouse, pp. 10-27. Cambridge: Cambridge University Press, 2005.

Heller, Agnes. "European Master Narratives about Freedom." In *Handbook of Contemporary European Social Theory*, edited by Gerard Delanty, pp. 257-65. London: Routledge, 2006.

Hepburn, Samantha. "Disinterested Truth: Legitimation of the Doctrine of Tenure post-Mabo." *Melbourne University Law Review* 29 (2005): 1-38.

———. "Feudal Tenure and Native Title: Revising an Enduring Fiction." *Sydney Law Review* 27/1 (2005): 49-86.

Herman, Judith. *Trauma and Recovery: The Aftermath of Violence from Domestic Abuse to Political Terror*. 2nd ed. New York: Basic Books, 1997.

Herzfeld, Michael. *Anthropology: Theoretical Practice in Culture and Society*. Malden, Mass.: Blackwell, 2001.

Heyne, Paul. "The Concept of Economic Justice in Religious Discussion." In *Morality of the Market: Religious and Economic Perspectives*, edited by Walter Block, Geoffrey Brennan, and Kenneth Elzinga, pp. 463-82. Vancouver: The Fraser Institute, 1985.

Hilton, Boyd. *The Age of Atonement: The Influence of Evangelicalism on Social and Economic Thought, 1785-1965*. Oxford: Oxford University Press, 1988.

Hirsch, E. D. "Meaning and Significance Reinterpreted." *Critical Inquiry* 11 (1984): 202-25.

Hirshman, Albert O. *The Passions and the Interests: Political Arguments for Capitalism before Its Triumph*. Princeton: Princeton University Press, 1977.

Hobbs, T. Raymond. "Hospitality in the First Testament and the 'Teleological Fallacy.'" *Journal for the Study of the Old Testament* 95 (2001): 3-30.

Hoffmeier, James K. *The Immigration Crisis: Immigrants, Aliens and the Bible*. Wheaton: Crossway, 2009.

Hogan, Linda. "A Different Mode of Encounter: Egalitarian Liberalism and the Christian Tradition." *Political Theology* 7/1 (2006): 59-73.

Honneth, Axel. "The Other of Justice: Habermas and the Ethical Challenge of Postmodernism." In *The Cambridge Companion to Habermas*, edited by Stephen K. White, pp. 289-323. Cambridge: Cambridge University Press, 1995.

Hopkins, Rob. *Localisation and Resilience at the Local Level: The Case of Transition Town Totnes*. PhD Thesis. Devon: University of Plymouth, 2010.

Horrell, David. *Solidarity and Difference: A Contemporary Reading of Paul's Ethics*. London: T & T Clark International, 2005.

Horsley, Richard, ed. *Paul and Empire: Religion and Power in Roman Imperial Society*. Harrisburg: Trinity Press International, 1997.

Horsley, Richard A. *Covenant Economics: A Biblical Vision of Justice for All.* Louisville: Westminster John Knox, 2009.

Houston, Walter J. *Contending for Justice: Ideologies and Theologies of Social Justice in the Old Testament.* 2nd ed. London: T&T Clark, 2008.

Huang, Yan. *Pragmatics.* Oxford: Oxford University Press, 2007.

Hudson, Michael. "The Archaeology of Money: Debt Versus Barter Theories of Money's Origins." In *Credit and State Theories of Money: The Contributions of A. Mitchell Innes,* edited by L. Randall Wray, pp. 99-127. Cheltenham: Edward Elgar, 2004.

————. "Debt Forgiveness and Redemption: Where Do the Churches Now Stand?" *Geophilos* 2 (2002): 8-33.

————. "How Interest Rates Were Set, 2500 BC–1000 AD." *Journal of the Economic and Social History of the Orient* 43 (2000): 132-61.

Hudson, Michael, and Baruch Levine, eds. *Privatization in the Ancient Near East and Classical World.* Cambridge, Mass.: Peabody Museum of Archaeology and Ethnology, 1996.

————. *Urbanization and Land Ownership in the Ancient Near East.* Cambridge, Mass.: Peabody Museum of Archaeology and Ethnology, 2000.

Human Rights and Equal Opportunity Commission, *Bringing Them Home: Report of the National Inquiry into the Separation of Aboriginal and Torres Strait Islander Children from Their Families.* Sydney: HREOC, 1997.

Huscroft, Grant, and Bradley W. Miller, eds. *The Challenge of Originalism: Theories of Constitutional Interpretation.* New York: Cambridge University Press, 2011.

Huston, James L. *Securing the Fruits of Labor: The American Concept of Wealth Distribution, 1765–1900.* Baton Rouge: Louisiana State University Press, 1998.

Ignatief, Michael. *The Needs of Strangers.* London: Vintage, 1984.

Jackson, Timothy. *Prosperity without Growth: Economics for a Finite Planet.* London: Routledge, 2011.

Jacobs, Mignon. "Parameters of Justice: Ideological Challenges regarding Persons and Practices in Leviticus 25:25-55." *Ex Auditu* 22 (2006): 133-158.

Janzen, J. Gerald. "On the Moral Nature of God's Power: Yahweh and the Sea in Job and Deutero-Isaiah." *Catholic Biblical Quarterly* 56 (1994): 458-78.

Japhet, Sara. *From the Rivers of Babylon to the Highlands of Judah.* Winona Lake, Ind.: Eisenbrauns, 2006.

————. "Periodization between History and Ideology II: Chronology and Ideology in Ezra-Nehemiah." In *Judah and the Judeans in the Persian Period,* edited by Oded Lipschits and Manfred Oeming, pp. 491-508. Winona Lake, Ind.: Eisenbrauns, 2006.

————. "Theodicy in Ezra-Nehemiah and Chronicles." In *Theodicy in the World of the Bible,* edited by Antii Laato and Johannes C. de Moor, pp. 429-69. Leiden: Brill, 2004.

Jennings, Willie James. *The Christian Imagination: Theology and the Origins of Race.* New Haven: Yale, 2010.

Johnson, Elizabeth. *She Who Is: The Mystery of God in Feminist Theological Discourse.* New York: Crossroad, 1993.

Jones, Gareth Stedman. *An End to Poverty? A Historical Debate.* London: Profile, 2004.

Joosten, Jan. *People and Land in the Holiness Code: An Exegetical Study of the Ideational*

Framework of the Law in Leviticus 17–26. Vetus Testamentum Supplements 67. Leiden: Brill, 1996.

Kang, Namsoon. "Toward a Cosmopolitan Theology: Constructing Public Theology from the Future." In *Planetary Loves: Spivak, Postcoloniality and Theology*, edited by Stephen D. Moore and Mayra Rivera, pp. 258-80. New York: Fordham University Press, 2011.

Kant, Immanuel. "Perpetual Peace: A Philosophical Sketch." In *Kant's Political Writings*, ed. H. Reiss. Cambridge: Cambridge University Press, 1971.

Kaplan, Ida. *Rebuilding Shattered Lives*. Parkville: Victorian Foundation for Survivors of Torture Inc., 1998.

Kaplan, Jonathan. "1 Samuel 8:11-18 as 'A Mirror for Princes.'" *Journal of Biblical Literature* 131 (2012): 625-42.

Keith, Michael, and Steve Pile. *Place and the Politics of Identity*. New York: Routledge, 1993.

Kelle, Brad E., Frank R. Ames, and Jacob L. Wright, eds. *Interpreting Exile: Displacement and Deportation in Biblical and Modern Contexts*. Society of Biblical Literature Ancient Israel and Its Literature, 10. Atlanta: SBL, 2011.

Keller, Catherine. *God and Power: Counter-Apocalyptic Journeys*. Minneapolis: Fortress, 2005.

Kenny, Robert. *The Lamb Enters the Dreaming: Nathanael Pepper and the Ruptured World*. Melbourne: Scribe, 2007.

Kesby, Alison. "The Shifting and Multiple Border and International Law." *Oxford Journal of Legal Studies* 21 (2007): 101-19.

Knaplund, Paul. *James Stephen and the British Colonial System, 1813-1847*. Madison: University of Wisconsin Press, 1953.

Knauf, Ernst A. "Grenzen der Toleranz in der Priesterschaft." *Bibel und Kirche* 58 (2003): 224-27.

Knohl, Israel. *The Sanctuary of Silence: The Priestly Torah and the Holiness School*. Minneapolis: Fortress, 1995.

Köckert, Manfred. "Das Land in der priesterlichen Komposition des Pentateuch." Pp. 147-62 in *Von Gott reden: Beiträge zur Theologie und Exegese des Alten Testaments*. Festschrift für Siegfried Wagner. Edited by Dieter Viewege and Ernst-Joachim Waschke. Neukirchen-Vluyn: Neukirchener Verlag, 1995.

Kolb, Robert W. *Sovereign Debt: From Safety to Default*. Hoboken, NJ: John Wiley & Sons, 2011.

Koole, Jan L. *Isaiah: Part III*. Translated by Anthony P. Runia. Historical Commentary on the Old Testament. Leuven: Peeters, 2001.

Kraemer, Joel L. "The Jihad of the Falasifa." *Jerusalem Studies in Arabic and Islam* 10 (1987): 288-324.

Kristeva, Julia. *New Maladies of the Soul*. New York: Columbia University Press, 1995.

Küng, Hans, and Jürgen Moltmann, eds. *The Ethics of World Religions and Human Rights*. London: SCM, 1990.

LaCocque, André. *The Trial of Innocence: Adam, Eve, and the Yahwist*. Eugene, Ore.: Cascade, 2006.

Lake, Marilyn, and Henry Reynolds. *Drawing the Global Colour Line: White Men's Countries and the Question of Racial Equality.* Melbourne: Melbourne University Press, 2008.

Lamey, Andy. *Frontier Justice: The Global Refugee Crisis and What to Do about It.* St Lucia: University of Queensland Press, 2011.

Langton, Marcia, Maureen Tehan, Lisa Palmer, Kathryn Shain, eds. *Settling with Indigenous People: Modern Treaty and Agreement-making.* Sydney: The Federation Press, 2006.

Levenson, Jon D. "Is There a Counterpart in the Hebrew Bible to New Testament Antisemitism?" *Journal of Ecumenical Studies* 22 (1985): 242-60.

———. "The Sources of the Torah: Psalm 119 and the Modes of Revelation in Second Temple Judaism." In *Ancient Israelite Religion: Essays in Honor of Frank Moore Cross,* edited by Patrick D. Miller, Paul D. Hanson and Sean D. McBride, pp. 559-74. Philadelphia: Fortress, 1987.

———. "The Temple and the World." *Journal of Religion* 64 (1984): 275-98.

———. "The Universal Horizon of Biblical Particularism." In *Ethnicity and the Bible,* edited by Mark G. Brett, pp. 143–69. Biblical Interpretation Series 19. Leiden: Brill, 1996.

Levinas, Emmanuel. *Otherwise than Being, or, Beyond Essence.* Translated by Alphonso Lingis. Dordrecht: Kluwer, 1991.

Levinson, Bernard M. *Deuteronomy and the Hermeneutics of Legal Innovation.* Oxford: Oxford University Press, 1998.

———. "The First Constitution: Rethinking the Origins of Rule of Law and Separation of Powers in Light of Deuteronomy." *Cardozo Law Review* 27 (2006): 1853-88.

———. *Legal Revision and Religious Renewal in Ancient Israel.* Cambridge: Cambridge University Press, 2008.

Levinson, Stephen C. *Pragmatics.* Cambridge: Cambridge University Press, 1983.

Lewis, Bernard. *Race and Slavery in the Middle East.* New York: Oxford University Press, 1990.

Lewis, Peter. *Acting in Solidarity? The Church's Journey with the Indigenous Peoples of Australia.* Melbourne: Uniting Academic Press, 2010.

———. "Terra Nullius Amnesiacs: A Theological Analysis of the Persistence of Colonisation in the Australian Context and the Blocks to Real Reconciliation." In *Colonial Contexts and Postcolonial Theology: Storyweaving in the Asia-Pacific,* edited by Mark G. Brett and Jione Havea, pp. 181-99. New York: Palgrave Macmillan, 2014.

Liedke, Gerhard. "שפט to judge." In *Theological Lexicon of the Old Testament,* vol. 3, ed. Ernst Jenni and Claus Westermann. Translated by Mark E. Biddle, pp. 1392-99. Peabody, Mass.: Hendrickson, 1997.

Lindbeck, George. "Postcritical Canonical Interpretation: Three Modes of Retrieval." In *Theological Exegesis: Essays in Honor of Brevard S. Childs,* edited by Christopher Seitz and Kathryn Greene-McCreight, pp. 26-51. Grand Rapids: Eerdmans, 1990.

Lipschits, Oded. "Achaemenid Imperial Policy, Settlement Processes in Palestine, and the Status of Jerusalem in the Middle of the Fifth Century BCE." In *Judah and the Judeans in the Persian Period,* edited by Oded Lipschits and Mandfred Oeming, pp. 19-52. Winona Lake, Ind.: Eisenbrauns, 2006.

————. "Demographic Changes in Judah between the Seventh and the Fifth Centuries BCE." In *Judah and the Judeans in the Neo-Babylonian Period*, edited by Oded Lipschits and Joseph Blenkinsopp, pp. 323-77. Winona Lake, Ind.: Eisenbrauns, 2003.

Lohfink, Norbert. "Opferzentralisation, Säkularisierungthese und mimetische Theorie." In *Studien zum Deuteronomium und zur deuteronomistischen Literatur III*, pp. 219-60. Stuttgarter biblische Aufsatzbände 20. Stuttgart: Katholisches Bibelwerk, 1995.

Long, D. Stephen. *Divine Economy: Theology and the Market*. London: Routledge, 2000.

Losonczi, Péter, and Aakash Sing, eds. *Discovering the Post-Secular: Essays on the Habermasian Post-Secular Turn*. Vienna: Lit Verlag, 2010.

Lyons, William John. *Canon and Exegesis: Canonical Praxis and the Sodom Narrative*. London: Sheffield Academic Press, 2002.

MacIntyre, Alasdair. *After Virtue*. Notre Dame: University of Notre Dame Press, 1981.

————. *Whose Justice? Which Rationality?* Notre Dame: University of Notre Dame Press, 1988.

Magowan, Fiona. *Melodies of Mourning: Music and Emotion in Northern Australia*. Crawley: University of Western Australia Press, 2007.

Mamdani, Mahmood. "Beyond Settler and Native as Political Identities: Overcoming the Political Legacy of Colonialism." *Comparative Studies in Society and History* 43/4 (2001): 651-64.

————. *When Victims Become Killers: Colonialism, Nativism, and the Genocide in Rwanda*. Princeton: Princeton University Press, 2001.

Manne, Robert, ed. *Whitewash: On Keith Windschuttle's Fabrication of Aboriginal History*. Melbourne: Black Inc., 2003.

Marlow, Hilary. *Biblical Prophets and Contemporary Environmental Ethics: Re-Reading Amos, Hosea, and First Isaiah*. Oxford: Oxford University Press, 2009.

Marr, David. *The High Price of Heaven*. St Leonards: Allen & Unwin, 1999.

Marshall, Christopher. *Beyond Retribution: A New Testament Vision for Justice, Crime and Punishment*. Grand Rapids: Eerdmans, 2001.

Marshall, I. Howard, Kevin J. Vanhoozer and Stanley E. Porter. *Beyond the Bible: Moving from Scripture to Theology*. Grand Rapids: Baker Academic, 2004.

Masalha, Nur. "Reading the Bible with the Eyes of the Canaanites: Neo-Zionism, Political Theology and the Land Traditions of the Bible." *Holy Land Studies* 8 (2009): 55-108.

McConville, J. Gordon. "'Fellow Citizens': Israel and Humanity in Leviticus." In *Reading the Law: Studies in Honour of Gordon J. Wenham*, edited by J. Gordon McConville and Karl Möller, pp. 10-32. Library of Hebrew Bible / Old Testament Studies 461. London: T&T Clark, 2007.

————. *God and Earthly Power: An Old Testament Political Theology*. London: T & T Clark, 2006.

————. "Law and Monarchy in the Old Testament." In *A Royal Priesthood? A Dialogue with Oliver O'Donovan*, edited by Craig Bartholomew, Jonathan Chaplin, Robert Song, Al Wolters, pp. 69-88. Scripture and Hermeneutics Series 3. Carlisle: Paternoster, 2002.

————. "Old Testament Laws and Canonical Intentionality." In *Canon and Biblical Interpretation,* edited by Craig G. Bartholomew Scott Hahn, Robin Parry, Christopher

Seitz and Al Wolters, pp. 259-81. Scripture and Hermeneutics Series 7. Milton Keynes: Paternoster, 2006.

McFague, Sallie. *Blessed Are the Consumers: Climate Change and the Practice of Restraint.* Minneapolis: Fortress, 2013.

McGrath, Alister E. *A Scientific Theology,* vol. 2. Grand Rapids: Eerdmans, 2002.

McKenna, Mark. "A History for Our Time? The Idea of the People in Australian Democracy." *History Compass* 1 (2003): 1-15.

McNeil, Kent. "Judicial Treatment of Indigenous Land Rights in the Common Law World." In *Indigenous Peoples and the Law: Comparative and Critical Perspectives,* edited by Benjamin J. Richardson, Shin Imai and Kent McNeil, pp. 257-58. Oxford: Hart, 2009.

McVicker, John. *Outlines of Political Economy.* New York: Wilder and Campbell, 1825.

Middleton, J. Richard. *The Liberating Image: The Imago Dei in Genesis 1.* Grand Rapids: Brazos Press, 2005.

Milbank, John. "The Midwinter Sacrifice." In *The Blackwell Companion to Postmodern Theology,* edited by Graham Ward, pp. 107-30. Oxford: Blackwell, 2001.

———. *Theology and Social Theory: Beyond Secular Reason.* Oxford: Blackwell, 1990.

———. *The World Made Strange: Theology, Language, Culture.* Oxford: Blackwell, 1977.

Milbank, John, Slavoj Žižek, and Creston Davis. *Paul's New Moment: Continental Philosophy and the Future of Christian Theology.* Grand Rapids: Brazos, 2010.

Milgrom, Jacob. *Leviticus 17–22.* Anchor Bible 3A. New York: Doubleday, 2000.

Miller, Robert, Jacinta Ruru, Larissa Behrendt, and Tracey Lindberg. *Discovering Indigenous Lands: The Doctrine of Discovery in the English Colonies.* Oxford: Oxford University Press, 2010.

Milstein, Sara J. "Expanding Ancient Narratives: Revision through Introduction in Biblical and Mesopotamian Texts." PhD dissertation. New York University, 2010.

Mitchell, Roger Haydon. *Church, Gospel and Empires: How the Politics of Sovereignty Impregnated the West.* Eugene, Ore.: Wipf & Stock, 2011.

Moellendorf, Darrel. "Persons' Interests, States' Duties, and Global Governance." In *The Political Philosophy of Cosmopolitanism,* edited by Gillian Brock and Harry Brighouse, pp. 148-63. Cambridge: Cambridge University Press, 2005.

Moltman, Jürgen. "God's Kenosis in the Creation and Consummation of the World." In *The Work of Love: Creation as Kenosis,* edited by John Polkinghorne, pp. 137-51. Grand Rapids: Eerdmans, 2001.

Monroe, A. S. "Israelite, Moabite and Sabaean War–ḥerem Traditions and the Forging of National Identity: Reconsidering the Sabaean Text RES 3945 in Light of Biblical and Moabite Evidence." *Vetus Testamentum* 57 (2007): 318-41.

Mooney, Harold A., and Paul R. Ehrlich. "Valuing Ecosystem Services: Philosophical Bases and Empirical Methods." In *Nature's Services: Societal Dependence on Natural Ecosystems,* edited by Gretchen C. Daily, pp. 23-48. Washington, DC: Island Press, 1997.

Moore, Stephen. "Paul after Empire." In *The Colonized Apostle: Paul through Postcolonial Eyes,* edited by Christopher D. Stanley, pp. 9-23. Minneapolis: Fortress, 2011.

Moore, Stephen D., and Mayra Rivera, eds. *Planetary Loves: Spivak, Postcoloniality and Theology.* New York: Fordham University Press, 2011.

Moores, Irene, ed. *Voices of Aboriginal Australia: Past, Present, Future.* Melbourne: Butterfly Books, Springwood, 1995.

Morrow, William. "'To Set the Name' in the Deuteronomic Centralization Formula: A Case of Cultural Hybridity." *Journal of Semitic Studies* 55 (2010): 365-83.

Morsen, Gary Saul, and Caryl Emerson. *Mikhail Bakhtin: Creation of a Prosaics.* Stanford: Stanford University Press, 1990.

Moss, Candida R., and Jeremy Schipper, eds. *Disability Studies and Biblical Literature.* New York: Palgrave Macmillan, 2011.

Motte, Standish. *Outline of a system of legislation, for securing protection to the aboriginal inhabitants of all countries colonized by Great Britain; extending to them political and social rights, ameliorating their condition, and promoting their civilization.* London: John Murray, 1840.

Murphy, Nancey. *Beyond Liberalism and Fundamentalism: How Modern and Postmodern Philosophy Set the Theological Agenda.* Valley Forge, Pa.: Trinity, 1996.

Myers, Ched, and Elaine Enns. *Ambassadors of Reconciliation*, Vol. 1: *New Testament Reflections on Restorative Justice and Peacemaking.* Maryknoll, NY: Orbis, 2009.

Nam, Roger S. *Portrayals of Economic Exchange in the Books of Kings.* Biblical Interpretation Series 112. Leiden: Brill, 2012.

Nan, Susan Allen, Zachariah Cherian Mampily, and Andrea Bartoli, eds. *Peacemaking: From Practice to Theory.* 2 vols. Santa Barbara, Calif.: Praeger, 2011.

Nandy, Ashis. *Bonfire of Creeds: The Essential Ashis Nandy.* New Delhi: Oxford University, 2004.

―――. "Cultural Frames for Social Transformation: A Credo." *Alternatives* 12 (1987): 125-52.

Nelson, Eric. *The Hebrew Republic: Jewish Sources and the Transformation of European Political Thought.* Cambridge, Mass.: Harvard University Press, 2010.

Nestor, Dermot. "If Not Now, When? The Ecological Potential of Isaiah's New Things." In *Creation Is Groaning: Biblical and Theological Perspectives*, edited by Mary Coloe, pp. 33-56. Collegeville, Minn.: Liturgical Press, 2013.

Newcomb, Steven T. *Pagans in the Promised Land: Decoding the Doctrine of Christian Discovery.* Golden: Fulcrum, 2008.

Newsom, Carol. "Bakhtin, the Bible and Dialogic Truth." *Journal of Religion* 76 (1996): 290-306.

Nihan, Christophe. *From Priestly Torah to Pentateuch: A Study in the Composition of the Book of Leviticus.* Forschungen zum Alten Testament II/25. Tübingen: Mohr Siebeck, 2007.

―――. "The Priestly Covenant, Its Reinterpretation and the Composition of 'P.'" In *The Strata of the Priestly Writings: Contemporary Debate and Future Directions*, edited by Sarah Shectman and Joel Baden, pp. 87-134. Abhandlundgen zur Theologie des Alten und Neuen Testaments 95: Zürich: Theologischer Verlag Zürich, 2009.

―――. "The Torah between Samaria and Judah: Shechem and Gerizim in Deuteronomy and Joshua." In *The Pentateuch as Torah*, edited by Gary N. Knoppers and Bernard M. Levinson, pp. 187-223. Winona Lake, Ind.: Eisenbrauns, 2007.

Noble, Paul. *The Canonical Approach: A Critical Reconstruction of the Hermeneutics of Brevard Childs*. Leiden: E. J. Brill, 1995.

Nobles, Melissa. *The Politics of Official Apologies*. Cambridge: Cambridge University Press, 2008.

Northcott, Michael. *An Angel Directs the Storm: Apocalyptic Religion and American Empire*. London: IB Taurus, 2004.

———. *A Moral Climate: The Ethics of Global Warming*. London: Darton, Longman and Todd, 2007.

———. *A Political Theology of Climate Change*. Grand Rapids: Eerdmans, 2013.

Novak, David. *Covenantal Rights*. Princeton: Princeton University Press, 2000.

———. "Oliver O'Donovan's Critique of Autonomy." *Political Theology* 9 (2008): 327-38.

Nurser, John. *For All Peoples and All Nations: Christian Churches and Human Rights*. Washington: Georgetown University Press, 2005.

Nussbaum, Martha. *Creating Capabilities: The Human Development Approach*. Cambridge, Mass.: Belknap, 2011.

———. *Frontiers of Justice: Disability, Nationality, and Species Membership*. Boston: Harvard University Press, 2006.

———. "Non-Relative Virtues: An Aristotelian Approach." In *Quality of Life*, edited by Martha Nussbaum and Amartya Sen, pp. 242-69. Oxford: Oxford University Press, 1993.

Oakeshott, Michael. *Lectures in the History of Political Thought*, edited by T. Nardin and L. O'Sullivan. Exeter: Imprint Academic, 2006.

Oblath, Michael D. "Of Pharaohs and Kings — Whence the Exodus?" *Journal for the Study of the Old Testament* 87 (2000): 23-42.

O'Donovan, Oliver. *The Desire of the Nations: Rediscovering the Roots of Political Theology*. Cambridge: Cambridge University Press, 1996.

———. "The Justice of Assignment and Subjective Rights in Grotius." In Oliver O'Donovan and Joan Lockwood O'Donovan, *Bonds of Imperfection: Christian Politics Past and Present*, pp. 167-203. Grand Rapids: Eerdmans, 2004.

O'Donovan, Oliver, and Joan Lockwood O'Donovan. *From Irenaeus to Grotius: A Sourcebook in Christian Political Thought 100–1625*. Grand Rapids: Eerdmans, 1999.

Ollenburger, Ben C. "Old Testament Theology: A Discourse on Method." In *Biblical Theology: Problems and Perspectives*, edited by Stephen J. Kraftchick, Charles D. Meyers and Ben C. Ollenburger, pp. 81-103. Nashville: Abingdon, 1995.

Olson, Dennis. "Biblical Theology as Provisional Monologization: A Dialogue with Childs, Brueggemann and Bakhtin." *Biblical Interpretation* 6 (1998): 162-80.

Olyan, Saul. "Exodus 31:12-17: The Sabbath according to H, the Sabbath according to P and H." *Journal of Biblical Literature* 124 (2005): 201-9.

———. *Rites and Rank: Hierarchy in Biblical Representations of Cult*. Princeton: Princeton University Press, 2000.

Oorschot, Jürgen van. "Hiob 28: Die verborgene Weisheit und die Furcht Gottes also Überwindung einer Generalisierten חקמה." In *The Book of Job*, edited by Willem

A. M. Beuken, pp. 183-201. Bibliotheca ephemeridum theologicarum lovaniensium 114. Leuven: Leuven University Press and Peeters, 1994.

Orlinski, Harry. "Nationalism-Universalism and Internationalism in Ancient Israel." In *Translating and Understanding the Old Testament. Essays in Honor of Herbert Gordon May*, edited by Harry T. Frank and William L. Reed, pp. 206-36. Nashville: Abingdon, 1970.

Oslington, Paul. "Natural Theology as an Integrative Framework for Economics and Theology." *St Mark's Review* 199 (2005): 56-65.

Oslington, Paul, ed. *Adam Smith as Theologian*. London: Routledge, 2011.

Osthathios, Metropolitan Geevarghese Mar. *The Sin of Being Rich in a Poor World: Holy Trinity and Social Justice*. Tiruvala: Christava Sahitya Samithi, 2004.

Otto, Eckart. "The Holiness Code in Diachrony and Synchrony." In *The Strata of the Priestly Writings: Contemporary Debate and Future Directions*, edited by Sarah Shectman and Joel S. Baden, pp. 135-56. Abhandlungen zur Theologie des Alten und Neuen Testaments 95. Zürich: Theologischer Verlag Zürich.

————. "Human Rights: The Influence of the Hebrew Bible." *Journal of Northwest Semitic Languages* 25 (1999): 1-14.

Papanikolaou, Aristotle. "Person, Kenosis and Abuse: Hans Urs von Balthasar and Feminist Theologies on Conversation." *Modern Theology* 19 (2003): 41-65.

Paradies, Yin C. "Beyond Black and White: Essentialism, Hybridity and Indigeneity." *Journal of Sociology* 42 (2006): 355-67.

Parpola, Simo. "Assyria's Expansion in the 8th and 7th Centuries and Its Long-term Repercussions in the West." In *Symbiosis, Symbolism and the Power of the Past*, edited by William G. Dever and Seymour Gitin, pp. 99-111. Winona Lake, Ind.: Eisenbrauns, 2003.

Paulson, Graham, and Mark Brett. "Five Smooth Stones: Reading the Bible through Aboriginal Eyes." *Colloquium* 45 (2013): 199-214.

Pearson, Noel, "Land Is Capable of Ownership." In *Honour Among Nations? Treaties and Agreements with Indigenous People*, edited by Marcia Langton, Maureen Tehan, Lisa Palmer, Kathryn Shain, pp. 83-100. Melbourne: Melbourne University Press, 2004.

Perdue, Leo. "Old Testament Theology since Barth's Epistle to the Romans." In *Biblical Theology: Introducing the Conversation*, edited by Leo G. Perdue, Robert Morgan and Benjamin D. Sommer, pp. 55-136. Nashville: Abingdon, 2009.

————. *The Sword and the Stylus: An Introduction to Wisdom in the Age of Empires*. Grand Rapids: Eerdmans, 2008.

Perkinson, James W. *White Theology: Outing Supremacy in Modernity*. New York: Palgrave Macmillan, 2004.

Perkinson, Jim. "A Canaanite Word in the Logos of Christ." In *Postcolonialism and Scriptural Reading*, edited by Laura Donaldson, pp. 61-85. Semeia 75. Atlanta: Scholars Press, 1996.

Perry, Michael J. "Is the Idea of Human Rights Ineliminably Religious?" In *The Idea of Human Rights: Four Inquiries*, edited by Perry, pp. 11-41. Oxford: Oxford University Press, 1998.

Philips, Gregory. "Healing and Public Policy." In *Coercive Reconciliation: Stabilise, Nor-*

malise, Exit Aboriginal Australia, edited by Jon Altman and Melinda Hinkson, pp. 141-50. Melbourne: Arena, 2007.

Philpott, Daniel. *Just and Unjust Peace: An Ethic of Political Reconciliation*. New York: Oxford University Press, 2012.

Polanyi, Karl. *The Great Transformation: The Political and Economic Origins of Our Time.* 2nd ed. Boston: Beacon, 2001.

Polkinghorne, John, ed. *The Work of Love: Creation as Kenosis.* Grand Rapids: Eerdmans, 2001.

Preston, Ron. *Religion and the Ambiguities of Capitalism.* Cleveland: Pilgrim Press, 1991.

Pury, Albert de. "Abraham: The Priestly Writer's 'Ecumenical' Ancestor." In *Rethinking the Foundations: Historiography in the Ancient World and in the Bible. Essays in Honour of John Van Seters*, edited by Stephen L. McKenzie and Thomas Römer, pp. 163-81. Beihefte zur Zeitschrift für die alttestamentliche Wissenschaft 239; Berlin: de Gruyter, 2000.

———. "Der priesterschriftliche Umgang mit der Jakobsgeschichte." In *Schriftauslegung in der Schrift. Festschrift für Odil Hannes Steck*, edited by Rainer G. Kratz, Thomas Krüger and Konrad Schmid, pp. 52-54. Beihefte zur Zeitschrift für die alttestamentliche Wissenschaft 300; Berlin: de Gruyter, 2000.

———. "Le tombeau des Abrahamides d'Hébron et sa fonction au début de l'époque perse." *Transeuphratene* 30 (2005): 183-84.

———. "Pg as the Absolute Beginning." In *Les Dernières Rédactions du Pentateuque, de L'Hexateuque et de L'Ennéateuque*, edited by Thomas Römer and Konrad Schmid, pp. 118-19. Bibliotheca ephemeridum theologicarum lovaniensium 203. Leuven: Leuven University Press, 2007.

———. "The Jacob Story." In *A Farewell to the Yahwist? The Composition of the Pentateuch in Recent European Interpretation*, edited by Thomas B. Dozeman and Konrad Schmid, pp. 51-72. Society of Biblical Literature Symposium Series 34. Atlanta: Society of Biblical Literature, 2006.

Rad, Gerhard von. *Die Priesterschrift im Hexateuch. Literarisch untersucht und theologisch gewertet.* Stuttgart: Kohlhammer, 1934.

———. "There Remains Still a Rest for the People of God." In *The Problem of the Hexateuch and Other Essays* pp. 94-102. London: Oliver & Boyd, 1966.

Rainbow Spirit Elders. *Rainbow Spirit Theology.* Melbourne: HarperCollins, 1997.

Rasmussen, Larry L. *Earth-Honoring Faith: Religious Ethics in a New Key*. Oxford: Oxford University Press, 2013.

Rawls, John. "The Idea of Public Reason Revisited." *University of Chicago Law Review* 64 (1997): 765-807.

Reed, Esther D. "Refugee Rights and State Sovereignty: Theological Perspectives on the Ethics of Territorial Borders." *Journal of the Society of Christian Ethics* 30 (2010): 59-78.

———. *Theology for International Law*. London: Bloomsbury, 2013.

Rendtorff, Rolf. *Canon and Theology: Overtures to an Old Testament Theology*. Translated by Margaret Kohl. Overtures to Biblical Theology. Minneapolis: Fortress, 1993.

Renger, Johannes. "On Economic Structures in Ancient Mesopotamia." *Orientalia* 18 (1994): 157-208.

Reynolds, Henry. *This Whispering in Our Hearts*. Sydney: Allen & Unwin, 1998.

Richard, Pablo. "Biblical Interpretation from the Perspective of Indigenous Cultures of Latin America (Mayas, Kunas and Quechuas)." In *Ethnicity and the Bible*, edited by Mark G. Brett, pp. 298-301. Biblical Interpretation Series 19. Leiden: Brill, 1996.

Rivera, Louis. *A Violent Evangelism: The Political and Religious Conquest of the Americas*. Louisville: Westminster John Knox, 1992.

Roberts, J. J. M. "The End of War in the Zion Tradition: The Imperialistic Background of an Old Testament Vision of Worldwide Peace." In *Character Ethics and the Old Testament*, edited by M. Daniel Carroll R. and Jacqueline E. Lapsley, pp. 119-28. London: Westminster John Knox, 2007.

Robertson, Lindsay G. *Conquest by Law: How the Discovery of America Dispossessed Indigenous Peoples of Their Lands*. New York: Oxford University Press, 2005.

Rogerson, John W. *According to the Scriptures? The Challenge of Using the Bible in Social, Moral and Political Questions*. London: Equinox, 2006.

Römer, Thomas. "Abraham Traditions in the Hebrew Bible." In *The Book of Genesis: Composition, Reception, and Interpretation*, edited by Craig A. Evans, Joel N. Lohr and David L. Petersen. Vetus Testamentum Supplements 152. Leiden: E. J. Brill, 2012.

———. "The Exodus Narrative according to the Priestly Document." In *The Strata of the Priestly Writings: Contemporary Debate and Future Directions*, edited by Sarah Shectman and Joel Baden, pp. 157-74. Abhandlundgen zur Theologie des Alten und Neuen Testaments 95. Zürich: Theologischer Verlag Zürich, 2009.

Rose, Deborah Bird. "Consciousness and Responsibility in an Australian Aboriginal Religion." In *Traditional Aboriginal Society*, edited by William H. Edwards, pp. 239-51. 2nd ed. Melbourne: Macmillan, 1998.

Rosendale, George. *Spirituality for Aboriginal Christians*. Darwin: Nungalinya College, 1993.

Rost, Leonhard. "Die Bezeichnungen für Land und Volk im alten Testament" (1934). In *Das kleine Credo und andere Studien zum Alten Testament*, pp. 76-101. Heidelberg: Quelle & Meyer, 1965.

Runzo, Joseph, Nancy M. Martin, and Arvind Sharma. *Human Rights and Responsibilities in the World Religions*. Oxford: Oneworld, 2003.

Rushton, Kathleen P. "The Cosmology of John 1:1-14 and Its Implications for Ethical Action in This Ecological Age." *Colloquium* 45 (2013): 137-53.

Sacks, Jonathan. *The Dignity of Difference: How to Avoid the Clash of Civilizations*. 2nd ed. London: Continuum, 2003.

Said, Edward. *The End of the Peace Process*. New York: Pantheon, 2000.

———. "Michael Walzer's Exodus and Revolution: A Canaanite Reading." In *Blaming the Victims: Spurious Scholarship and the Palestinian Question*, edited by Edward Said and Christopher Hitchens, pp. 161-78. New York: Verso, 1988.

———. "Reflections on Exile." In *Reflections on Exile and Other Literary and Cultural Essays*, pp. 173-86. London: Granta, 2000.

Samos, Mark. "Secularization in De Iure Praedae: from Bible Criticism to International Law." *Grotiana* 26-28 (2005-2007): 147-91.

Sanneh, Lamin. *Translating the Message: The Missionary Impact on Culture.* Maryknoll: Orbis, 1989.

―――. *Whose Religion Is Christianity? The Gospel beyond the West.* Grand Rapids: Eerdmans, 2003.

Saunders A. C. de C. M. "Legal and Philosophical Justifications of the Slave Trade." *A Social History of Black Slaves in Portugal, 1441-1555,* pp. 35-46. Cambridge: Cambridge University Press, 1982.

Schluter, Michael, and David Lee. *The R Factor.* London: Hodder and Stoughton, 1993.

Schluter, Michael, and John Ashcroft, eds. *Jubilee Manifesto: A Framework, Agenda and Strategy for Christian Social Reform.* Leicester: InterVarsity Press, 2005.

Schmid, Konrad. *Genesis and the Moses Story: Israel's Dual Origins in the Hebrew Bible.* Translated by James D. Nogalski. Siphrut 3. Winona Lake, Ind.: Eisenbrauns, 2010. Translation of *Erzväter und Exodus: Untersuchungen zur doppelten Begründung der Ursprünge Israels in den Geschichtsbüchern des Alten Testaments.* Wissenschaftliche Monographien zum Alten und Neuen Testament 81. Neukirchen-Vluyn: Neukirchener, 1999.

―――. "Judean Identity and Ecumenicity: The Political Theology of the Priestly Document." In *Judah and Judeans in the Achaemenid Period: Negotiating Identity in an International Context,* edited by Oded Lipschits, Gary N. Knoppers, Manfred Oeming, pp. 3-26. Winona Lake: Eisenbrauns, 2011.

Schmitt, Carl. *Political Theology: Four Chapters on the Concept of Sovereignty.* Translated by George Schwab. Chicago: University of Chicago Press, 2005.

Schwartz, Baruch J. "Reexamining the Fate of the 'Canaanites' in the Torah Traditions." In *Sefer Moshe: The Moshe Weinfeld Jubilee Volume,* edited by Chaim Cohen, Avi Hurvitz and Shalom M. Paul, pp. 151-70. Winona Lake, Ind.: Eisenbrauns, 2004.

―――. "Torah from Zion: Isaiah's Temple Vision (Isaiah 2.1-4)." In *Sanctity of Time and Space in Tradition and Modernity,* edited by Alberdina Houtman, Marcel Poorthuis and Joshua J. Schwartz, pp. 12-26. Leiden: Brill, 1998.

Scott, Bruce R. *Capitalism: Its Origins and Evolution as a System of Governance.* New York: Springer, 2011.

Searle, John R. *Speech Acts: An Essay in the Philosophy of Language.* Cambridge: Cambridge University Press, 1969.

Secher, Ulla. "The Doctrine of Tenure in Australia post-Mabo: Replacing the 'Feudal Fiction' with the 'mere Radical Title Fiction'– Part 2." *Australian Property Law Journal* 13 (2006): 140-78.

Sen, Amartya. *The Idea of Justice.* London: Allen Lane, 2009.

Sherword, Yvonne. "Francisco de Vitoria's More Excellent Way: How the Bible of Empire Discovered the Tricks of [the Argument from] Trade." *Biblical Interpretation* 21 (2013): 215-75.

Shils, Edward. "Primordial, Personal, Sacred, and Civil Ties." *British Journal of Sociology* 8 (1957): 130-45.

Shiva, Vandana. *Earth Democracy.* Cambridge, Mass.: South End, 2005.

―――. *Staying Alive: Women, Ecology, and Development.* London: Zed, 1989.

Silver, Morris. *Economic Structures of the Ancient Near East.* London: Croom Helm, 1985.

————. *Prophets and Markets: The Political Economy of Ancient Israel.* Boston: Kluwer Nijhof, 1983.

Ska, Jean-Louis. *Exegesis of the Pentateuch.* Tübingen: Mohr-Siebeck, 2009.

Smith, Anthony D. *Chosen Peoples.* Oxford: Oxford University Press, 2003.

Smith, Kay Higuera, Jayachitra Lalitha, and L. Daniel Hawk, eds. *Evangelical Postcolonial Conversations: Global Awakenings in Theology and Practice.* Downers Grove: Inter-Varsity Press, 2014.

Smith-Christopher, Daniel. *A Biblical Theology of Exile.* Minneapolis: Fortress, 2002.

Sommer, Benjamin D. "A Jewish Approach to Reading Scripture Theologically." In *Biblical Theology: Introducing the Conversation,* edited by Leo Perdue, Robert Morgan, and Benjamin D. Sommer, pp. 1-53. Nashville: Abingdon Press, 2009.

————. "Unity and Plurality in Jewish Canons." In *One Scripture or Many? Canon from Biblical, Theological and Philosophical Perspectives,* edited by Christine Helmer and Christof Landmesser, pp. 108-50. Oxford: Oxford University Press, 2004.

Southwood, Katherine. *Ethnicity and the Mixed Marriage Crisis in Ezra 9–10: An Anthropological Approach.* Oxford Theological Monographs. Oxford: Oxford University Press, 2012.

Speiser, Ephraim A. "'People' and 'Nation' in Israel." *Journal of Biblical Literature* 79 (1960): 157-63.

Sperber, Dan, and Dierdre Wilson. *Relevance: Communication and Cognition.* 2nd ed. Oxford: Blackwells, 1995.

Spina, Frank. *The Faith of the Outsider: Exclusion and Inclusion in the Biblical Story.* Grand Rapids: Eerdmans, 2005.

Spivak, Gayatri Chakravorti. *A Critique of Postcolonial Reason: Toward a History of the Vanishing Present.* Cambridge, Mass.: Harvard University Press, 1999.

Stanley, Brian, ed. *Missions, Nationalism and the End of Empire.* Grand Rapids: Eerdmans, 2003.

Stanley, Christopher D., ed. *The Colonized Apostle: Paul through Postcolonial Eyes.* Minneapolis: Fortress, 2011.

Stavrakopoulou, Francesca. *Land of Our Fathers: The Roles of Ancestor Veneration in Biblical Land Claims.* Library of Hebrew Bible / Old Testament Studies 473. London: T & T Clark, 2010.

Stephen, James. "Colonization as a Branch of Social Economy." Reprinted in Paul Knaplund, *James Stephen and the British Colonial System, 1813-1847,* pp. 281-98. Madison: University of Wisconsin Press, 1953.

Steymans, Hans Ulrich. *Deuteronomium 28 und die* Adê *zur Thronfolgeregelung Asarhaddons: Segen und Fluch im Alten Orient und in Israel.* Orbis Biblicus et Orientalis 145. Göttingen: Vandenhoeck & Ruprecht, 1995.

Stiver, Dan R. "Felicity and Fusion: Speech Act Theory and Hermeneutical Philosophy." In *Transcending Boundaries in Philosophy and Theology,* edited by Kevin J. Vanhoozer and Martin Warner, pp. 145-56. Aldershot: Ashgate, 2007.

Stone, Lawson G. "Ethical and Apologetic Tendencies in the Redaction of the Book of Joshua." *Catholic Biblical Quarterly* 53 (1991): 25-35.

Stout, Jeffrey. *Democracy and Tradition.* Princeton: Princeton University Press, 2003.

Strawn, Brent A. "On Vomiting: Leviticus, Jonah, Ea(a)rth." *Catholic Biblical Quarterly* 74 (2012): 445-64.

―――. "'A World under Control': Isaiah 60 and the Apadana Reliefs from Persepolis." In *Approaching Yehud*, edited by Jon L. Berquist, pp. 85-116. Atlanta: Society of Biblical Literature, 2006.

Strelein, Lisa. *Compromised Jurisprudence: Native Title Cases since Mabo*. Canberra: Aboriginal Studies Press, 2006.

Tambiah, Stanley. *Magic, Science, Religion and the Scope of Rationality*. Cambridge: Cambridge University Press, 1990.

Taylor, Charles. *Modern Social Imaginaries*. Durham: Duke University Press, 2004.

―――. "The Politics of Recognition." In *Multiculturalism and "The Politics of Recognition,"* edited by Amy Gutman, pp. 25-73. Princeton: Princeton University Press, 1992.

―――. *A Secular Age*. Cambridge, Mass.: Belknap Press, 2007.

―――. *Sources of the Self: The Making of Modern Identity*. Cambridge, Mass.: Harvard University Press, 1989.

Terrien, Samuel. "Quelques Remarques sur les affinités de Job avec le Deutéro-Esaïe." In *Volume du Congrès: Genève, 1965*, pp. 295-310. Vetus Testamentum Supplements 15. Leiden: Brill, 1966.

Thiselton, Anthony. "Dialectic in Hermeneutics and Doctrine: Coherence and Polyphony." In *The Hermeneutics of Doctrine*, pp. 119-44. Grand Rapids: Eerdmans, 2007.

Tierney, Brian. *The Idea of Natural Rights*. Atlanta: Scholars Press, 1997.

Tinker, George E. *American Indian Liberation: A Theology of Sovereignty*. Maryknoll, NY: Orbis, 2008.

United Nations High Commission on Refugees. *Asylum Trends, First Half of 2014*. Geneva: UNHCR, 2014.

―――. *Global Trends 2013*. Geneva: UNHCR, 2014.

Uyangoda, Jayadeva. "Understanding Ethnicity and Nationalism." *Ecumenical Review* 47/2 (1995): 225-31.

Van Hecke, Pierre J. P. "Searching for and Exploring Wisdom." In *Job 28: Cognition in Context*, ed. Ellen Van Wolde, pp. 139-62. Biblical Interpretation Series 64. Leiden: Brill, 2003.

Vanhoozer, Kevin. *The Drama of Doctrine: A Canonical-linguistic Approach to Christian Theology*. Louisville: Westminster John Knox, 2005.

―――. "From Speech Acts to Scripture Acts: The Covenant of Discourse and the Discourse of the Covenant." In *After Pentecost*, edited by Craig Bartholomew, Colin Greene and Karl Möller, pp. 1-49. Carlisle: Paternoster, 2001.

―――. "Imprisoned or Free?" In *Reading Scripture with the Church: Toward a Hermeneutic for Theological Interpretation*, edited by Andrew K. M. Adam, Stephen E. Fowl, Kevin J. Vanhoozer, and Francis Watson, pp. 51-93. Grand Rapids: Baker, 2006.

―――. *Is There a Meaning in This Text? The Bible, the Reader and the Morality of Literary Knowledge*. Grand Rapids: Zondervan, 1998.

―――. "One Rule to Rule them All?" in *Globalizing Theology: Belief and Practice in an Era of World Christianity*, edited by Craig Ott and Harold A. Netland, pp. 85-126. Grand Rapids: Baker Academic, 2006.

————. *Remythogizing Theology: Divine Action, Passion and Authorship.* Cambridge: Cambridge University Press, 2010.

Van Ittersum, Martine Julia. *Profit and Principle: Hugo Grotius, Natural Rights Theories and the Rise of Dutch Power in the East Indies, 1595-1615.* Leiden: Brill, 2006.

Vattel, Emmerich de. *The Law of Nations; or, Principles of the Law of Nature, applied to the conduct and affairs of Nations and Sovereigns.* London: G. G. and J. Robinson, Paternoster-Row, 1797.

Veling, Terry. "In the Name of Who? Levinas and the Other Side of Theology." *Pacifica* 12 (1999): 275-92.

Veracini, Lorenzo. *Settler Colonialism: A Theoretical Overview.* Houndmills: Palgrave Macmillan, 2010.

Volf, Miroslav. *Exclusion and Embrace: A Theological Exploration of Identity, Otherness, and Reconciliation.* Nashville: Abingdon, 1996.

————. *A Public Faith: How Followers of Christ Should Serve the Common Good.* Grand Rapids: Brazos Press, 2011.

————. "The Social Meaning of Reconciliation." *Interpretation* 54 (2000): 158-72.

Vorster, Jakobus M. "The Ethics of Land Restitution." *Journal of Religious Ethics* 34 (2006): 685-707.

Waldron, Jeremy. *God, Locke and Equality: Christian Foundations of John Locke's Political Thought.* Cambridge: Cambridge University Press, 2002.

————. "The Image of God: Rights, Reason and Order." In *Christianity and Human Rights: An Introduction*, edited by John Witte Jr. and Frank S. Alexander, pp. 216-35. Cambridge, UK: Cambridge University Press, 2010.

Wallace, Howard N. "Jubilate Deo omnis terra: God and Earth in Psalm 65." In *The Earth Story in the Psalms and the Prophets*, edited by Norman C. Habel, pp. 51-64. The Earth Bible 4. Sheffield: Sheffield Academic Press, 2001.

Walzer, Michael. *In God's Shadow: Politics in the Hebrew Bible.* New Haven: Yale University Press, 2012.

Wan, Sze-kar. "Does Diaspora Identity Imply Some Sort of Universality? An Asian-American Reading of Galatians." In *Interpreting Beyond Borders*, edited by Fernando Segovia, pp. 107-33. Sheffield: Sheffield Academic Press, 2000.

Watson, Blake A. "The Impact of the American Doctrine of Discovery on Native Land Rights in Australia, Canada and New Zealand." *Seattle University Law Review* 34 (2011): 532-35.

Watson, Francis. *Text and Truth: Redeeming Biblical Theology.* Edinburgh: T&T Clark, 1997.

Watson, Rajula Annie. *A Christian Understanding of Land Ethics.* Delhi: ISPCK, 2004.

Weaver, Alain Epp. *States of Exile: Visions of Diaspora, Witness and Return.* Scottdale: Herald Press, 2008.

Weinfeld, Moshe. *The Place of the Law in the Religion of Ancient Israel.* Vetus Testamentum Supplements 100. Leiden: Brill, 2004.

————. *Social Justice in Ancient Israel and in the Ancient Near East.* Jerusalem: Magnes, 1995.

Weiser, Artur. *Das Buch Hiob*. Das Alte Testament Deutsch 13. Göttingen: Vandenhoeck & Ruprecht, 1951.

Weithman, Paul. *Religion and the Obligations of Citizenship*. Cambridge: Cambridge University Press, 2002.

Welker, Michael. "Habermas and Ratzinger on the Future of Religion." *Scottish Journal of Theology* 63 (2010): 456-73.

Westermann, Claus. *Isaiah 40-66*. Translated by David Stalker. Old Testament Library. London: SCM, 1969.

Weyland, Francis. *The Elements of Political Economy*. 4th ed. New York: Leavitt, Lord, 1854.

Whybray, R. Norman. *The Good Life in the Old Testament*. London: T&T Clark, 2002.

————. *Isaiah 40-66*. NCB. London: Marshall, Morgan & Scott, 1975.

Wilkinson, Katherine K. *Between God and Green: How Evangelicals Are Cultivating a Middle Ground on Climate Change*. Oxford: Oxford University Press, 2012.

Williamson, H. G. M. "The Composition of Ezra 1-6." *Journal of Theological Studies* 34/1 (1983): 1-30.

————. *Studies in Persian Period Historiography*. Forschungen zum Alten Testament 38. Tübingen: Mohr Siebeck, 2004.

Wilson, Eric. *Savage Republic: De Indis of Hugo Grotius, Republicanism and Dutch Hegemony within the Early Modern World System, c.1600-1619*. Leiden: Brill, 2008.

Wilson, Erin K.. "Be Welcome: Religion, Hospitality and Statelessness in International Politics." In *Hospitality and World Politics*, edited by Gideon Baker, pp. 145-70. Basingstoke: Palgrave Macmillan, 2013.

Windschuttle, Keith. *The Fabrication of Aboriginal History*, Vol. 1, *Van Dieman's Land 1803–1847*. Sydney: Macleay Press, 2002.

Winkle, Dwight van. "The Meaning of *yad wašem* in Isaiah LVI 5." *Vetus Testamentum* 47 (1997): 378-85.

Wire, Antoinette. *The Corinthian Women Prophets*. Minneapolis: Fortress Press, 1990.

Wolterstorff, Nicholas. *Divine Discourse: Philosophical Reflections on the Claim That God Speaks*. Cambridge: Cambridge University Press, 1995.

————. *Justice in Love*. Grand Rapids: Eerdmans, 2011.

————. *Justice: Rights and Wrongs*. Princeton: Princeton University Press, 2008.

————. "Reading Joshua." In *Divine Evil? The Moral Character of the God of Abraham*, edited by Michael Bergmann, Michael J. Murray, and Michael C. Rea, pp. 236-56. New York: Oxford University Press, 2010.

————. "A Response to Trevor Hart." In *Renewing Biblical Interpretation*, edited by Craig Bartholomew, Colin Greene, and Karl Möller, pp. 335-41. Grand Rapids: Zondervan, 2000.

————. "The Unity behind the Canon." In *One Scripture or Many? Canon from Biblical, Theological and Philosophical Perspectives*, edited by Christine Helmer and Christof Landmesser, pp. 217-32. Oxford: Oxford University Press, 2004.

Wöhrle, Jakob. "Abraham amidst the Nations: The Priestly Concept of Covenant and the Persian Imperial Ideology." In *Covenant in the Persian Period*, edited by Richard J. Bautch and Gary N. Knoppers, pp. 23-39. Winona Lake, Ind.: Eisenbrauns, 2015.

————. *Fremdlinge im eigenen Land: Zur Entstehung und Intention der priesterlichen Passagen der Vätergeschichte.* Forschungen zur Religion und Literatur des Alten und Neuen Testament 246. Göttingen: Vandenhoeck & Ruprecht, 2012.

————. "The Integrative Function of the Law of Circumcision." In *The Foreigner and the Law: Perspectives from the Hebrew Bible and the Ancient Near East,* edited by Reinhard Achenbach, Rainer Albertz, and Jakob Wöhrle, pp. 71-87. Beihefte zur Zeitschrift für Altorientalische und biblische Rechtsgeschichte 16. Wiesbaden: Harrassowitz, 2011.

————. "The Un-Empty Land: The Concept of Exile and Land in P." In *The Concept of Exile in Ancient Israel and Its Historical Contexts,* edited by Ehud Ben Zvi and Christophe Levin, pp. 189-206. Beihefte zur Zeitschrift für die alttestamentliche Wissenschaft 404. Berlin: de Gruyter, 2010.

Woodley, Randy S. *Shalom and the Community of Creation: An Indigenous Vision.* Grand Rapids: Eerdmans, 2012.

Wright, Jacob L. "The Commemoration of Defeat and the Formation of a Nation in the Hebrew Bible." *Prooftexts* 29 (2009): 433-73.

————. "Writing the Restoration: Compositional Agenda in the Role of Ezra in Neh 8." *Journal of Hebrew Scriptures* 7 (2007): 19-29.

Wright, Jacob L., and Michael Chan. "King and Eunuch: Isaiah 56:1-8 in Light of Honorific Royal Burial Practices." *Journal of Biblical Literature* 31 (2012): 99-119.

Wright, John W. "Remapping Yehud: The Borders of Yehud and the Genealogies of Chronicles." In *Judah and the Judeans in the Persian Period,* edited by Oded Lipschits and Manfred Oeming, pp. 67-89. Winona Lake: Eisenbrauns, 2006.

Wright, N. T. *The Resurrection of the Son of God.* Minneapolis: Fortress Press, 2003.

————. *Surprised by Hope: Rethinking Heaven, the Resurrection, and the Mission of the Church.* New York: HarperCollins, 2008.

Wright, Tom. "Paul and Caesar: A New Reading of Romans." In *A Royal Priesthood? A Dialogue with Oliver O'Donovan,* edited by Craig Bartholomew et al., pp. 173-93. Grand Rapids: Zondervan, 2002.

Wykes, Michael. "Devaluing the Scholastics: Calvin's Ethics of Usury." *Calvin Theological Journal* 38 (2003): 27-51.

Wyschogrod, Michael. *The Body of Faith: Judaism as Corporeal Election.* Minneapolis: Seabury-Winston, 1983.

Yoder, John Howard. *The Royal Priesthood.* Grand Rapids: Eerdmans, 1994.

Yoder, Perry B., and Willard M. Swartly, eds. *The Meaning of Peace: Biblical Studies.* 2nd ed. Elkhart, Ind.: Institute of Mennonite Studies, 2001.

Young, Iris M. *Justice and the Politics of Difference.* Princeton: Princeton University Press, 1990.

Zevit, Ziony. *The Religions of Israel: A Synthesis of Parallactic Approaches.* New York: Continuum, 2001.

Žižek, Slavoj. *The Fragile Absolute, or, Why Is the Christian Legacy Worth Fighting For?* London: Verso, 2000.

Index

Scripture Index